CW00662769

A COLONIAL BOY

the soundtrack of an african childhood

Chris Cocks

Also by Chris Cocks:
Fire Force: A Trooper's War in the Rhodesian Light Infantry (1989)
Survival Course (1998)
The Cheetah magazine (2011)
Africa's Commandos (co-author) (2012)
Deslocado Redemption (2018)

Copyright © Chris Cocks, 2024
chriscocks8@gmail.com
Book designed by Acepub
Back cover photo courtesy of Robyn Norris
Set in Bembo Book MT Std 11.5/ 14.25
ISBN: 9798872551850
ASIN: B0CQR9D4RK

All rights reserved. No part of this publication may be reproduced, distributed or transmitted in any form or by any means, including photocopying, recording, or other electronic or mechanical methods, without the prior written permission of the author.

A COLONIAL BOY

FOR MY PARENTS

CONTENTS

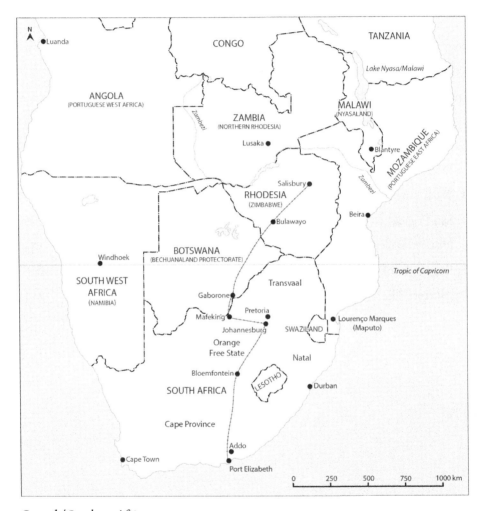

Central / Southern Africa

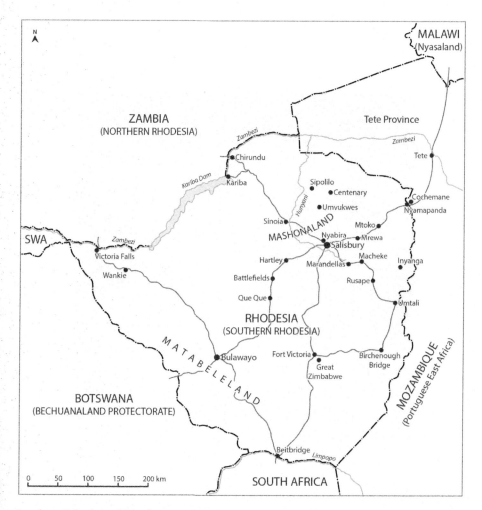

Southern Rhodesia / Rhodesia

Prologue
The Carnival is Over—The Seekers, 1965

It is shortly after 1 o'clock—11 o'clock GMT—on Thursday, 11 November 1965, a typical hot Rhodesian summer's day. It is two days before my eighth birthday but the anticipation of the very real possibility of a *Beezer* annual and a platoon of Britains model soldiers as a birthday present is overshadowed by the slightly nasal, toneless voice of the prime minister on the wireless in the staff room. I am struggling to hear what he is saying, craning my head round the corner of the open staff room door. I try and peer in, afraid that the assembled teachers will shoo me away. But they don't see me or if they do, they ignore me, too engrossed in Mr Smith's words to bother with a small Standard 1 boy hanging about in the doorway.

There is another boy at the door, on the other side. He is bigger than me and I only vaguely know him. He doesn't seem to mind me being there. Some boys are still filtering out from the stuffy prefab classrooms, shoes scuffing on the concrete walkways, satchels hanging awry off their shoulders; others have dashed off to the field to finish their interrupted breaktime games of open gates, stingers or marbles; and some slouch toward the carpark outside the school gate, munching half-eaten sandwiches, crusts curling, without interest, waiting for their mothers to collect them. None appears interested in what our teacher Mrs Lewis had said would be a very important announcement from Mr Smith.

She'd even let us off five minutes early—unheard of—with the words: "The prime minister, Mr Ian Smith, is going to be making a very, very important announcement at a quarter past one. Mr Hickman thinks that he will be declaring U … D … I," she said in a measured manner, not because we were children— she never patronized us—but I believe to impress upon us the gravity of the occasion. "UDI," she continued, "is a unilateral declaration of independence. This means that Mr Smith will be telling the Queen that Rhodesia shall be an independent country without any ties to Britain."

Could this be true? I'd gasped. This was devastating news. I'd stuffed my slate, my chalks and *Dick and Jane* books into my satchel and scurried off to the staff room, hot on Mrs Lewis's heels. The staff room had the only wireless in the

1

school. I'd heard the teachers listening to it during breaktimes when they had their tea. I still had one apricot ball secreted away in my satchel, which I hadn't eaten at break. It had been too dangerous to produce it—the other boys would have spotted it and stolen it.

"Now therefore, we, the Government of Rhodesia, do hereby declare: That it is an indisputable and accepted historic fact that since 1923 the Government of Rhodesia have exercised the powers of self-government and have been responsible for the progress, development, and welfare of their people …" Mr Smith's voice drones. It irritates me slightly the way he pronounces the country—'Rhodeeseeya'.

I have no idea what he is talking about and he does seem to be taking a long time to get to the point. I am waiting to hear those all-important words: 'unilateral', 'declaration' and 'independence'. I do not know what 'unilateral' means but I guess it is something serious.

"That the people of Rhodesia fully support the request of their Government for sovereign independence and have witnessed the consistent refusal of the Government of the United Kingdom to accede to their entreaties …"

I steal a glance at the boy opposite me. He is a lanky youth with a mop of straggly blond hair hanging across his face. It looks annoying. He is absorbed with Mr Smith's lengthy speech so I slide the satchel off my shoulder and, shielding it behind my right hip, squirrel my hand into the bowels of it. There! That's it! I feel the hard, round apricot ball next to my lunchbox and clutch it tightly. I withdraw my hand, all the while my gaze fixed firmly on the boy. He is bigger than me and, without doubt, if he has an inkling of what I'm up to he'll snatch the prize away in a flash, regardless of the huddle of teachers not three yards from our position by the door.

"That the Government of Rhodesia have for a long period patiently and in good faith negotiated with the Government of the United Kingdom for the removal of the remaining limitations placed upon them and for the grant of sovereign independence …"

There! That word! Independence! But still no unilateral. I slowly manoeuvre my hand out from the satchel and bring it to my mouth, my gaze still rigidly but discreetly on the boy. I lift my hand to my mouth and pretend to wipe my nose, at the same time popping the apricot ball into my mouth. Triumph!

"Now therefore we, the Government of Rhodesia, in humble submission to Almighty God, who controls the destiny of nations, conscious that the people of Rhodesia have always shown unswerving loyalty and devotion to Her Majesty the Queen and earnestly praying that we the people of Rhodesia will not be hindered in our determination to continue exercising our undoubted right to demonstrate the same loyalty and devotion in seeking to promote the common good so that dignity and freedom of all men may be assured, do by this proclamation adopt, enact, and give to the People of Rhodesia the Constitution annexed hereto …"

"Hey! You!" the boy hisses at me. "What are you sucking?" He is glaring at me.

I start, my heart races. To lie might anger him. It must be obvious I have something in my mouth … like a sweet. It's not beyond reason that afterwards he might take me round the back of the classrooms where the veld is and beat me up. I decide to face him off and open my mouth wide, my tongue out, the apricot ball now white with saliva perched dexterously on top.

"Apricot," I whisper loudly, in a so-there tone.

"I want one. Got any more?"

"Uh uh."

He glares at me. "Next time, new boy!" he rasps.

Mr Smith is rambling on … and on. And then, suddenly, I hear him say: "God save the Queen."

What? What does that mean—'God save the Queen'? I am confused: one minute he's talking about independence, presumably being mean to the Queen and the next he's being nice to her.

There is movement in the staff room, chairs scraping. Mr Smith is still talking but a couple of the teachers are standing and chatting quietly. Things seem tense. Mrs Scrase, the Standard 2 teacher, is leaving. I see her shaking her head. She's very strict but she's nice and I like her. You know where you stand with her. She'll be my teacher next term and I am nervously looking forward to the challenge. I heard some parents talking one day, saying she's the best teacher in the school. She strides out the staff room with an air of disgust, shaking her head and muttering to herself, a light sheen of sweat on the trace of her moustache.

I back away, making myself small, but she sees me and stops. "Why, hello Christopher! Have you been listening?"

I nod vigorously, "Yes, Mrs Scrase. But … but did he do the UDI declaration?"

She smiles at me. "Yes, Christopher. He damned well did. We're for it now. Oh yes." She pats my head and strides off toward her classroom.

We're for what now? I know she is not telling me everything, but I do know quite clearly that Mrs Scrase doesn't think UDI is a good thing. And Mrs Scrase

3

is never wrong. For a fleeting moment I feel a sense of isolation, a sense of abandonment. Does this mean the Queen is not our queen anymore? I don't know how it will happen but I have a visceral sense of impending trouble. Not doom perhaps but bad things. I feel angry with Mr Smith. Why did he do this? Why has he done this to the Queen? My queen! I have always stood up in the cinema when they play 'God Save the Queen', I have always stood up at cricket matches and rugby matches when they play 'God Save the Queen'. She is my queen and I am immensely proud of her. I am proud to be part of the British Empire. I know about Agincourt and Trafalgar and Waterloo and Rorke's Drift. Nelson and Wellington, Francis Drake, Warwick the Kingmaker and Henry V are my heroes and now we won't share the same monarch, Her Majesty Elizabeth the Second, by the Grace of God, of the United Kingdom of Great Britain and Northern Ireland.

Little do I know, that with the flourish of the twelve signatures on the UDI document, my life will change irrevocably. It signals the end of *la belle époque Rhodesienne*.

The bigger boy has thankfully disappeared. The other teachers are talking more loudly now, agitated, excited, animated. I shlurp on the dying remnants of the apricot. Clouds are building up for the afternoon thunderstorm. It is very close. The sun vanishes behind a bank of towering cumulus clouds as the omnipresent crows swirl and squabble and peck at bits of discarded tuck under the plane tree in the quad. The cicadas momentarily stop their incessant chorus in the veld behind the classrooms.

I suddenly realize the time and glance at the carpark. Sure enough, my mother's blue and white Opel station wagon is there, waiting for me.

★

The following morning—12 November, which happens to be my auburn-headed friend Mark Bushnell's birthday—I am trying to listen to what my parents are talking about in the dining room next door. We children—my younger-by-sixteen-months twin sisters, Sarah and Caroline,* and I—are eating our breakfast of Jungle Oats porridge and herrings at the kitchen table, a sturdy, pale green piece of furniture with a chipped laminated top that doubles as the

---

*My sisters, twins Sarah and Caroline, were born on 25 July 1959. I don't remember the event but I apparently registered my dismay by depositing a voluminous turd in the middle of the verandah.

ironing board. The beautiful *Elizabethan Serenade** is playing on the wireless, light and gay.

"I dunno, Bets. I don't have a good feeling about this UDI," says my father. "People are talking of leaving."

Sarah is kicking me under the table, deliberately and irritatingly so.

"Such a bloody bore, isn't it, darling," responds my mother vaguely. Her priority is to ensure she gets us to school on time.

"One thing for certain, I'm not going back to bloody England," my father snaps. "Too depressing for words."

"There's always South Africa, Mike."

"Stop kicking me Sarah," I hiss.

"Full of bloody *jaapies*, Bets," my father snaps almost irrationally." I don't speak Afrikaans and anyway, I reckon their time is coming."

I know that *jaapie*—loosely an inbred redneck in Afrikaans—is derogatory and a word commonly used by my father and Granma Teddy, as is navvy which they use to describe working-class white people.

"We know what your birthday present is," Caroline teases me in a singsong lilt, but I don't bite.

"I know, dear, but it's always an option … and mama's there so we'd have a good, solid base."

"Teddy?" my father snorts. "The last thing we need is to be beholden to her!" he says, ignoring the fact that most of the furniture in the house has been supplied by Granma Teddy. Even my favourite toy, Charlie—a limp, sparsely furred dog with an unserviceable squeak—was given to me by Granma Teddy when she learned, with some dismay, that the only toy I had at the time was a wooden cotton reel.

I feel the nausea rising. It's the herrings. I start gagging and the twins start sniggering.

"Christopher!" my father's voice booms from the dining room.

"It's the herrings, daddy. They make me sick."

"Don't be ridiculous! Pull yourself together!"

I simply don't understand the reason, but herrings—clearly a North Sea luxury for my father during the war—always make me sick. Kippers—or smoked herrings—don't; in fact, I adore kippers. The bile is rising as I make

---

*An exquisite light classical piece written by Ronald Binge on Queen Elizabeth II's coronation, first performed by Mantovani and his orchestra. Until well into adulthood, I always believed it had been written in the Tudor era for Queen Elizabeth I. Had it, it would have been a Tudor chart topper.

a dash for the kitchen door, running the gauntlet of the twins' sniggers and vomit into the hydrangeas, with Pluto the Dalmatian—who is quite partial to regurgitated herring—on hand. Pluto—with one blue eye and one green—knows the drill, his tail whipping dangerously like a *sjambok*.* Ashen-faced, I resume my place at the kitchen table, hoping against hope that my father hasn't heard my little contretemps.

He hasn't: he's up brusquely from the table, grabbing his briefcase. "I'm off, Bets. I'll be late tonight. Nets at Sports Club."

Now it's the final curtain on the morning ritual: a tablespoon of cod liver oil thinly disguised as malt. Again, I feel the bile rising but the ice-clear soprano of Judith Durham of The Seekers—the voice of an angel is the only way to describe it—singing 'The Carnival Is Over' on the wireless momentarily distracts me. Is she singing to me? Is she singing to Rhodesia? Unaccountably, emotion washes over me. It is all such a curious business. "Lamentable, Christopher," Mrs Scrase had said. "Lamentable."

And for a fleeting instant I have an inkling of what she meant.

---

*a heavy leather whip (Afrikaans)

Introduction
Catch a Falling Star—Perry Como, 1957–1959

A part from Perry Como hogging the airwaves, November 1957 was a relatively innocuous month for the fifties. The Cold War was getting frostier with the Soviets unveiling their latest intercontinental missile, and the baby boom was in full swing. And how. Not that there weren't any outstanding events. On 10 November the Soviets launched Sputnik II (Russian for 'Travelling Companion II') into space with a dog, Laika, at the helm while the American space programme was still firmly grounded.

On the music front, the godfather of punk, James Osterberg, aka Iggy Pop, was a bright fourth grader in Ann Arbor, Michigan, diligently being steered towards a career in politics—as was his young contemporary William Clinton down south in Arkansas. Buddy Holly and the Crickets topped the UK charts in November with 'That'll Be the Day', while Elvis Presley held the number 1 slot on the Billboard Hot 100 across the Atlantic with 'Jailhouse Rock' in the same month. Rock 'n' roll, however, wasn't quite yet king with Debbie Reynolds's 'Tammy' selling the most records for the year, followed closely by Pat Boone's 'Love Letters in the Sand'. (Elvis only appeared at number 8 with 'All Shook Up'.)

With the trashing of music, so too with books. Mickey Spillane, tough guy from Brooklyn, sold twenty-seven million copies of his racy crime thrillers in the second part of the decade. On the non-fiction list in the US, *The Holy Bible*—Revised Standard Edition, naturally—held the top position in the years 1952, 1953 and 1954 with annual sales of 2,000,000, 1,100,000 and 710,000 respectively. Dan Dale Alexander's *Arthritis and Common Sense* (also a revised edition) gripped America, and top spot, in 1956, but 1957 (and 1958) belonged to Art Linkletter with *Kids Say the Darndest Things*. People were lightening up— as witnessed by the fact that Pat Boone's *Twixt Twelve and Twenty* sold 260,000 copies in 1959 (with the engaging sub-title of 'Pat Talks to Teenagers').

Certainly not lightening up were Eisenhower and Khrushchev. Undaunted, however, in November 1957, *Playboy* celebrated its fourth birthday, having given the world the likes of Marilyn Monroe, Jayne Mansfield, Brigitte Bardot, Gina

Lollobrigida, Sophia Loren, Anita Ekberg and June 'The Bosom' Wilkinson.

In Africa, things were a wee bit slower and not quite as vibrant. As to be expected. In March 1957, the Gold Coast was granted independence from Britain, grandiosely taking the name Ghana from the eponymous ancient empire. Kwame Nkrumah, still regarded as one of the founding fathers of African nationalism and 'pan-Africanism', became the country's first prime minister, though he wasn't to last too long, being overthrown in a 1966 coup while on a state visit to Vietnam, of all places. Ghana's fortunes declined significantly under Nkrumah's rule when the liberation hero nationalized industry, censored the media and gaoled anyone who complained, thus setting the benchmark for the plethora of forthcoming African leaders. Francophone Guinea followed soon after, with its new prime minister, Sékou Touré, opting for independence from France, thereby incurring de Gaulle's wrath, with France immediately severing all political and economic ties. Sékou Touré saw his new role as a job for life—literally—retaining power for twenty-seven years until his death in 1984. Guinea's fortunes declined significantly under Sékou Touré's rule.

In Algeria, the French were battling it out with the Algerian independence movement FLN in a civil war, with both sides guilty of the most horrible atrocities. On the equator, Kenyan independence loomed with Jomo Kenyatta's Mau Mau having committed unspeakable acts of savagery in the name of liberation, though Kenyatta was always crafty enough to distance himself from the Aberdare bandits. It would be more than fifty years before the facts emerged of Britain's equally heinous response to the insurgency. Across the continent on the western side the Belgians had only a couple of decades earlier stopped chopping off the hands of recalcitrant Congolese, a gruesome act widely emulated by RUF rebels half a century later in Sierra Leone.

Farther south on the subcontinent, Edward L. Ward-Petley of Bellville, Cape Town, won the 1957 South African open singles croquet championships as the Treason Trials entered their second year, with Nelson Mandela et al. on trial for their lives. Prime Minister J. G. Strydom, a barrel of laughs if ever there was, entrenched further the National Party's grip on power, steadily advancing its policy of apartheid which had seen its naissance in the Group Areas Act of 1950. Two years earlier, in 1955, Strydom's Minister of Native Affairs, Dutch-born and Bulawayo-educated Dr Hendrik Verwoerd, had achieved lasting infamy by callously evicting 60,000 non-whites from the vibrant Johannesburg township of Sophiatown, a multi-ethnic melting pot of jazz and Jozi-chic (it was here that the likes of Miriam Makeba, Hugh Masekela and Dolly Rathebe first performed). Bundled into police transports in the grey dawn, amid the dust and roar of the bulldozers, the *swarts* were unceremoniously dumped in the burgeoning black townships of Meadowlands and Soweto. To add insult to injury the 'Nats', in a moment of sublime crassness, renamed Sophiatown Triomf (Triumph). This of course paled into insignificance when, on 21 March 1960, some 7,000 black protestors marched on Sharpeville police station in the Vaal Triangle where jittery white policemen opened fire, leaving sixty-nine protestors dead on the dusty veld. But South Africa was still the world's largest gold producer, so such matters were neither here nor there, really.

Farther north again, in the territories across the Limpopo, Zambezi and Shire rivers, the Federation of Rhodesia and Nyasaland, a colonially inspired experiment comprising the colonies of the two Rhodesias—Southern and Northern—and Nyasaland, was seemingly flourishing, in spite of black nationalist mutterings from, primarily, Dr Hastings Kamuzu Banda, the leading nationalist of the time—in a well-crafted outburst he'd referred to the Federation as "stupid", which it probably was. However, Dr Banda, ignoring the pleas of his Nyasa co-nationalists to return home to foment unrest and spoil for independence, was skulking in the Gold Coast, having fled his medical practice in London under the cloud of an adulterous affair with his receptionist, Mrs French. He eventually returned to Nyasaland in 1958.

In the Rhodesias, two months earlier, on 12 September 1957, the Southern Rhodesia African National Congress (SRANC) was formed under Joshua Nkomo, a union of black labour and black political parties, the City Youth League and the more-or-less dormant African National Congress. It was not a coincidence that the date fell on Pioneers' Day—formerly Occupation Day but judiciously name-changed in 1929—as white settlers celebrated sixty-seven years of occupation. (In 1890, Rhodes's Pioneer Column had arrived in Fort Salisbury and raised the Union Flag in what was to become Cecil Square.) It was not long before SRANC meetings in rural areas were banned, and the SRANC was dissolved.

Under the leadership of the Federal prime minister, Sir Roy Welensky—a Lithuanian Jew, engine driver and pugilist of some repute—it was boom time in the Federation. Copper production on the Northern Rhodesian Copperbelt couldn't keep pace with world demand, Nyasaland flourished as tea became the colony's major export and Southern Rhodesia, the economic and political hub of the Federation because of its relatively sophisticated infrastructure, was quickly establishing itself as the world's foremost tobacco producer, ably abetted with significant exports of iron ore, coal, chrome, nickel, asbestos, gold, manganese, cotton, wheat, maize and beef.

With the boom immigrants poured into the Federation, mainly from a dreary postwar Britain and such Mediterranean countries as Portugal, Italy, Greece and Lebanon. These new settlers were an eclectic mix of educated middle-class families, barely literate working-class navvies, not a small sprinkling of remittance men, bounders and cads, a smattering of aristocrats and a host of ex-servicemen—all seeking their fortune and a better life. The latter were afforded special treatment, with many eligible, at a shilling an acre, for the virgin farms in Southern Rhodesia that were being allocated in newly proclaimed white farming areas such as the Horseshoe and Centenary 'blocks' in the north and northeast of the country. (The Centenary block was opened in 1953, so named after the centenary of Cecil John Rhodes's birth.) Fortunately for the whites, the Land Apportionment Act of 1930, amended in 1940, ensured there was more than enough prime land for the white settlers—fifty per cent in fact, or forty-five million acres, with the blacks taking up a third and the balance unallocated. (This act was redrafted in 1969 to become the Land Tenure Act when land allocation for blacks increased to near fifty per cent, or forty-four million acres, with the balance set aside for national parks.)

My parents were two such immigrants. They were married in the Anglican chapel in Addo, in the Sundays River Valley of the Eastern Cape in January 1956. Shortly thereafter, they migrated to Salisbury, the capital of the booming colony of Southern Rhodesia, where I was born a year and a bit later, on 13 November 1957.

What quirk of fate had decreed that I should have been born in such a place? In a country that promised so much but ultimately took everything? After all, my father, like thousands of postwar immigrants, could easily enough have settled in Australia, New Zealand or Canada. What a different story it would have been. Perhaps today he'd be sitting in a wicker chair on the lawn of a comfortable retirement village with a white picket fence in Adelaide or Toronto or Auckland with his great-grandchildren squealing happily about him.

Apart from being born in a Salisbury hospital, the Lady Chancellor Maternity Home, what defined me as a Rhodesian, if in fact that's what I was? Obviously, I had no choice in the matter, but if I had, would I have wanted to be a Rhodesian? Over the years, to establish some form of self-identity, I embarked on a quest to find out more about my ancestors, because, if I could establish who they were then surely it would tell me who I was? After all, without them I was nothing. Or so I thought at the time. So, untangling a complex network of lineage that spans generations and centuries, this is how I came to be born in that whites-only hospital on North Avenue in Salisbury.

I
Theme from *A Summer Place*—Percy Faith Orchestra, 1960–1962

My mother was born in April 1932 in Johannesburg as Betty Short. That's it. No middle name and Betty—not Elizabeth—just plain, economical Betty. At the time her parents were living at 'The Kraal' on Louis Botha Avenue in Orange Grove, Johannesburg. Her birth certificate records that her father, Clifton Max Short, was a 35-year-old European, a medical practitioner from the Transvaal and her mother, 29-year-old Hilda Elizabeth Edmunds, was from the Cape Province, also a European, but without any profession listed.

My father, Michael George Cocks, was also born in 1932, in Ealing, England. It's an unfortunate surname, especially for a schoolboy and I have no doubt that my father, and his father before him, endured the same name-calling and teasing as had I and, as I'm sure, my children faced. (My English cousin Andrew recently changed his name to Cox for the sake of his children.) It took me most of my high-school days to finally wear without shame my nickname of Chiloga (Shona for penis).

The name Cocks is something of an enigma, and other than being of Old English roots, I cannot state with any clarity as to its origin. Apparently, there are several variations, including Cockton, Cockspur, Cockcroft, Cockburn, Cockson, Cockrill, Cocklin, Cock and Cockhead, among many. Apart from Cock and Cockhead, I would have given anything to have been born with any one of these variants. Which, in fact, as it transpires, I could have. My great-great-great-grandfather, Edward Cock (1816–51) was the last of the line who died (in Wandsworth) without the plural form. His eldest son, James Cock, was born, also *sans* 's', in Broadstairs, Kent, in 1841. An itinerant carpenter, he and his wife Susan (née Eagles, a splendid surname) moved to London where my great-grandfather, Edward George Cock, also *sans* 's', was born in 1865. It was during the 1891 national census that James had the presence of mind to sharply inform the young census-taking official that the family name did indeed have an 's' on the end. So that was that—with the stroke of a quill, singular Cock became singular Cocks and the plural became the Cockses. Although, had James been slightly quicker off the mark, he could quite easily have changed us to Cook.

The Historical Research Centre goes on to speculate that the name might derive from the Old English *cocca*, meaning a hillock or a clump. It further speculates that my father's forbears might well have hailed from the villages of North Cockerington or South Cockerington in Lincolnshire. However, the explanation I prefer is that the name derives from the poultry slaughterers who once plied their trade in the Cockes Lane of medieval London.

It's not really important, though it was once.

My father's paternal grandfather, Edward George Cocks (1865–1935), was an Anglican vicar. Born in Suffolk, he lived and worked in Croydon before moving to Argentina, to a parish in Rosario, about 300 kilometres northwest of Buenos Aires. Here Jorge (as he was now commonly known) brought out his bride-to-be, Lottie Sarah French (perhaps related to Dr Banda's mistress), a farmer's daughter from England; they were married on 8 May 1895 by the Anglican Bishop of the Falklands, before relocating to a parish in Buenos Aires. The couple then returned to England where in 1922 Jorge (now back to George) became the vicar of Cornwood, a small parish on the southern edge of Dartmoor. He died in Plympton in 1933, with Lottie following him in 1938.

My paternal grandfather, Adrian Cocks, however, was different kettle of fish. He was an RAF pilot! Born in 1904, he joined the RAF in the mid-1920s and saw action on the North West Frontier in the Afridi and Red Shirt rebellions of 1930/1, flying Airco DH.9A biplane bombers. During the Second World War, he worked in radar and reached the rank of group captain; in early 1945 he was dispatched to Alamogordo, New Mexico, as the RAF attaché on the A-bomb project, the so-called Manhattan Project. The first atom bomb in the United States was successfully tested at the 'Trinity' site, Alamogordo, on 16 July 1945. Adrian was also something of an amateur thespian and had a small speaking part in the 1949 Gregory Peck movie, *12 O'Clock High*. My father's younger half-brother, Ian, remembers he and his siblings watching the movie at a drive-in in the New Mexico desert near Alamogordo but had all fallen asleep by the time their father uttered his immortal lines. My father, who spent a school holiday in Alamogordo, rarely mentioned his parents and their divorce. Of course, one doesn't talk about such things, but from what I can glean, during the upheaval of wartime Britain, there were whisperings of infidelity in the marriage. From my grandfather's disgruntlement, which I got a hint of many years later, I can only assume that it was my grandmother Esmé who'd been unfaithful. This was confirmed when I overheard my father telling my mother that when Esmé, he and Sally (his sister) were living in Swindon, there was a steady stream of strange men in and out the house. With all those good-looking American airmen in England at the time, with a plethora of chocolate and nylon stockings, I suppose it wasn't too difficult to sweep a pretty, young Scottish lass off her feet—even if she was married to a senior RAF officer.

★

I guess about my earliest memories. They are defined by the songs of the time, certain smells, like the smell of the roses in my mother's garden after a summer thunderstorm, and from faded photographs that perhaps do not evoke, but manufacture, a memory.

Percy Faith's 'Theme from *A Summer Place*', a Billboard Hot 100 hit in 1960—a blockbuster number 1 in fact—is my clearest earliest musical memory. I was three. There are no time-and-place associations with this song, other than a distant, misty recall of a time of hope, now melancholic and gone. 'Sukiyaki', a year or two later, takes me back to a winter's evening, sitting on my father's leather pouf by the fire, eating tomato soup and croutons. It is a happy, cozy memory: by the fireside on the pouf was my safe place. Edith Piaf's 1959 hit 'Milord' transposes me directly to languid picnic lunches on the Shavanoia River beyond the Ewanrigg Botanical Gardens northeast of the city of Salisbury, with hot summer days and the ever-present threat of crocodiles in the muddy waters. Bryan Hyland's 'Itsy Bitsy Teenie Weenie Yellow Polkadot Bikini' from the same year and his smash hit 'Sealed with a Kiss' of three years later are redolent of my father's Benson & Hedges cigarettes, my mother's cat's-eye sunglasses and her swirling chiffon skirts. They evoke Granma Teddy's stylish Stuttafords outfits, her veiled pillar-box hats and her chic Italian leather purse and handbag. It was a time of 'cool'.

I was only a few days' old when my parents bought the house at 4 Chiromo, Midvale Road, in the Salisbury suburb of Highlands. Having taken his passage on a Union Castle liner to Port Elizabeth in 1954 (paid for by Granma Teddy), my father started work with Lawson's, a South African firm of insurance brokers. In 1956, a position with Lawson's embryonic Salisbury office became available. It was offered to my father, and he took it, a decision he was to bemoan half a century later.

On 29 February 1959, 500 SRANC nationalists were arrested by the BSAP, the British South Africa Police (Southern Rhodesia's police force) and detained under one of three Acts—the Law and Order (Maintenance) Act, Emergency

Powers Act and Unlawful Organizations Act—that provided basis to restrict Africans, particularly those engaged in civil disorder, violence and intimidation in townships and rural tribal areas. It spelled the death knell of the SRANC, but other nationalist parties would soon sprout. At the same time Royal Rhodesian Air Force (RRAF) squadrons—English Electric Canberra bombers and de Havilland Vampire jet fighters—were deployed to Cyprus, Aden and Kuwait.

★

Midvale Road was almost Salisbury's easternmost thoroughfare, off the Enterprise Road, in what was known as the Highlands TMB or Town Management Board. To me it was frontier territory. The Enterprise Road was the main artery from Salisbury to the northeastern rural areas of Enterprise and Mtoko, and ultimately the Tete Province of Portuguese East Africa, the mighty Zambezi River and Nyasaland. Of course, I didn't know of these places, but I was vaguely aware that beyond Midvale Road lay a scary place where jungles teemed with lions and elephants and perhaps savage tribes who used small white boys in sacrificial rituals.

The Enterprise Road was tarred to the five-mile peg at the Midvale Road turnoff on the left at the bottom of the dip just before the *vlei*, or marsh, 200 yards after Lewisam Garage. The road started its journey in town, at the intersection of Jameson Avenue near the Park Lane Hotel and the Khaya Nyama (House of Meat) Steakhouse. On the two-mile peg, just after you passed David Livingstone Primary School and Salisbury Central Prison on your left and the Gremlin drive-in restaurant on your right, you came to Newlands shopping centre.

Newlands was our big shopping centre. Here my mother got her car serviced and filled up with petrol at T&D Motors, the Shell garage, owned by her friend Vernon Dickinson. Next to T&D was Jowett's Cycles, run by Mr Jowett, a dour man from the north of England but who sure knew his bikes. Part of Newlands was taken up by Murandy Square, backed up against the garage. Here my mother did her banking at the Standard Bank on the corner. It was also here that she began her charity collections for the Shearly Cripps Children's Homes and the SPCA, shaking a green money tin on Saturday mornings outside the bank. In later years she moved into town, with its more lucrative spots outside Barbours or Greatermans department stores.

Following the 'U' of the square inward was the florist, next to which was the Dairy Den, where for fifteen years we'd buy our ice-cream cones on Saturday mornings. A hairdressing salon and the Highlands post office made up the centre of the 'U'. Brain Brothers, the hardware shop owned by Derek Brain who played hockey and cricket with my father at Salisbury Sports Club, was in the one corner next to Supreme Butchery—although my mother bought her meat at Premier Butchery across the road. Then came the Enterprise Bookshop and a shoe shop where my mother bought my Clarks shoes.

Leaving Newlands, still heading northeast, past the Seventh-day Adventist church, you came to Governor's Lodge on the corner of Glenara Avenue. This was where Sir Humphrey Gibbs lived. He was the most important man in the country and my mother told me that he was a friend of the Queen's. It was a very smart red-brick building with a red-tiled roof, at least two storeys' high. A Union Jack fluttered from a pole on the roof. Behind the high, red-brick walls, if you peeked through the gates, you would see a driveway sweeping up over manicured lawns between avenues of palm trees to the neo-Grecian arches that marked the entrance to the residence. Quite often there was a Rolls-Royce parked in front. It was always exciting to drive past Governor's Lodge because the sentries at the gate were always very smart, standing rigidly to attention outside their pillar boxes with their .303 rifles at the slope. When it rained, they were allowed inside the sentry boxes. Mostly they were black BSAP police constables in khaki uniforms of tunic and shorts, khaki puttees and mirror-glimmering brown boots; as headgear they wore a royal-blue fez with gold tassles.

Across the Glenara intersection, on the left were the Highlands TMB offices where I was later to witness a spectacular accident while riding my bike to choir practice. A young black man was cycling furiously down the hill on the bike track towards me when a car came tearing out from the TMB offices to get onto the Enterprise Road and collided with the cyclist. With a sickening crunch the man was flipped some fifteen or twenty feet into the air and after several impressive somersaults, landed with an equally sickening thud in the storm drain, which fortunately was grass and not concrete. The driver—it could have been Mrs Gillespie for all I knew—was in a high state of agitation as she got out the car to attend to her victim. I realized I was a witness, the only witness, and knew instinctively this was not a good thing, so as unobtrusively as I could, I wheeled my bike up to St Mary's Anglican church, next door to the TMB, where I dashed inside, sacrilegiously I'm sure, to seek out Father Neahum. I was afraid of Father Neahum, convinced he didn't like me or children in general. He could stare right into your soul and I'm sure he knew all my secrets, almost as if he believed I was hosting the devil inside me and that if he stared hard enough, I'd be obliged to release whatever evil I was surely harbouring. I never submitted, even though his neck twitched uncontrollably as the curtain raiser to spewing forth fire and brimstone from out under his flowing white beard. I breathlessly told him what I had just witnessed and please could he come in case the cyclist was dead. I could see he was sceptical, but he nonetheless followed me out, cassock billowing, as we ran onto the cycle path. And … nothing. No car, no Mrs Gillespie, no cyclist, no wrecked bike, not even a pool of blood. The only sign of humanity was another African, a pedestrian wearing sunglasses, hands in pockets, whistling and sauntering down the cycle track with his penis hanging out, urinating hands-free, the jet of urine tracing a strangely hypnotic circular pattern in front of him. The priest's neck twitching intensified but no words came forth.

The TMB was where my mother paid the rates—the electricity, water and rubbish-removal accounts. Behind the TMB offices were the public swimming baths where Joy Morby taught me how to swim and Highlands Junior School.

From the church it was all gently downhill to Midvale Road. Just after the Presbyterian church on the right—a modernist, vaguely unattractive edifice (with probably the same architect as had been used for the Seventh-day Adventist church)—the one landmark of any import on this final two-mile stretch was the Catholic church and Nazareth House, an old-age home in the grounds of the church where all the old Catholics went to die. This was what my mother told me. My mother didn't like Catholics. She called them "bloody Catholics" and said they were "meddling do-gooders". Nazareth House was therefore to be avoided.

From the Catholic church, down the hill, the road was lined on the left by massive fir trees that appeared to touch the sky, blocking out the afternoon sun and casting deep shadows across the road. I always felt the hint of a chill when I passed. Across the road was the Lewisam shopping centre; hardly a shopping centre, it boasted a BP garage and a general store, but we didn't go there because my mother said "that's where the Africans do their shopping". It was an old-fashioned art-deco building with a lean-to verandah in front, supported by large, round pillars grimy from the handprints of milling picannins—derived from the Portuguese *pequeño*, meaning small—as they were known. On the verandah, always with a ragtag crowd about, were a few greasy pinball and mini-soccer machines and where for a decade Millie Small's 'My Boy Lollipop', the seven single irredeemably scratched, blasted out at passing motorists from a portable gramophone disguised as a valise. Behind the store, I was warned, was a shebeen where the *skollies** congregated to drink an illicit brew called *skokiaan* and smoke

---

*a petty criminal, a hoodlum (South African/ Afrikaans)

16

stuff called *dagga*, moonshine and marijuana respectively.

Over the road from the turnoff to Midvale Road was a large grassy *vlei* where horses grazed. This was the property of Lewisam Riding School, but I never did see anyone riding—just horses grazing, always. In the bottom of the *vlei* was a scraggly stand of poplar trees. My mother warned that this was a dangerous place where the skollies hid from the police during the day before sneaking out at night to the shebeen to make mischief.

If you drove past Midvale Road, you hit the gravel road almost immediately, which took you through the *vlei* and up a slight incline toward the frontier suburb of Chisipite. On the left was Wood's nursery, recently relocated from Steppes Road, where Mr Wood grew all sorts of plants and flowers. The Woods were friends of my parents, and their eldest son Dean was the same age as me. His sister Jo Jo was the same age as my sisters. On the right-hand side of the road were some very old houses, dark and dilapidated. I'm certain the double-storey one was haunted. Half a mile on, opposite Drew Road on the left, you turned right into Hindhead Avenue and the Chispite shopping centre. Like Lewisam though, it consisted only of a garage—Caltex—and a shop. But this shop we frequented because it was the Délice Bakery where my mother bought her bread—always hot and fresh, straight from the oven. The French rolls were as tall as me and I'd nibble at the ends before we got to the car. It was not only a bakery, more of what is known in Africa as a café, a place where you could also buy milk, sweets, cigarettes, ice-creams, cool drinks, penny-cools, crisps, Chelsea buns and doughnuts and other stuff like shoe polish, matches and candles. I didn't like the owners. They were Greek and regarded me like a thief. Although of course they gushed whenever my mother came into the shop. It was always, "How can we help you, Mrs Cocks? Nice fresha French bread?" but with the owner, Mr Somethingopoulis, looking at me sideways like I was about to steal something. He'd undoubtedly give me a sharp clip round the ear if my mother weren't there. He was a short, fat, dark man with a moustache who wore a stained, open, white shirt over a stained, white vest. His trousers were supported by cooking-oil-shiny braces. His wife was also short, fat and dark with a moustache, but she was kindlier, although she ruffled my hair and called me 'Sonny'. The whole family worked in the shop. The eldest son was called Spiro and he dressed like a Teddy boy—"one of those bloody duckies," my mother said—with a greasy Elvis hairstyle, tight denim jeans and an open-neck shirt that revealed a bush of thick, black chest hair and a barely visible medallion with an emblem that looked curiously like a vagina dangling on a fat-linked gold chain. He always had a Peter Stuyvesant cigarette hanging languidly from his puffy lips and drove a Lambretta scooter that was generally parked on the pavement. I touched it once and was immediately reprimanded by a voice from nowhere: "Hey! You boy! Donna touch that!" He was constantly winking at my mother which I somehow found distasteful. I loathed Spiro. His time would come …

The Enterprise Road was to play a pivotal role in my childhood: I would get to know every signpost, every mile peg, every culvert, every house, every church, even every tree along its way. It was the axis of my world.

Midvale Road, in many respects a microcosm of the Enterprise Road, *was* my world. It was a dirt road, about 400 yards long with a sharp left-hand bend at the end where the road then continued between avenues of bauhinia trees for a further hundred yards into a cul-de-sac. Our house was the second on the right of this dog's-leg bit. I could never fathom our address—4 Chiromo, Midvale Road—surmising perhaps (many years later) that Chiromo had once been a farm and our house was on lot 4 of the erstwhile farm. A few years later, when the TMB eventually got round to tarring Midvale Road, they decided, in their council wisdom, that our portion of the road, the cul-de-sac, was *not* in fact part of Midvale Road and that it warranted not lane but close status. In the blink of a town-planning eye our address changed to 4 George Talbot Close. The reaction from my parents was explosive.

"Who the bloody hell is George Talbot?" ranted my mother.

"Why weren't we, the residents, consulted about this?" pontificated my father.

"Like bloody Nazis; just do what they want. I'm going to go up to the TMB—RIGHT NOW—and give that Mrs Gillespie a piece of my mind."

"Steady on, Bets. Mrs Gillespie is just the secretary. You need to write to the councillor. There are channels, y'know."

"Bugger the channels. That councillor's a ghastly wet anyway."

A brouhaha in tandem also occurred a decade or so later when the PTC—the Posts and Telecommunication Corporation—decided, unilaterally (like UDI), to change our phone number from Salisbury 42663 to Salisbury 45175. I was particularly aggrieved as 42663 had become part of my DNA (an anachronistic analogy), perplexed that a number change could be instituted without an extra digit being added, which was the fashion and which even I could understand.

However, such matters were all in the future.

The Midvale Road of the early sixties boasted six houses, two on the long bit and four in the cul-de-sac. The first house as you turned left off the Enterprise Road, after the vacant plots on either side—gloomy properties lined with huge fir trees—was No. 4 on the right, half of which (like a semi) was owned by Jack and Beryl Dent, delightful Cockneys who had immigrated after the Second World War. Jack, a professional pianist, played dinner music—strictly songs from the thirties and forties of the 'White Cliffs of Dover' and 'A Nightingale Sang in Berkeley Square' ilk—at Tiffany's Restaurant in the Jameson Hotel situated at the western end of Jameson Avenue in town. On the rare occasion that my parents treated us to a dinner at Tiffany's, I was struck by the hushed tones of the diners, the unobtrusive padding of waiters' feet on the plush pile, the tinkle of silver cutlery and the tinkling of Jack's equally muted ivories. Jack and Beryl's house was partitioned by makeshift timber boarding up the passage, a bit like that brand-new Berlin Wall, random and indifferent. The reason for this—according to Meg Davies who lived over the road at No. 3—was that the house was haunted. My sisters and I well believed this, as one evening, while my parents were having sundowners with the Dents in their overgrown garden—the lawn had reverted to bush grass in keeping with the vast expanse of open veld on the other side of the sagging four-foot wire-mesh fence—we sneaked into the equally unkempt, dilapidated vacant portion of the house, a relic from the thirties with pseudo-Dutch gables, to flirt with the supernatural. Tiptoeing along the creaking wooden floorboards of the passage, we came to the division. Prying loose a plank, we slithered through into darkness, dank and musty, to be assaulted by a cloak of cold. That there was a presence was undoubted, as indicated by the hairs bristling on the back of my neck and an icy shiver down my spine. I turned to my sisters to suggest withdrawal, but they had already scuttled back into the realm of humanity, as did I, in haste.

In contrast to the Dents' house, across the road lived the Davies. Also a house from the thirties, almost identical in architectural style, it was immaculately maintained, with a circular driveway that swept up to the front verandah round a sunken rose garden worked into exquisite stonework with a Grecian birdbath in the middle. Meg and Forbes, a childless couple in their early fifties who bickered endlessly, were friends of my parents. Meg—known by my parents as 'the little woman' because of her less-than-five-foot height—was always perfectly groomed and had the most beautiful, piercing blue eyes I had ever seen, marred only by the voluminous amounts of pink G&Ts that she consumed (the blue eyes went red), starting at elevenish, or even tenish (she didn't work). With her cigarette holder habitually smeared with bright red lipstick, she chain-smoked—Consulate, a menthol cigarette—so she had that raspy, dowager voice and a husky, guttural laugh. In 1958, when Meg first heard that my parents had a son, she snapped at them: "Well, I hope he doesn't ride a bloody motorbike."

Forbes—a good sixteen inches taller than Meg, but deceptive because he stooped, probably to talk to her—worked for Lonrho and was every inch the Dickensian accountant, with leather elbow patches on his cardigans and spectacles on a string round his neck. He berated Meg continually, but she'd long since learned to carry off blasé-chic with aplomb.

"Oh, do shut up, Meg. We've all heard the story a thousand times of how you swam the Bosporus," Forbes would snigger dismissively. It was a queer snigger, punctuated with a series of mini-snorts.

With a conspiratorial smile, Meg winked at me and the twins. "Pay no attention to him; he's a miserable old so-and-so ... Forbes, oh do get me another drink."

"You've had quite enough, Meg."

"I'll decide that, Forbes, thank ... you ... very ... much. And while you're there [the drinks cabinet was incorporated into a mammoth Grundig gramophone], you can switch Nat ... bloody ... King ... bloody ... Cole ... off."

"Language, Meg. The children!" Forbes was a Nat King Cole groupie and, invariably, either 'Those Lazy, Hazy, Crazy Days of Summer'—those days of soda and pretzels and beer, redolent of happy all-American family summers benignly overseen by Ike—or his all-time favourite, 'Rambling Rose', was on the turntable.

We spent much time at the Davies's house because a) they had a television (which they kindly lent us when they took their annual six weeks' leave at Christmas, a very exciting period for the family), b) they had a swimming pool and c) both Forbes and my father were avid golf fans and every Sunday evening—too late to swim—we were obliged to witness Arnold Palmer's, Gary Player's and Jack Nicklaus's every drive, every iron and every putt on the PGA tour, while Meg and my mother sat yakking and drinking in the sitting room. No amount of playing with Bedlam the Bedlington terrier—with his severe paucity of fur—averted the harrowing experience.

Into the cul-de-sac lived the Whites in the first house on the right, our eastern neighbours. The property opposite was vacant, save—bizarrely—a tennis court, crumbling and overgrown with shoulder-high weeds, the net having long since vanished into the bush where the black people came from, to be used as a fishing net. The Whites, of similar age to my parents, had two daughters, Shona and Sally-Anne. Shona, a pretty, curly-haired imp with a smattering of freckles across her perky nose, was the same age as me and I was deeply in love with her. Sally-Anne was my sisters' age and, in a curious daily ritual, played hostess to my sister Caroline who crawled through the straggly thatching-grass fence that separated the properties—every morning at 7 o'clock on the dot—to an awaiting Sally-Anne who presented her with an ice-cold bottle of Coca-Cola at the kitchen door. Both the Whites—Graham and Jan—and my parents were quite aware of this sacramental routine and clearly condoned it. Sarah and I, on the other hand, remained wholly nonplussed: we were only allowed one Coke a week, on a Saturday lunchtime—which Caroline was also entitled to—and failed to come to terms with the injustice of it all. It had crossed our minds that we should perhaps accompany Caroline one morning and see if we didn't get given a Coke too, but Caroline, understandably not wanting to jeopardize her daily boon, was adamant that this was her personal domain and would not hear of it, so we deferentially, and grudgingly, backed off.

Politically, stuff had been happening, which would account for my father's Police Reserve accoutrements. The National Democratic Party (NDP) had been formed, replacing the banned SRANC, with Michael Mawema as president. The Monckton Commission, or more properly, the Advisory Commission for the Review of the Constitution of the Federation of Rhodesia and Nyasaland, was set up by the British government under the chairmanship of Walter Monckton, 1st Viscount Monckton of Brenchley, to investigate and make proposals for the future of the Federation of Rhodesia and Nyasaland: simply, it recommended eventual majority rule for the three Federation states. British Prime Minister Harold MacMillan made his 'wind of change' speech in the South African Parliament in Cape Town, which went down like a lead balloon with the white parliamentarians. South Africa withdrew from the Commonwealth not long after that.

1961 was a busy year. The London Constitutional Conference was convened where a new constitution was enacted that widened the franchise to include African representation. This was rejected by the NDP. The Congo Border crisis erupted and Southern Rhodesia sent troops. In December, the NDP was banned and instantly replaced by the Zimbabwe African People's Union (ZAPU) under Joshua Nkomo, Herbert Chitepo and Ndabaningi Sithole.

1962 was equally busy with the white anti-Federation Dominion Party reconstituted as the Rhodesian Front, winning the white general election later in the year. Nyasaland seceded from the Federation (to become Malawi in 1965), followed by the first arrests of armed black nationalists in Southern Rhodesia, which in turn saw ZAPU banned.

★

One evening the Whites came over to break the devastating news that they were leaving.

"I've got a good job lined up in Jo'burg, Mike. Top insurance brokers. I'd be a fool to turn it down," announced Graham, a shorter version of Roger Moore but without the mole.

"So, when are you leaving?" asked my mother, an ever-so-muted quiver in her voice; she was very fond of the Whites and had something of a soft spot for Graham, which my father did go on about.

"End of the month," replied Jan, peering over her black-rimmed cat's-eye spectacles. "We've already booked the removals people."

"Oh dear, this is sad news," said my mother with the hint of a tear in her eye. "What a dreadful bore."

"We'll see them often enough, Bets," my father consoled with some sincerity. "It's not like we never go to Jo'burg."

I felt what could only equate to an anxiety attack coming on: Shona was leaving! My beloved Shona! The hole in the pit of my stomach was tangible and I wanted to be sick.

"CAROLINE!" my father bellowed above the sudden atomic blast of Helen Shapiro's 'Walkin' Back to Happiness' on the wireless: Caroline had a penchant for turning up the volume—full—whenever she happened to pass the gramophone, which was frequently. "TURN THAT BLOODY RACKET OFF!"

Other than Caroline's stifled giggle, there was instant silence before Graham continued: "Y'know, we've been thinking of leaving for some time now … ever since all this trouble in the townships. I mean, what kind of life is it, Mike, with all this Police Reserve stuff every other night?"

Graham was referring to the paramilitary duties that he and my father undertook as BSAP reservists. With reverential awe, I regularly inspected my father's police uniform and paraphernalia: a navy-blue set of overalls, a white NATO-type helmet with POLICE RESERVE stencilled on in navy blue in front, a very long truncheon with a leather thong on the handle and a whistle attached to a plaited lanyard. (The truncheon lived under my father's side of the bed and the whistle in the drawer of his bedside table alongside several rubberized balloons, uninflated and knotted at the one end to retain an unidentifiable yellowy-white, gooey substance. Equally distasteful was the glass of water on top of his bedside table which acted as a spittoon for the nicotine-induced phlegm that he expectorated over the course of several nights.) I had no idea whether he was on the front line facing off hordes of rioters in the black townships of Harari and Highfields armed only with a truncheon and a whistle, though perhaps—if the pictures in the newspaper were anything to go by—German shepherds and teargas canisters were quite possibly issued in situ.

"A couple of nights a week is hardly onerous, Graham," quipped my father. "It's not like we're on the front line in the townships ... a gentle stroll round the local neighbourhood looking for skollies is about it."

"Still ... it's the thin end of the wedge," Graham justified, unwisely, as does everyone who emigrates. "I reckon this could be a second Congo." He was referring to the Congolese independence of 1960 and the ensuing massacres, mutilations and mass rapes of Belgian colonists—nuns and priests were not exempt—with traumatized, bewildered survivors being airlifted out by RRAF DC-3s to a makeshift refugee camp in the Salisbury showground.

My mother, despite her feelings for Graham, took admirable exception. "We still have to live here, Graham ... and anyway, things aren't so rosy in South Africa what with those bloody Nats. Just look at Sharpeville."

"At least Verwoerd and the Nationalists have things firmly under control. South Africa's far too powerful to go the way of the rest of Africa."

My mother *humphed* and my father looked sheepish; he didn't like confrontation. The discussion was at an end and the Whites rose to leave. I took a last, wistful look at Shona and retired to my bedroom where I closed the door and wept.

So that was the end of the Whites.

The house was then purchased by a Mrs Roos, a bantamesque, full-breasted, middle-aged woman—either divorced or widowed, we never established which—who drove a modified Austin Metropolitan, with the back part of the cab converted into a pickup-truck-type arrangement with a canvas covering. It always struck me that if Big Ears ever graduated from a bike this would be the perfect car for him. With Mrs Roos came her splenetic, bloodshot-eyed gardener, a scary Manyika tribesman called James, who moved into the servants' quarters—a one-roomed 'house', or *khaya*—positioned on our common boundary down toward the river. James would prove to be a worthy opponent in the years ahead.

Opposite our entrance, the penultimate property in the cul-de-sac, bar ours, accommodated a pleasant young couple called the Bachelors—he wore his hair in a Beatles mop and drove a beaten-up VW Beetle—but their rambling, ramshackle house, more of a cottage really, was set among a dark, dank wood where a straggly kikuyu lawn grew knee-height, its runners clawing ineffectually at an insipid sun under a canopy of oaks and mulberry trees, the latter shedding a squishy, purple carpet underfoot. I was afraid to visit and only did so under sufferance when my mother had cause to pop over.

"Now, wipe your feet, Christopher," she would admonish when we got home. "I do wish they'd do something with all those frightful mulberries; the stains are such a bloody nuisance."

I didn't know who lived in the house at the end of the road, the one between a pair of imposing white gateposts with coach-lanterns on top. I had never visited, having only ever caught the briefest of glimpses of a very smart house at the culmination of a long, brick-paved driveway that wound its way between perfectly trimmed shrubs and an immaculately maintained lawn. It was a house that exuded affluence. In a few years' time, the Saunders—North Country immigrants—would become our western neighbours when they moved in, but for now it was out of bounds. Norman Saunders—a dentist—was well to do.

Our property, or garden—referred to as a 'yard' by the common people, the navvies, south of the railway line—was set on two and a half acres that sloped gently down to the Umwindsi River. The name Umwindsi, a white-settler attempt to deal with the tricky conjoined consonants of the Shona language,* was later and more correctly named the Mubvinzi and constituted our northern boundary. It was a narrow piece of land, with the three-and-a half-bedroomed house—the half-bedroom being more of a large broom cupboard where Granma Teddy stayed when she came to visit from South Africa—positioned on the upper slope, protected from winter frost and summer flood, but with only ten yards freeboard on the western boundary and some twenty on the eastern. It was likely that the house was built sometime in the forties and equally likely that the architect had misdirected visions of art-deco grandeur. With white imitation-stucco walls, an unpainted asbestos-sheeting roof and navy-blue trimmings— the window frames, gutters and fascia boards—it was, nonetheless, a functional house that only leaked in the dining room, formerly the verandah, because the roof sloped the wrong way: inward instead of outward. In due course my father would paint all the trimmings yellow which would brighten the entire aspect and upgrade the house from blue almost-art deco to yellow almost-art deco.

The one notable interior feature was the parquet flooring, shined to a dull buff by George the gardener, with residual globs of white polish between the blocks, some of which had come adrift of the tacky bitumen adhesive with a resultant array of splinters. Another feature was the split-level sitting room— referred to as a 'lounge' by the common people—which boasted a slate-lined

---

*more properly chiShona

fireplace and the rosewood gramophone. The two steps where the levels split—caused not by architectural genius but by topographical necessity—proved handy for additional seating when my parents hosted their dinner parties.

At the one end of the steps, like a solid full stop, was the built-in drinks cupboard-cum-bookshelf-cum-telephone table. Things tended to get quite busy there, especially if someone was on the phone and someone else wanted a drink. Above the telephone was a random picture, always askew, of Talleyrand-Périgord, Prince of Benevuntum,* cockeye because it had been hung a few inches too low and every time someone picked up the phone, the handpiece knocked the picture out of kilter (my mother never was one for that feng shui malarkey). The book collection consisted of the likes of *Everybody's Pepys*, Neville Shute's *On the Beach* and *A Town Like Alice*, Alan Paton's *Cry the Beloved Country*, several Dickenses such as *Martin Chuzzlewit*, *Oliver Twist*, *Hard Times* and *A Tale of Two Cities*, *The Virginians* by Thackeray, *Les Feuilles d'Automne* by Victor Hugo, *The Cruel Sea* and *The Tribe That Lost Its Head* by Nicholas Monsarrat, *The Robe* by Lloyd C. Douglas, *How Green Was My Valley* by Richard Llewellyn and of course Paul Gallico's *The Snow Goose: A Story of Dunkirk*. I do believe that in the eighteen years that I shared the house with the books, that I was the only one to ever lay a hand on them. One gem I later discovered as a teenager was *The Atonement of Ashley Morden* by Fred Bosworth which still rates in my Top 10.

The bulk of the furniture—all courtesy of Granma Teddy—comprised a once-primrose settee (it's not a sofa or a couch, heavens!), two matching armchairs, an antique rocking chair (stinkwood), an antique chest of drawers (Georgian, walnut), an antique foldout card table with the original felt and an inlaid chess board (Queen Anne, rosewood), an antique coffee table (stinkwood again), two Persian rugs, an excruciatingly beautiful antique kist with ornate brasswork that Granma Teddy had inveigled from the Sultan of Zanzibar, and the leather pouf. Not supplied by Granma Teddy but by the Treasure Trove—the pawn shop in town on the corner of Second Street and Baker Avenue opposite Cecil Square—was a brace of dowdy stained-pine side tables and the standard lamp with the frilly shade, the fabric partially blackened from an overzealous light bulb.

★

I was sitting on my bed, the strains of Bert Kaempfert's 'Swinging Safari' filtering through from the transistor radio that my mother had with her in the

---

*published by T. Kinnersley, 1 May 1815.

kitchen. It was a happy tune—"very gay" as Granma Teddy would say—that supposedly, from the white man's vantage point at any rate, captured the essence of Africa. However, the fledgling black nationalists might view it as yet another painful, colonial imposition, this one by a Dutch big-band conductor flailing his baton thousands of miles away across the seas, Still, I found myself abstractedly humming along as I waited.

"I'll be there in a minute, Christopher," my mother shouted. "I'm nearly finished."

She had just finished patching up one of the Tessa's victims—the dog, a boxer, Tessa would occasionally extract a chunk of flesh from an innocent passerby on Midvale Road—and was now busy preparing the staff's month-end ration packs that supplemented their wages. ("We try not to call them servants," she always said.) It was apparently common practice, "otherwise," as my mother's cousin Di Edmunds would say phlegmatically, "if you don't give them food, they'd just piss their wages against the wall."

We had three black servants: Theresa, a wholesome young woman with a lovely, kind face under a colourful *doek*, a headscarf, who doubled as the cook and the nanny; George who split his duties between the garden and the house— "too clever for his own good, that one; better watch him," was Di's assessment— and Peter, a dedicated gardener who was hired to help my mother develop her rose garden which was fast turning into a lucrative little business and whom Di called "the local kraal idiot" because he was a simple chap. All three were Shonas—despite the popular fashion to employ Nyasa 'boys' who supposedly had an astonishing work ethic when compared to our local slovens—and all three came from the Mtoko district, undoubtedly from the same clan as is the nature of job-market nepotism in Africa.

Each monthly ration pack consisted of a 20-lb bag of *mielie* meal, or maize meal, to make their staple diet, the stodgy *sadza*, 5 lb of brown sugar, 5 lb of brisket, two tins of pilchards in tomato sauce, a 1-lb packet of Tanganda tea, 2 lb of powdered milk, two bars of Lifebuoy soap and a slab of blue soap for laundry.

Still I waited. I heard the general hubbub of chatter from the kitchen above the captivating voice of Françoise Hardy singing 'Tous les Garçons et les Filles'. I knew it was French, something foreign, which surely augmented her haunting allure. Her photo was on a record cover at the White's house, the most beautiful creature I had ever seen and I craved more than anything in the world that my parents might buy the record, but they never did: it was too avant-garde for their taste, too Beatnik for their LP collection that stretched to *Irma la Douce*, *My Fair Lady*, *South Pacific*, *West Side Story*, *The Boyfriend*, *Kismet*, Acker Bilk's

Stranger on the Shore, Noël Coward at Las Vegas, Never on a Sunday starring the sultry Melina Mercouri and Jules Dasin, and Julius Katchen reciting Rachmaninoff's Piano Concerto No. 2. They had one 7 single: Bing Crosby's 1956 'Heat Wave' written by Irving Berlin; the flip side was 'Mountain Greenery'. My love affair with Françoise Hardy would endure for more than a generation.

I don't think it was, but my bedroom was simple and austere. The bed on which I was sitting—another acquisition from the Treasure Trove—was an evil, steel-framed tank-trap, ready to cut and bruise small shins clambering aboard. The springs, looped hexagonally across the frame and untightened since the Blitz, supported a lumpy, three-inch-thick coir mattress that harboured needle-sharp fibres ready to escape at night through the ticking to prick me unmercifully. In years to come the bed would be used by my sisters and me as a landing zone as we launched ourselves like lemmings from the top of the semi-built-in cupboard, causing not a few broken springs and cracked skulls, with the beleaguered bed assuming the appearance of a hammock. The pillow, equally hideous, was a block of hard industrial foam rubber that seemed to have been left in the sun too long. My mother tried to convince Granma Teddy that it was of an ergonomic design—though the phrase was yet to be invented—that "it's very good for one's neck" but Granma Teddy would have none of it: "Don't talk nonsense, Bets. It's a cheap offcut from the Dunlop factory. Goodness! The poor child!"

My bedside table was in fact two wooden gin cases nailed together—probably scrounged from Meg Davies—to create the allusion of an open-sided cupboard. GILBEY'S was still vaguely discernible through the poorly applied white enamel paint. (Following on with the alcoholic theme, the household cat, a friendly black female with a white star on her forehead, was called Giah, Haig spelled backward.) My bedside lampstand was a Vat 69 whisky bottle, most certainly a two-and-six bargain from the Treasure Trove. My carpet, apparently once Persian, was threadbare and had the texture of a cricket mat.

There were four small pictures on the wall, the first two, a matching pair, by courtesy of His Majesty the King: a Drum Major of the Royal Marines, 1829, and a Bugler of the 3rd Foot Guards, 1830, framed by J. Vaughan of 61 Rissik Street, Johannesburg. The third picture was a dreary old print of Louis XVIII landing at Calais and the fourth an even gloomier print of Lord Exeter's fleet bombarding the city of Algiers. Other than a porcelain washbasin in the corner of the room, a curious feature, this was the sum of my furnishings, until 1965 when a desk would be procured from the Treasure Trove so that I could do my prep, aka homework.

I heard the kitchen door slamming.

"DON'T SLAM THE BLOODY DOOR!" yelled my mother at the departing staff as they bustled off to their respective *khayas*—a single room for Theresa and a larger room that George and Peter shared—to make inroads into their rations.

She appeared at my door momentarily, clutching Big Ted, looking flustered and with a cigarette dangling from her lips. I watched mesmerized at the tail of untapped ash about to drop onto the carpet. "There! That's done. Thank god."

I had been aware for some time that the Big Ted presentation was imminent as I'd happened to overhear my mother and Granma Teddy talking about it.

"Dear me, Bets; it's just a teddy bear. What good is it doing stashed away in your cupboard stinking of mothballs?"

"It's *my* teddy bear, mama. I've had Big Ted since I was three … he's very special to me," my mother retorted with a hint of petulance.

"Well, Christopher is almost five and all he's got is Charlie. It's high time he had another toy."

"I'll give it to him when he's six. He's too young." My mother was almost whining.

"You most certainly will not, Bets! You will give Big Ted to him right now, d'you hear? I've never heard such nonsense. Just plain, damned selfish!"

So that was that. Of course, I'd always known about Big Ted; I'd glimpsed him often enough in my mother's cupboard sitting jammed into the top shelf—the one above the corsets and the two-ways—with a wistful, thousand-yard stare and a red bandana round his neck.

The handover ceremony was brief. My mother sat next to me on the bed with Big Ted on her lap.

"Christopher. This is Big Ted. I want you to understand that he's very special to me. I've had him since, umm … nineteen … thirty … five. If you promise to look after him, you can have him. Do … you … understand?"

I nodded vigorously, reverentially.

"Right … there you go." She got up to leave. "I've got to go to the shops. These bloody servants are eating us out of hearth and home."

I introduced Big Ted to Charlie prostrate on the Dunlop chunk and decided that Big Ted needed to view the outside world, starting with the garden.

★

As was the custom of the times, most white Rhodesian families took an annual four-week holiday, or longer. Black people 'went home', back to the reserves in the bush to see their families, plant their *mielies*, tend their cattle and sit under a tree and drink traditional beer. For whites a seaside holiday was *de rigeur*, normally in Beira on the central coast of Portuguese East Africa—PEA or Mozambique—where, in their thousands, they would gorge themselves on *camarão, cervejas, vinho* and *galinha piri-piri*: respectively cheap prawns, 2M and Manica beer, Lagosta Vinho Verde and Graça, and chicken piri-piri, generally at Johnny's Place, Restaurante Pic-Nic or Clube Náutico. (A similar scenario played itself out in Lourenço Marques, the capital city at the southern tip of the country, with the inundation of South African tourists, unkindly dubbed 'Banana Boers' by the locals because of their proclivity for the ubiquitously cheap bananas, cheap cashew nuts and cheap black *putas*.*) I'd always wanted to go to Beira because many of my friends holidayed there and, more importantly, it was only a six-hour drive from Salisbury.

"Revolting bloody place," my mother would state. "Filthy sea, filthy town and full of Rhodesian oiks."

"A bit like Butlin's," my father would add as an addendum that apparently said it all.

So we never went, instead visiting Granma Teddy in the Eastern Cape, a good three-day drive, where she'd rent a holiday house: somewhere like 'Schoenies', or Schoenmakerskop, near Port Elizabeth, a quaint row of old fishing cottages overlooking a rocky, windswept coastline and the wreck of the *Sacramento*—it was here a few years later, while poking around in the sandy backyard of our holiday cottage that I stumbled upon the partially interred skeleton of what had obviously been the household tabby, which I exhumed, confirmed it was in fact a cat from the anatomical reference book on pets that I took out from the Queen Victoria Library on my return to Salisbury, identified and named all the bones, reconstructed the skeleton on a piece of plywood and submitted it as a school science project for which I was awarded a Highly Commended—or a more sedate beach house in Summerstrand on Port Elizabeth's Marine Parade.

For our 1962 annual holiday my parents decided that we'd embrace Africa and spend the month at a Monkey Bay resort on the shores of tropical Lake Nyasa in Nyasaland. 'Resort' conjures up images of Club Med; however, Monkey Bay in 1962 was anything but, being whimsically African, with thatched *bashas*— probably called *cabanas* today—lining the water's edge on pristine beaches kissed by the gentle lapping of waves, an ideal spot for children. This was before the lake was renamed Lake Malawi on the country's independence from Britain in

---

*whores (Portuguese)

1965—when Dr Banda returned, presumably *sans* Mrs French—and before overfishing depleted the once-abundant stocks of chambo, a type of bream that is delicious, and before bilharzia became a pervasive shoreline menace.

The journey from Salisbury to Blantyre and on north up the lake to Monkey Bay was an immense undertaking—on wholly dirt roads—as the family piled into my father's Austin Cambridge, with my sisters and I squabbling in the back before we'd even come to the Enterprise Road. In short time we passed through the white farmlands of Enterprise, with monstrous crops of tobacco and maize lining the road like an emerald-green carpet as level and precise as a billiard table that stretched from horizon to horizon. Then on through the African rural areas, the traditional native homelands—to be known as Tribal Trust Lands as of 1965—of Mrewa and Mtoko, the eponymous settlements languid, dusty hamlets with a sprinkling of general dealer's stores, a petrol station or two, dusty picannins playing with old car tyres and bony, flea-infested, yellow-eyed mongrels snapping angrily at lazy blue flies in the shade of rusted signboards advertising Coca-Cola, Five Roses tea, Lux soap and Peter Stuyvesant cigarettes with the tagline 'The international passport to smoking pleasure' across the faded image of attractive young white jet-setters living it up in Acapulco somehow indecorous.

Then on through Mtoko to Nyamapanda on the PEA border, with encroaching, jungle-like bush attempting to devour the road, in places throttling it with a canopy that blocked out the sun. Occasional clearings revealed dishevelled crops of maize, sorghum and sunflowers among the weeds, with be-*doeked* tribeswomen in frowzy, colourless dresses, hems hanging loosely below their knees, leaning casually on their *badzas*—their hoes—in the baking heat and observing with indifferent interest the passing Austin Cambridge and its *murungu* passengers. Barefoot children, their clothes tattered, came rushing onto the verges, grinning big white-teeth smiles, squealing, cartwheeling, laughing and calling out in time-honoured African fashion, "*Murungu! Murungu!* Sweets … *dinoda* sweets!"* Wondering distractedly whether these children might be related to Theresa, George or Peter, I tossed a handful of sweets—grabbed hastily from a communal bag on the back seat that my mother kept topping up in a vain attempt to shut us up—out the window and watched through the back as the children scrabbled delightedly in the dust.

Nyamapanda, the border and far-flung outpost of Empire, housed the Department of Customs and Immigration, with its smart white officialdom

---

*"White man! White man! Sweets … give me sweets!"

in white naval-type uniforms, a police station and the Native Commissioner's office. Seamlessly clearing the Rhodesian side by 12.05 p.m., we discovered that the Portuguese side, the settlement of Cochemane, closed entirely between midday and 3 p.m. for the traditional siesta. Nerves frayed, voices whined and irritated parents smoked indignantly while we waited for the servants of the Império Português (Empire), also known as the Ultramar Português (Overseas), to return to their posts.

Eventually descending into the Zambezi valley along what was to become known as the Tete Corridor during the not-so-far-off (read imminent) Portuguese–Frelimo bush war, we were assaulted by a wall of scorching heat, something like 125° Fahrenheit in the shade of a baobab which would become 50° Centigrade when we converted from imperial to decimal some years later. The heat and humidity cloyed in our throats and by the time we reached Tete on the Zambezi River, once a Swahili trading post, now the last Portuguese town upstream and the navigable limit, our stocks of cool drinks and water, as hot as they were, were almost exhausted. The impressive one-kilometre-long Tete suspension bridge had yet to be built—it was completed in 1973 to link Rhodesia and the southern Tete Province with Malawi—so travellers were obliged to make use of a rickety ferry that had, that blistering summer afternoon, broken down.

So began a three-hour ordeal. Without a breath of wind and a tree in sight at the ferry station down by the river—the word station is inappropriate: it was the riverbank—the heat intensified inexorably as the afternoon progressed. My father had tuned the car radio in to LM Radio broadcasting from Lourenço Marques—a trendy, pop-music-only radio station with trendy English-speaking disc jockeys, mainly South Africans—but no amount of The Tornados, Elvis Presley, Frank Ifield or The Four Seasons could relieve the torture, exacerbated by preposterous swarms of mosquitoes and mopane flies, extremely irritating midges that attack like miniscule vampires any exposed moisture—principally eyes, nose and mouth—on a human body. By the time the ferry was mended, the thrill and excitement of the river-crossing had long since dissipated as the Austin Cambridge disembarked and made its weary way up the escarpment and into the relatively cooler climes of Blantyre, Nyasaland, in darkness.

The holiday was idyllic with lazy, sultry days spent building sandcastles on the beach and endless swimming in the gentle waters of the lake, to the holiday soundtrack of 'Rhythm of the Rain' by The Cascades (Listen to the rhythm of the falling rain ... ahh ... that one). My parents appeared to relax and there was an unusually overt closeness between them, not that they held hands or anything quite so giddy, but it pleased me, warmly so, to see it.

"Very friendly these natives, aren't they, Mike?" my mother suggested, sipping on some sort of long-glassed cocktail with Angostura bitters lurking at the bottom.

"Not surprised. They all seem to smoke that *dagga*."

"Really? Cannabis? I thought it was illegal."

"It is, but it doesn't seem to deter them," replied my father, wiping beer froth from his mouth. "In fact, Nyasaland's apparently renowned for the stuff. They call it *chamba* here."

"Isn't that the fish?"

"No, Bets, that's chambo."

There was a moment's silence as my mother's straw made slurping noises plumbing the Angostura depths. "No wonder! I asked a chap on the beach yesterday—y'know, those chaps who sell those gorgeous fabric prints— whether he had any chamba. He said he did indeed and pulled out this funny-looking *mielie* cob from his basket. Wanted half a crown for it. Silly man, I told him, 'That's not fish!'"

My father smiled, genuinely amused. "Well, lunchtime and then a bit of a lie-down."

"I wonder if they'll have chambo on the menu today," mused my mother. "It *is* rather good."

"Hope they've DDT'd the hut. Damned mosquitoes are a menace. The manager said they were spraying today."

★

The garden tour was an enormous success, the solitude—if you didn't count Big Ted, Pluto (who had replaced the flesh-eating Tessa who vanished one day, never to be seen again) and the new dog, Sam, a wire-haired mongrel of terrier descent and a recent acquisition from the SPCA which cost my father a £2 donation—blissful. Lunch over, my father had gone back to work, the twins were having their afternoon nap and my mother was having her lie-down, reading the newspaper with Giah curled up next to her on the bed. First stop was 'the boys' *khaya*' which backed up onto the road at the top of the property in front of a rampant jasmine creeper clambering across a declining trellis that provided a modicum of privacy from the public eye but no security: not that security was too much of an issue, the one common crime being an occasional 'fisherman' dangling a stick with a string and a hook through an open window at night and seeing what household item he might acquire.

Peter and George were squatting on the swept-clean, hard, bare earth outside their door over a modest fire, cooking their ration meat in a battered aluminium pot. I squatted down beside them, eying the cobs of maize that had been thrown directly onto the coals, the kernels blackened, crunchy and delicious, at the same time attempting to keep Pluto and Sam a respectable distance from the stewing brisket.

Peter laughed, an expansive guffaw that emanated from deep within his belly. He laughed easily, always with a smile beaming across his face. "You want some mielies, *mustah*?"

"Yes please, Peter," I nodded, indefinably uncomfortable with the form of address. My father was also addressed as 'master', pronounced *mustah* (white farmers were addressed as *baas*, as in 'boss'), my mother as 'madam', pronounced *medem* and my sisters as 'miss', pronounced *missi*.

Peter hooked a hot cob from the embers with a piece of wire and placed it on an enamel plate to cool. Still a young man, he was prematurely bald. His pate, which merged effortlessly into his forehead, gleamed black in the sun as if it has been shined to a high gloss with Nugget shoe polish, which I think it might. He spoke with what sounded like a speech impediment, but I suspect it was the relic of a stutter combined with his poor grasp of English. George, who spoke fluent English, was not as welcoming, almost sullen as he stared fixedly into the fire without a word. His eyes were bloodshot again, perhaps from the smoke of the fire.

The maize cob had cooled. Peter took a knife and sliced off the kernels. Grabbing a handful, I took my leave, as George looked up, unsmiling, inscrutable. The sky was clouding over, the pressure rising palpably and building up for the regular afternoon thunderstorm. A large shadow swept by a vast unseen hand crossed the top lawn under the jacaranda tree as the sun disappeared momentarily from view.

Down the slope from the top lawn below where the cars were parked, was another lawn adjacent to the new patio that my father and Peter had built to replace the old verandah, now the dining room. The patio, with its slasto floor, Roman-pillar pergola, grapevines and wrought-iron furniture, was where my parents—during clement weather—took their sundowners and entertained their friends. In front of the house looking north to the river was another lawn partially bordered by a three-foot brick wall covered with tickey creeper, a bed of cannas and agapanthus and a magnificent Pride of India as a full stop.

On the other side of the wall were my mother's roses which took up a good half an acre that effectively bisected the property in an explosion of colour. My mother had contracts to supply three hotels in town: Meikle's, The Ambassador and The Hotel Elizabeth. In time I would become familiar with every bush and every variety: Queen Elizabeth, Montezuma, King's Ransom, Super Star, Peace, Iceberg and many more.

Below the rose garden—other than an impressive stand of bamboo that seemed as tall as a skyscraper and which my father harvested for poles for his compost-heap project—stubbly, untamed bush claimed the final acre down to the Umwindsi. The soil here was jet-black clay, as hard as concrete in winter and in summer a bog that sucked you in up to your knees. Lined with poplars and willows—as well as old paint tins, car tyres, rusted bicycle frames, bottles and other such detritus—the river here, barely several paces across, was only a few hundred yards downstream from its source, but it could nevertheless come down in a raging deluge quite capable of sweeping away a child, as African rivers tend to do every summer. Mingling among the willows and poplars were outbreaks of Lantana camara, an invasive, noxious weed with striking yellow and amber flowers that is toxic to livestock, particularly cattle. My parents' farming friends regularly pointed this out—"It's illegal, y'know, Mike. Better get it taken out or you'll have the vet department down your neck"—even though the nearest cow was no closer than several miles away. Nevertheless, the fact that my father was breaking the law—with apparent criminal intent—was alarming.

Across the river, virgin bush climbed gently up the valley for a mile or so until it reached Steppes Road, Drew Road and the burgeoning suburb of Colne Valley. Periodically, Granma Teddy took me and my sisters for walks in the veld, along the web of tracks—some human, some game—that crisscrossed the valley, regaling us with stories of how lions would lie in wait behind the large boulders to leap onto unsuspecting passersby and gobble them up. We'd believe her and huddle into the folds of her pleated skirt.

2
The End of the World—Skeeter Davis, 1963–1964

The Edmunds family, Granma Teddy's family, can trace their lineage to the early thirteenth century—to one Edmund de Bawdewyn aka John Edmunds of Bayliff's Court. (Today, Bailiffscourt is a hotel in Climping, near Littlehampton, West Sussex, which was lovingly rebuilt and renovated by Lord Moyne in 1948.) Edmunds is of Anglo-Saxon origin but the surname, de Bawdewyn, would indicate Norman ancestry, so perhaps the Edmunds ingratiated themselves with their Norman conquerors to become the Anglo-Norman land barons they apparently were. (Sometime between then and now, the impressive land holdings disappeared.)

My grandmother, Hilda Elizabeth Edmunds, was born in Beaufort Street, Grahamstown, in 1902. Her mother, the feisty Jamaican-born Beatrice Louise Hayden, as a vivacious 16-year-old Irish girl had jumped ship in Port Elizabeth in 1897—while en route from India to Ireland—to elope with her lover, Guy William Edmunds, who met her at the docks. At the time, the age of consent in South Africa was 18, so the couple caught the nearest Zeederberg Royal Mail coach, via Mafeking, to Bulawayo in the fledgling colony of Rhodesia where they were married.

Guy, Hilda's father, had been born in India where he was to meet his future bride. It does appear that the pair had carefully planned the romantic elopement, but quite why Port Elizabeth was chosen as the disembarkation port is unclear. In 1898, the happy couple returned to the Eastern Cape to begin their married life; however, the Second Anglo-Boer War, which broke out in 1899, disrupted their plans. Guy immediately enlisted with the Border Mounted Rifles and was transferred with the regiment to the Natal front. His military career was to be short-lived, very: he was critically wounded in the opening weeks of the war, at the Battle of Elandslaagte, explained away as a reconnaissance by the losing British commander. Guy took a Mauser bullet in the thigh, which tumbled up his body, through a lung before exiting through his shoulder. Left for dead on the battlefield, the Boers were looting the corpses when a young Boer noticed one move. He called out, "*Kommandant, die een beweeg*" ("this one's moving") to which the kommandant replied, "*Los hom.*" ("Leave him"). The next day the British returned to collect their dead and noticed Guy still breathing. Transferred to a hospital marquee in the besieged town of Ladysmith, he contracted pneumonia. During a violent thunderstorm, he was clinging on to a brass tentpole, which got struck by lightning. He survived.[*]

I have from the siege of Ladysmith an auctioneer's brochure (Joe Dyson Auctioneer Feb 21, 1900) and in it are listed the items Guy bought on behalf of his mess mates:

1lb Beef Fat	11s.
1 dozen Eggs	£2 8s.
1 Fowl	18s. 6d.
1 small plate Grapes	£1 5s.
1 dozen Matches	13s. 6d.
¼-lb Tin Capstan Navy Cut Tobacco	£3

He writes on the one blank page: "These were paid for by our mess which consisted of five. I wasn't allowed to smoke for a few days until the cash [was paid]. I had to pay £3 for the Tobacco."

After the Boer War the couple finally managed to settle down—in a manner of speaking. Guy had itchy feet and was forever starting a new farming venture—somewhere in the wild hinterland of South Africa—all the while breeding prolifically. The couple had six children, five boys and a girl. The girl, the eldest of the siblings, was my grandmother, Teddy, as she came to be known from an early age. She abhorred the name Hilda—"sounds like a bloody aphid"—and with five younger brothers to 'boss up', she was something of a tomboy. Teddy, derived from Edmunds, became her name for life.

During the early years of the twentieth century, the Edmunds family farmed on the banks of the Limpopo River, near Alldays in the Northern Transvaal (now Northern Province), not far from what is today Mapungubwe National Park. Ox-wagons were the only form of transport and at a very young age Teddy became adept at inspanning the beasts and manoeuvring the wagons over the rutted tracks of the dry bushveld. Aged 5, she swam across the Limpopo

---

[*]An alternative version to this story is that Beatrice, my great-grandmother-to-be, was in fact a nurse in Ladysmith during the siege and tended to Guy, which is how they met. This is perhaps more plausible, although they did get married in Bulawayo.

to Rhodesia—and back again—unafraid of the crocodiles lurking in wait. Her younger brothers regarded her with a kind of awe, something which was to persist throughout their lives.

However, the harsh conditions and poor rainfall ensured failure of the Limpopo venture. So, the family inspanned their wagons and moved—this time to the Eastern Transvaal (now Mpumalanga Province)—to the banks of the Crocodile River in the Loskop area, where Guy grew citrus with some success. Again, in 1914, war loomed, and Guy signed up once more and disappeared to the Western Front for four years.

In the early 1920s, the Edmunds family again relocated—this time to Kirkwood in the Sundays River Valley, near today's Addo Elephant Park in the Eastern Cape, where Percy Fitzpatrick was in the process of developing a large citrus irrigation scheme. It was here that Teddy met Sir Percy's daughter, Cecily, who was to become a lifelong friend. Again, bad luck dogged the family and, in 1927, the farmhouse was burned to the ground with all the family silver and heirlooms incinerated.

Teddy eventually left home and with her new husband, Clifton Short, settled in Johannesburg where my mother Betty was born. However, Clifton's death in 1935 left Teddy in financial straits, exacerbated by the Depression of the mid-thirties. By the time the Second World War broke out in 1939, Teddy was essentially destitute, having tried several ventures, including a small seamstress business in Rosebank—next door to Sid James's mother, herself a seamstress—as well as a florist in Melville. She was forced to take a job in a munitions factory on the Rand for the duration of the war, but struggled to make ends meet. Robert, the eldest of her brothers, offered to help raise Betty and took her in. Robert, or Bob, or 'Boy' as he was most known, had done well in life. Having qualified in accountancy, he became Ernest Oppenheimer's personal accountant, was a senior partner in Howard Pim's accountancy firm (Pim was a well-known liberal philanthropist after whom the Soweto suburb of Pimville is named) and was chairman of Standard Bank South Africa, the Argus Press and the Johannesburg Turf Club, among others—so he wasn't short of cash. He lived on a stud farm in the Sandown area north of Johannesburg; in the late sixties he sold the property to the Sandton City developers.

The young Betty was happy here, growing up with Boy's two daughters, Diana and Dawn, both accomplished horsewomen. In 1946, Boy dispatched Betty to St Mary's Diocesan School for Girls, in Kloof, near Durban, as the coastal climate was considered more amenable for the sinus problems that were to hound her for the rest of her life. In the same year, Teddy's fortunes changed.

She met Roy Matthews, a brigadier in the Indian Army and they were married a few years later in 1950 when Roy retired. Roy, a dashing cavalryman of the old school, had spent the war running the Indian Army's Remount Depot (ARD), responsible for the supply of horses and mules to the Indian Army in the Burma Campaign (for which he was awarded an OBE). South Africa was an obvious source of supply, so he was to spend much of his time procuring mounts and transport animals in Natal and the Cape. The saddest moment of his military career occurred when a shipload of his mules was torpedoed by a German U-boat outside Durban harbour.

After a brief spell running a stud farm in Nottingham Road in the Natal Midlands, Roy and Teddy, in 1951, purchased 'Nutcombe', a citrus farm at Addo in the Sundays River Valley. Teddy had effectively 'come home' and was to spend the next forty years in this valley.

★

1963 was ushered in by Skeeter Davis and a thunderstorm of epic proportion, the intensity rivalling that of the opening artillery barrage of the Somme offensive and sending the twins and the pets scuttling under beds, howling and mewing in paroxysms of terror. With something like two inches of rain in half an hour, the leaking dining room was not up to the task as my mother and I frantically grabbed any receptacle to hand—buckets, pots, pans, the twins' potties—to trap the gushers before serious damage was done to the parquet.

My father was nowhere to be seen.

"MIKE!" my mother shouted ineffectually above the combined din of the storm and the twins' and the pets' wailing. "WHERE THE BLOODY HELL ARE YOU?"

It transpired that my father was trapped in his car, on his way out to buy some cigarettes at Délice.

The storm suddenly abated, not in anticipation of tapering off but in preparation for the final onslaught. My mother and I knew it was coming as the sky darkened further, with a malevolent deep-orange hue painted by the devil himself enveloping the world as we knew it. Rapidly emptying what buckets we could into the lavatory—"we don't call it a toilet, now do we", although PK, *picannin khaya* ('the 'small house') was acceptable—we hurried back to replace them under the leaks already staining the ceiling board.

And then it came. Hailstones the size of golf balls assaulted 4 Chiromo, Midvale Road in a fearful bombardment, smashing against the asbestos roof-sheeting and glancing off the windows like rifle shots as the under-bed banshee caterwauling from within the bowels of the house increased to a crescendo. I looked out the dining-room window and could see nothing but a wall of whiteness.

Then it stopped, as suddenly as if the devil had flicked a switch, sweeping the storm away and northward over Colne Valley where it could make its mischief. My father staggered in, bedraggled and visibly shaken, with the sonorous roar of the Umwindsi in flood assailing our senses through the open door.

"Christ! You should see the cars, Bets. Absolutely hammered by the hail. Thanks goodness they're insured."

But my mother wasn't listening; she was distractedly surveying her rose garden, or what was left of it. A foot or so under water, with muddy rivulets hurrying to join the torrent downslope, it was a sorry sight. What an hour before had been vibrant, healthy rosebushes were now mournful skeletons, flowerless and leafless, the devastation utter.

"Look at my roses, Mike."

My father said nothing; there was nothing to say.

She was crying as she stooped to take a bucket.

"There, there, Bets. Buck up. We've got guests arriving in a couple of hours."

And indeed, we had. New Year's drinks—elevenses—at the Cockses was becoming something of an annual ritual. RSVP'd for 11 o'clock were Meg and Forbes Davies, Di and Joy—my mother's lesbian cousin Di Edmunds and her partner Joy Morby—and farmers Bruce Thoms, Bob Smith, Pat Matthews—all single—and John and Evadne Sandys-Thomas.

The cleanup began as the sun emerged from behind heavy banks of cloud, at first nervously then more boldly as the cumulonimbi began to dissipate, fading to shades of mauve and lilac and then to white ponytails, light and fluffy, pasted whimsically against the sky. And with the sun came the heat, baking and sweating, sucking at the wetness and creating curtains of steam while we dealt with the aftermath of the storm.

Theresa, having a day off but unfortunate enough to be in her *khaya*, was duly shanghaied, with a yard broom thrust into her hand to attend to the leaves, broken branches and mangled grapevines littering the patio. Barefoot and looking quite comely out of her starched maid's uniform and white *takkies*, or plimsolls, and wearing a floral cotton frock just above the knees that accentuated her figure, she set to the task with gusto, uncomplaining as always. Peter was still back home in Motko on his Christmas leave, which left George, supposedly on duty but nowhere to be found.

My father had a most peculiar call for summoning the staff from afar, a type of *errpp*, issued in a near-falsetto that did indeed carry some distance. Whether he thought this was some ancient tribal form of communication—I was always bemused, even a mite embarrassed when I heard an *errpp*—I don't know, but it came across as the mating call of an unwell aardvark. With no response, the *errpps* increased in annoyance and intensity until my father approached Theresa.

"Where's that George? He's meant to be on duty."

"He go to clinic, *mustah*," Theresa replied with the bob of a curtsey.

"What's the matter with him? He was at work yesterday and there was nothing wrong with him."

Theresa did not reply, her eyes downcast.

"He's gone to that bloody shebeen, hasn't he?" my father snapped.

Again, Theresa failed to respond, her silence a sure indication that George was drinking it up with the skollies at the back of the Lewisam shops.

I was given a jute sack with instructions to clean up the jacaranda pods, branches, sticks and other such detritus carpeting the driveway, a job I approached with little enthusiasm. The twins, being exempt from such physical chores, were simpering at my mother's skirt tails. I was still at it when Meg and Forbes arrived, picking their way down the drive—they had walked—with Meg in front, placing precisely each high-heeled patent-leather shoe to avoid the puddles, accompanied by a series of clipped utterances, "*dip … dip … dip … dip*", in time with each step.

"Oh Meg, must you?" niggled Forbes, folding his umbrella and clearly irritated with the *dip, dip, dips*.

"You … are … a … curmudgeon, Forbes!" Meg chuckled huskily in that staccato tone of hers, her blue, blue eyes dancing in anticipation of the frivolity, and G&Ts, ahead and clicking her fingers in time to the strains of 'Telstar' by The Tornados emanating loudly from the sitting room.

"Really, Meg! You're not a teenager. I do wish you'd grow up."

I never really did see Meg unhappy. She was simply a vivacious *bonne vivante* and if she did have her first G&T an hour or so earlier than the accepted elevenses, what of it?

Next to arrive and a kindred *bon vivant* was Pat Matthews—my Uncle Pat and my mother's stepbrother through Granma Teddy's second marriage to Brigadier Roy Matthews, OBE, late of the Indian Army and this world—driving a brand-new silver Jaguar. Clandestinely nicknamed 'Cottontail' by my parents, Uncle Pat alit from the car in a flourish of blue cigarette smoke, his overly sincere smile revealing gapped teeth stained yellow—despite the accessorized cigarette holder—from his three-pack-a-day Matinée cigarette habit. He wore a navy-blue, double-breasted sports jacket, a red satin cravat supporting a set of premature jowls, white slacks and gleaming Oxford brogues, his thick, blond hair falling rakishly across his face in a contrived coiffe.

"Christofaah! My dear boy!" he announced grandly, patting me on the head. "And Betty, my dear! How *are* you?"

Mwa, mwa, peck, peck.

Always pleasant to me, I liked Uncle Pat, although he was barely tolerated by most of my parents' friends. His wife Miranda, however, hadn't tolerated him at all and had recently left him, perhaps because of his flamboyant Happy Valley sort of lifestyle. (Miranda had done an oil painting of Lamorna Cove for my father which hung in the sitting room; it wasn't very good) A wealthy tobacco grower, superficially at least, Pat farmed up in Sipolilo, a hundred miles or so north of Salisbury toward the Zambezi escarpment, where he entertained lavishly, his all-night parties at times extending to several days, punctuated with his renowned Noël Coward repertoire—he was an accomplished pianist—and weekend trips to the fleshpots of Beira and Lourenço Marques in his Cessna 172 Skyhawk that was technically owned by the Land Bank.

The Sandys-Thomases, who arrived just after Pat in a battered 1953 Ford F-100 pickup truck directly from Raffingora—west across the Hunyani River from Sipolilo—were the very antithesis of Uncle Pat: they lived frugally in a pole and *daga* house, essentially a mud hut under thatch, with cow-dung floors and the windows frameless and glassless. The cab, crammed with John (aka 'Sandy'), a pregnant Evadne and two wailing infants somewhere under the thick cloud of cigarette smoke, was matched by an equally chaotic truck bed at the back, jammed to the gunwales with prams, old leather suitcases and sundry agricultural implements that had been brought into town for repair.

"Sandy! My dear boy!" Pat gushed. "And Evadne, my dear! How *are* you?"

Mwa, mwa, peck, peck.

"We're fine, thank you Patrick," Evadne replied breathlessly, lumping the two children with her husband. "I simply *must* go to the loo."

"So, how's the tobacco, old boy?" Pat inquired of Sandy who plonked the infants on the ground to attend to their necessary accoutrements of prams, pushchairs and bags of nappies wedged under a faulty knapsack sprayer leaking DDT in the back of the truck.

"Not bad, Patrick. Could be better. A bit too much damned rain," Sandy responded in his trademark monotone as the youngest child, Peter, started crying because a jagged jacaranda pod—an oversight on my part—had infiltrated his soiled nappy and lodged itself up his soiled bottom. The elder child, Michael, had crawled off round the back of the pickup to inspect the exhaust pipe. "And your crop, Patrick?"

"Capital! A splendid season, old chum."

All the adults knew that this was little more than Pat's grossly misguided optimism, that his tobacco crop, resembling more a stand of cabbages gone to seed, was not going to amount to much, having been ravaged by aphids, red spider mites, alternaria, mildew—both types, downy and powdery—and poor-to-non-existent management.

"But I reckon I might diversify next season … into market gardening. There's a fortune to be made in onions, I'm told."

"I'm pleased for you, Patrick," retorted Sandy unconvincingly. "Still flying?"

Michael was in anguish, crying lustily from an exhaust-pipe burn on his hand.

"Absolutely, old chap. Off to LM next weekend. Booked out a suite in the Polana. Would simply *love* to have you and Evadne along. Easy enough to pop over to Raff and pick you up at your nearest airstrip."

Evadne, a tall, willowy, no-nonsense woman, came striding out the house and swept up the children. "Come, come, John. Can't stand here yakking all day. Betty!" she called, "Might you have any Savlon? Michael's burnt himself … silly boy."

The rest of the guests all arrived directly and within minutes the patio was a sea of social hubbub, increasing in proportional intensity as the crystal decanters of Scotch diminished and wooden beer crates filled with empty Lion Lager bottles. Theresa, who had kindly offered to stay on to assist my mother—something I considered strangely gratifying as I found myself mesmerized by the sway of her hips and the rhythmic rise and fall of her buttocks under the cotton frock—brought through tray after silver tray of snacks: platters of Camembert, Gruyère and Roquefort, chipolata sausages skewered onto toothpicks with pickled onions and small cubes of cheddar, crystal bowls of crisps with creamy chive and avocado dips, anchovies and olives and bowls and bowls of salted peanuts.

Bruce Thoms, a bow-legged rancher and big-game hunter of the Robert Ruark tradition, was there chatting to Di and Joy. In his trademark khaki shirt, khaki shorts, khaki stockings and khaki *veldskoene*—Boer bush shoes of suede leather—he was dwarfed by Di and Joy, both tall women (with Di being bigger-boned than Joy) and both wearing cropped hairstyles, blue denim jeans, check shirts, *veldskoene* and, paradoxically, super-bright red lipstick.

"Why don't you kids fuck off and play somewhere else?" Di suggested fondly to me and my sisters hovering about underfoot. "And take the damned dog with you, too," she added, referring to Pluto who thought the whole event had been laid on primarily for his entertainment, mingling as he was with the guests, snout probing up crotches and under skirts, with his tail belting lipstick-smeared crystal glasses and bottles of beers off tail-height side tables and all the while snarling that insane, happy smile of his.

So off we duly fucked, to the driveway to play on Bruce's short-wheel-base II-series Land Rover, an open jeep painted with black and white zebra stripes and with the windshield folded down onto the bonnet so that Bruce could shoot a charging bull elephant at 50 mph while still in fourth gear. In the gun rack affixed to the top of the dashboard lay two rifles: a .308 and .22 Hornet. I gasped, awestruck, as had surely a host of attractive women—some single, many not—who had fallen for Bruce's rugged charm in a haze of khaki fever.

"Bit of a roué, that Bruce," my father always said, with a hint of envy.

Bruce had recently, in farming speak, 'gone on his own'; that is, he'd progressed from farm assistant to farm manager to owner. For the past few years, he had been managing one of 'Boss' Lilford's ranches but had scraped enough money together to put a down-payment on a ranch near Battlefields on the Umniati River, midway between Gatooma and Que Que in the Midlands Province. He was vastly relieved to have left the employ of Boss Lilford, a hard man who owned dozens of farms and ranches across the country; in fact, Boss Lilford probably owned Rhodesia—he even had a town named after him— Lilfordia— and he most certainly owned the Rhodesian Front, a party he'd started the previous year together with his retainer, Ian Smith. Speaking of the devil, the conversation on the patio had inevitably turned to politics.

"So, Bob, what do you make of this fellow Winston Field?" Di was asking.

"As a tobacco farmer or as a prime minister?" Bob, a portly Welshman who grew tobacco out in the Umvukwes on one of the myriad Bentley farms, was, like Bruce Thoms, a bachelor, though perhaps not quite as eligible.

Di laughed. "Well, he wouldn't be prime minister if he wasn't a good tobacco farmer."

"Yes, but that doesn't necessarily make for good prime minister, does it?" quipped Joy.

"Doesn't matter," interjected Bruce Thoms. "The RF is owned by Lilford and Smith, and Field does what he's told. Nothing more than a puppet."

"They're all ghastly, bloody right-wingers," stated my mother.

43

"Well, they do seem to be keeping the nationalists in check," added John Sandys-Thomas unexcitedly. "That's got to count for something. The last thing we need is the likes of Sithole and Nkomo starting up all this terrorist nonsense like Mandela." Sandy was a Rhodesian Front supporter though he would be unlikely to openly admit it in such company.

"Sithole and Nkomo will damned well declare an armed struggle if Mandela hangs," warned Di.

Uncle Pat, in a moment of inspiration and extricating himself from Forbes's golfing monologue, something my father was unable to do, explained: "These treason trials in Pretoria have been dragging on forever. Under the law Mandela is a terrorist and should hang but Verwoerd knows he can't hang him. If he does there'll be a black revolution. But on the other hand, he's got his hard-core *verkramptes* in the Nats threatening to oust him if he doesn't."

"You mean far-right-wingers? I didn't think there was anyone right of Verwoerd," said Joy.

"*Ja*, there is: Boss Lilford," quipped Bruce.

Everyone laughed, unaware that Nkomo and Sithole had already dispatched their initial cadres to the Soviet Union for military training, as Bruce continued, "Don't laugh ... and I shouldn't be saying this because I'm a farmer myself, but the problem with the RF is that it's run by white farmers *for* white farmers. It's nothing more than a self-serving old boys' country club. There isn't a politician among them."

"They're all ghastly right-wingers," stated my mother matter-of-factly.

Picking distractedly at a chipolata sausage, I had long since lost the thread of the conversation when Meg bent down to talk to me, the slightest hint of a slur on her smoky breath.

"Chris ... ta ... fah! Your mother tells me you're starting kindergarten in a few days."

I nodded, frowning. It was a terrifying prospect.

"Well, you will learn Latin and Greek and become a clever little bunny like your father."

I nodded again.

"*Inter urinas et faeces nascimur* is what I always say," she rasped, ruffling my hair. "Oh Forbes! My ... glass ... is ... strangely ... empty! I think I'll switch to Haig."

I had no idea what language Meg was talking but suspected it might be Afrikaans. I actually fancied myself as something of an Afrikaans linguist, being fluent in such phrases as '*Als is beter met groot, groot Coke*' and '*Oompad Voor*', respectively 'Things go better with big, big Coke' and 'Detour Ahead'. It had taken some time, but I had also mastered *Pasop Snelstrik* (Beware of Speed Traps) and *Na die Strand* (To the Beach), not to mention the ubiquitous *Net Blankes* (Whites Only) signs that seemed to be riveted to everything in South Africa from public toilets (*Here* for men and *Dames* for women) to park benches and public beaches.

But the adult chat was becoming tedious, loud and repetitive. Picking my way through a forest of legs, spilled beer and cigarette ash, I decided to join my sisters on the lawn eating oxalis, a succulent weed with a bitter-sweet taste, as I overheard Bruce upbraiding my father—"It's illegal, y'know, Mike. Better get that lantana taken out or you'll have the vet department down your neck"—and Forbes berating Meg: "Good gracious, woman! We are most certainly NOT born between urine and faeces! Whatever possessed you to say something like that to a child?"

★

A few days came and went and before I knew it, I had been enrolled in KG1 at Highlands Kindergarten, the feeder school to Highlands Junior School next to the TMB offices just off the intersection of the Enterprise Road and Glenara Avenue. I was not at all happy about it, the newness of it all, the bigness of everything and, above all, the apparent abandonment by my parents. I somehow knew that I had been sucked into a system that would expect me to conform, inexorably and forever: there would be no escape until death.

The feelings of abandonment—it had all started with Shona White—began with the lift-club that my mother had arranged with Grace Wood, mother of Dean, and Cynthia Brewer, mother of Simon. The fourth boy in the lift-club was Oliver Grey who lived next door to the Brewers on Newton Spicer Drive, a cul-de-sac off Kent Road, south across the Enterprise Road from Nazareth House. Quite why Oliver's mother was not involved in the driving roster was a mystery, though I secretly suspected that Oliver had killed her which was the only logical reason why we never met her, why she was never mentioned. It all added up: Oliver, a bespectacled, lanky boy with a sullen demeanour, had something intangibly dark about him. The fact that he always got to sit in the front passenger seat—even in my mother's Opel, something I found particularly galling—only added to the conspiracy theory that he had some evil aura about him, and the three mothers would do anything to accommodate him for fear of a hex.

So, Dean Wood, Simon Brewer—we'd met at the Treetops Nursery School sandpit the previous year—and I had to sit in the back seat. Dean, a studious boy, always sat on the left, reading a book, and never uttering a word: I suspected that he found our conversation inanely tedious. Simon, a garrulous, ginger-headed boy full of *bonhomie*, sat in the middle and I on the right, jammed up against the door because Simon exceeded his space quota because of his robust chubbiness—his inner thighs oozing out of his grey khaki shorts appeared welded together—and his flamboyant armography. Cynthia Brewer drove a shiny black Morris Minor with wooden panels and indicators that clicked outward at ninety degrees just below roof height, like one of Mr Geppeto's fabrications and which truly fascinated me.

Grace Wood's car was a barely roadworthy station wagon of indeterminate make, model and vintage. The seating configuration for us four boys remained the same as in the Opel and the Morris Minor but with several addenda: Dean's younger siblings, headed up by his sister Jo Jo, were crammed into the back, the boot space, to be deposited at nursery school or just along for the ride because Grace, being the earth mother that she was, didn't have a nanny with whom to leave the infants. I never knew how many infants, toddlers and babies were wedged into the back—the Woods had a lot of children—and tended to avoid turning round to look for fear of making eye contact with one of them who might wail irrationally.

The kindergarten playground was dominated, naturally, by the KG2 boys, rowdy louts who monopolized the swings, the roundabout and especially the jungle gym. The KG1 children barely got a look-in but on the rare occasion that we did, things inevitably ended up in blood and tears. Simon Brewer, once in his haste to claim his spot on the jungle gym, was vigorously manhandled by some older boys while precariously balanced on a slippery cross-beam and plummeted earthward—his inner thighs so coated with a sheen of sweat that left them incapable of purchase—and broke his right arm: this restricted his armography in the lift-club but was an added protuberance into my ribcage.

I made friends with Jimmy Scott, a tousle-haired *gamin* with a twinkle in his eye and a lisp on his lips. During a play-acting session of the Old Testament, the book of Genesis to be precise, Jimmy found himself cast as Esau—or Eethaw—and one of his lines was to ask his brother Jacob (played by the omnipresent Simon Brewer) for some soup. Not only did his lisp prove an encumbrance to the pronunciation of the word soup but he pronounced the word in a most peculiar manner, as in 'sop' instead of 'soop': "Jacob, pleathe may I have thum thop."

With that, the entire class would erupt in raucous laughter, urging, "Say it again, Jimmy! Say it again!"

So Jimmy duly obliged—"Jacob, pleathe may I have thum thop"—until the penny dropped that he was having the mickey taken. A frown creased his brow, and I could sense a deep, atavistic fury rising within him.

Jimmy's revenge was not long in coming—three days in actuality—and I was to become an unwitting accomplice. It was quite apparent that it had not been planned, that Jimmy had not stewed over it for days, but was an opportunistic example of *carpe momentum temporis*. The break bell had just gone, and the children were all filing back into class. Jimmy and I needed to pee and were lingering at the urinal when Jimmy decided to let loose with a powerful jet of urine aimed carelessly at the window.

"Come on. Leth thee if we can wee out the window!"

The hitch was that the window, open though it was, was some two feet above our head height. Undaunted, Jimmy made a valiant attempt, reinforced by the pint of Mazoe orange juice he'd consumed over break. I have no idea what prompted me to join the fray but join I did and with reckless abandon we seemed to urinate forever, with vigorous streams of pee lacing the walls, the floor, the doors of the cubicles and our clothes ... but none out the window. Eventually, sated, the floor awash, the reality of what we'd just done began to sink in when the door burst open and in stormed Mrs Johnson, the headmistress, who took one look at the bladder carnage in front of her. "Both of you! Come with me!" she hissed. "This very instant." Her voice was barely audible, as if an exorcist was at work on her. Grabbing each of us by an ear, she yanked us out the toilets and down the corridor.

Jimmy, all sense of vengeance—and dignity—dissipated in a flash, was wincing, cringing, simpering: "Pleathe, Mithith Johnthon ... it wath a mithtake ... it wath hith idea."

I thought my ear was about to be severed entirely from my head by the time we arrived at the back of the kitchens. Mrs Johnson thrust us into a broom cupboard where we were confronted by an array of brooms, mops, dusters, cloths, buckets and cleaning liquids.

"You ... have ... half ... an ... hour." There, that exorcist voice again. "Those toilets better be spotless. Otherwise, you *will* be expelled."

I gasped: this was the ultimate indignity. Oh, the shame. Needing no further encouragement, we grabbed mops and buckets and slunk back to the toilets in the hope that no one would see us. No one did: they were all in class and the classroom windows onto the corridor were all above desk height.

Mopping away, I was more concerned about what my parents' reaction would be than Jimmy's shameless treachery. The first hurdle would be my mother, but I need not have worried. Cynthia Brewer was picking us up today and the only reaction in the Morris Minor was Simon's "Jeepers, you stink."

The affair was never mentioned by my parents, although I was on tenterhooks for several days, assuming that they knew and were just playing me in a form of perverted, silent sadism. And nor did Mrs Johnson revisit the matter: she had bigger fish to fry in the form of two scandals that broke shortly after the lavatory desecration. The first concerned Henry Rudd who had been overseeing a ring of upskirters, until one of his cohorts took things a bit too far by trying to ascertain what was under one set of knickers. The second was a KG2 boy who had been caught gluing his egg to his spoon.

It was during kindergarten that my love affair with the stage was kindled. It started with a school fancy-dress competition and my mother, in consultation with my father, decided that I would be Lawrence of Arabia, which I felt was a clever choice: all the other boys would likely go as the Lone Ranger, Davy Crockett, Captain Hook or the Mad Hatter, with perhaps a Tonto or two thrown into the mix. The costume itself was simple enough: an old sheet with holes cut out for the neck and the arms and pulled together at the waist with the knotted-rope belt from my father's burgundy dressing-gown. The keffiyeh headdress, fashioned from an old red-check dish towel, was nicely held in place by one of my sisters' Alice bands. The *pièce de résistance*, however, was the life-size, cardboard-cutout camel that my mother had diligently spent several days making. The problem of course came when we had to get it into my father's Austin. Running late, nerves were fraying.

"Oh, for god's sake, Bets! Do hurry up. We're going to be late for this bloody thing." My father had had to sacrifice his weekly nets practice at Sports Club.

"Well, how do you suggest we get it into the car without damaging it?"

"You should have thought about that beforehand, shouldn't you? You'll just have to fold it in half … here … at the hump."

"Mike! Stop it! You'll break it!"

He did not break it but as I made my grand entrance into the school hall, the camel flopped over at the offending crease. Nevertheless, the Lawrence part of the duo was enough to ensure a Highly Commended and a red rosette. I was very pleased and so was my mother, rightly so as she'd put a lot of effort into the ensemble.

Not pleased at all were all the unplaced entrants. As I was leaving the hall, trying vainly to keep the limp camel upright, I was confronted by a posse of Lone Rangers—and a single Tonto whom I identified as Jimmy Scott—led by

48

Simon Brewer, his ridiculously small cardboard Stetson perched rakishly on his head like an angry pimple.

"He's wearing an Alice band!" one Lone Ranger yelled exultantly.

"He's a girl!" said another.

"Girl … girl … girl!" they all chanted gleefully.

Hiding my keffiyeh behind the camel's hump, I tried to ignore the taunts as my mother grasped me firmly by the arm: "Walk up, Christopher. Ignore the little brutes. They're just jealous."

And so I did. I was proud of my mother.

My big break came when I was cast as Peter Pan. Almost predictably, when our teacher, Mrs Hess,* asked who wanted to play the part of Peter Pan every boy in the class almost leaped onto his desk, arms thrashing wildly and howling "Me, me, me" at Mrs Hess in a sharklike feeding frenzy. Every boy that is, except me. With some rather clever reverse psychology, I did not climb onto my desk, I did not put up my hand and I did not clamour "Me, me, me." Instead, I stayed seated—demurely—with the hint of a knowing smile on my face as if to impart to Mrs Hess, "You really want to pick me, Mrs Hess. Jimmy Scott cannot do the part because of his lisp and Simon Brewer's physique is unsuitable, not being requisitely elfin. So … do the right thing and pick me. You know you want to. Secretly, I'm one of your favourites, aren't I?"

The class went silent as Mrs Hess slowly scanned the room. After what seemed an eternity, her gaze came to rest on me: "Peter Pan will be played by Christopher," she announced with finality.

"There! Got it!" I said to myself as the hint of a knowing smile broadened into a self-satisfied beam that was accompanied by a universal groan from all the other boys.

The next plum role was that of Wendy which went to a pretty little blonde called Nicola. We exchanged coy glances before Simon Brewer landed the glorious role of Captain Hook. Jimmy Scott could only manage 6th Pirate, reduced to muttering "Ahoy, me heartieth" in the background.

Yet again my mother excelled in the wardrobe department, and I suspect J. M. Barrie would have approved. With a green tunic, green tights, green slippers and plastic sword, all topped off with a green pixie bonnet, I certainly looked the part. The problem, again, was that tights were considered female attire and once more I came in for much malicious abuse from the pirates, not helped by the bright red lipstick that I was obliged to wear. Still, I found the

---

*Mrs Hess's daughter, Susan, was my parents' electrician many years later.

outfit curiously sensual and anticipated with relish the scene when I would be required to cuddle up to the lithe and lissom Wendy in her oh-so-slightly-revealing nightie. Wendy's ardour, however, did not match mine and although on opening night—the only night actually—her passion was satisfactory (acted of course), we parted ways at the end of the play with nary a word, let alone a peck on the cheek: she was simply inscrutable. Such was my introduction to the coldness—and power—of the fairer sex, something that left me confused and unable to identify that I had clearly been jilted. The play was nevertheless an astonishing success and subject to a standing ovation. Simon Brewer shone as Captain Hook—his hook was a lethal butcher's-hook contraption at the end of a cardboard wine-bottle casing that plugged onto his arm—although he did tend to overact and, on a few occasions, threatened to usurp the leading man. Jimmy Scott tried desperately to get noticed with some clumsy attempts at scene-stealing but had to contend with five other pirates who didn't lisp.

★

In June 1963, the Profumo Scandal broke. I wasn't quite sure what all the fuss was about other than it involved—disappointingly—a Conservative MP, John Profumo, who had conducted some sort of illicit dealing with a Christine Keeler, a call girl, and who was consequently in big trouble. I assumed a call girl was someone who called on people—which they do—and failed to comprehend quite what the problem was. However, what struck me most about the whole affair was Miss Keeler's legs—the photos in the newspapers and in *LIFE* magazine (to which my parents subscribed) of her alighting from a car with her skirt hitched up to the top of her long, stockinged legs—which had me absolutely mesmerized. Not to mention that insanely risqué photoshoot of her naked in a chair which was banned in South Africa and then belatedly in the Rhodesias.

"Christopher! What are you reading?" my mother peered over my shoulder. "Good gracious! Not that little hussy!"

Miss Keeler's legs were of the same ilk—long and shapely—as those of the principal boy in *Dick Whittington*, last year's pantomime at Reps Theatre, though Dick had worn fishnet stockings with a black seam down the back that had me riveted to my seat, my mouth agape in total awe of such wondrous things. I vaguely connected the sensuality of my Peter Pan tights to Christine's legs but was puzzled as to what I might do about it, if in fact there *was* anything that could be done. Perhaps such things would one day come clear, like the words of the hit by Ruby and The Romantics, 'Our Day Will Come'.

The songs of the time were as equally lustrous as Miss Keeler and I was particularly drawn to Little Peggy Marsh's 'I Will Follow Him', Perry Como's 'I Love You and Don't You Forget It' and even The Singing Nun's 'Dominique'. Of course 'Summer Holiday' by Cliff Richard and The Shadows eclipsed everything and became an unofficial Rhodesian anthem—"What a gay little tune," Granma Teddy said of it—although I found it a bit contrived and unnecessarily happy, all a bit twee.

But 1963 belonged to Skeeter Davis—born in 1931 in Dry Ridge, Kentucky and nicknamed 'Skeeter' by her grandfather because of her exuberant energy (skeeter is Appalachian slang for mosquito)—and I felt she belonged to me. I first saw her performing, by accident, on the Davies's television. The SRBC had somehow managed to lose the PGA tour transmission—much to the incandescent rage of Forbes and the marginal annoyance of my father—and, of all things, were using a Grand Ole Opry show as a filler. And there she was, this winsome little blonde thing with a par-beehive hairdo held up with an Alice band, wearing a plain frock and singing 'The End of the World', a song I'd heard dozens of times on the wireless and the signature song of the age. Seeing Skeeter Davis in person, almost-live on stage, was something special: I felt she was singing to me and only to me and I would have reached out and caressed the screen had it not been for Forbes's latent fury. The words, hauntingly nihilistic, pierced my core, as they had millions.

Two months after Christine Keeler flashed her legs to the world, Dr Martin Luther King gave his 'I have a dream' speech to over a quarter of a million civil rights supporters at the Lincoln Memorial in Washington DC. My frame of reference—*LIFE* magazine, again—showed pictures of a sea of people, mainly black people, listening to Reverend King, who was apparently both a doctor and a priest, outlining his vision for the future in biblical rhetoric. The photographs ignited in me a sense of curiosity: were black people in America—negroes, they were called, or coloured folk, as opposed to natives as my mother and Granma Teddy referred to them—also excluded as they were here in Africa? I could not identify exactly what it was they were excluded from, but I knew— I thought I knew—that they were in every respect unequal to us whites. I accepted that in Africa this was the way things were—although I knew innately that it was not quite right—but it really struck me that this was seemingly also the case in the United States. Progressive America, land of the free, land of the brave, land of John Fitzgerald Kennedy, but also unequal.

Closer to home, the British established the 'five principles' for Southern Rhodesia, the first being no independence before majority rule. Northern

Rhodesia seceded from the Federation. There was trouble in the nationalists' camp and a split. On 8 August 1963, the Zimbabwe African National Union (ZANU) was formed by Sithole from disaffected ZAPU factions. Two days later, Nkomo formed the People's Caretaker Council (PCC) to replace the proscribed ZAPU and the first significant batch of nationalists, led by ZANU's Emmerson Mnangagwa, was shipped to the People's Republic of China for military training.

★

In the spring of 1963, my parents decided that our annual holiday would be confined to the borders of Southern Rhodesia, principally the eastern border area. So once again we set off in the Austin Cambridge, the twins and I squabbling between blurted stanzas of 'Summer Holiday' before we'd even come to the Enterprise Road, and headed south, skirting the municipal boundary on the dusty Salisbury Drive, the grand ring road that circled the entire city and which took two decades to complete and three to macadamize, till we arrived at the drive-in cinema on the Umtali road. Then east for several hours along the strip road—two nine-inch-wide strips of tarmac for a car to straddle—through the sleepy farming villages of Bromley, Marandellas, Macheke, Headlands, Rusape, Odzi and eventually to Umtali where the Austin Cambridge broke down and where I witnessed my parents' first public fight, the public being my sisters and me.

Stranded on the verge halfway down Christmas Pass overlooking the border town of Umtali carpeted in mauve jacaranda blossom—tantalizingly close but still a good few miles down the pass—I reckoned that our planned night stop, the White Horse Inn in the Vumba mountains just south of Umtali, might perhaps be postponed to tomorrow's night stop.

"So why have we broken down?" my mother inquired of no one in particular, lighting up a cigarette.

"I've no idea, Bets," replied my father testily, tapping out a Benson & Hedges. "I'm not a bloody mechanic."

"Well, don't you think you should at least open the bonnet and have a look?"

"At what? As I said, I'm not a mechanic."

"Maybe there's something obvious. Maybe it'll jump out at you. So much for bloody Car Mart: I thought they'd just serviced it."

"Oh, for God's sake, Bets …," my father exhaled angrily, the smoke clouding the back seat as my sisters gagged and retched in exaggerated fashion.

I distractedly started humming 'Summer Holiday' but *pianissimo* for fear of antagonizing my father: I could sense that the situation was escalating. But I had a vested interest in a satisfactory resolution: I was hungry and had no desire to sleep in the car on the side of the road.

"I know!" I piped up from the back. "Why don't I get out and get a lift to a garage and they can send a mechanic and I can get a lift back with him?" I thought this a very sensible suggestion and so it seemed did my father.

"Mike! You're not serious! Christopher is six years old, for goodness' sake!" fumed my mother as she flicked her cigarette butt into the dry grass on the side of road.

"Well, you go then, Bets."

"I bloody well will too. There's a Car Mart in Umtali, isn't there? They can send a bloody mechanic." She adjusted her headscarf, wiped the smudges from her cat's-eye Ray-Bans, had a quick check of her lipstick in the vanity mirror and got out the car, slamming the door behind her to the accompaniment of Sarah and Caroline's spontaneous crying that this was perhaps the last they'd ever see of their mother. They still had a further five minutes of her, well, the back of her at least, as she furiously flagged down the next passing car.

An hour and six Benson & Hedges later, the twins' caterwauling reduced to a simper, the Car Mart breakdown truck hove into view with my mother in the passenger seat. It pulled up in front of the Austin as the mechanic—in other circumstances my mother would have referred to him as an oik—got out the driver's seat and sauntered up to my father's window, resting his elbow nonchalantly on the wing mirror like James Dean.

"Pop it, will you, china."

"Pop what?" asked my father, nonplussed, at the same time attempting to deal with the proximity of the mechanic's breath.

"The bonnet, my *boet*."*

"Oh."

My parents had yet to exchange a word as the mechanic scoured the inside of the bonnet. Not two minutes later he dropped it with a clang, shaking his head ominously.

"Camshaft, my china," he stated matter-of-factly.

"Camshaft?" asked my father.

"*Ja*, it's fucked. You aint goin' nowhere, my *boet*."

"The nice man told me on the way up that if there's a problem then he'll tow us down to Car Mart."

---

*my brother (Afrikaans)

I was greatly relieved that my mother had regained the use of her voice.

"S'true, china. I'll hook you up and get you back to the shop."

And so it was that he hooked us up, not with a simple rope but with a heavy-duty towbar. This was extremely exciting and, what's more, we'd get to ride in the car with my father handling the steering and braking, though I suspect he had no idea what was expected of a towee driver.

"Ma'am, why don't you ride up front with me?" James Dean winked at my mother.

Clearly finding a greasy duckie mechanic marginally less distasteful than my father's company, my mother duly obliged and clambered back into the tow truck as we jolted off in a cloud of exhaust fumes.

As we rounded the bend at the bottom of the pass, with the Wise Owl Motel on the right, a convoy of fire engines came hurtling by, sirens wailing, heading up the way we'd just come.

"Looks serious," muttered my father.

At Car Mart, the workshop manager—in charge of 'the shop'—reinforced what James Dean had told us but in less colourful language: that the camshaft was well and truly finished and what with the Rhodes and Founders long weekend looming, it would take at least a week to get a new part down from Salisbury; however, the good news was that we could use the Car Mart pool car, an ageing VW Beetle, for a nominal rental.

A VW Beetle! With the engine in the boot! I was thrilled but my mother clearly wasn't, grumbling that Beetles were "terribly common" and very "non-U". Nevertheless, we had little choice and to give the Beetle its due it never let us down over the next fortnight, chugging up hill and down dale, through the Vumba, Melsetter, the Chimanimani mountains and over Birchenough bridge across the Sabi River to the Zimbabwe Ruins a few miles east of Fort Victoria.

It was at breakfast the following morning at the Wise Owl Motel that I happened to be reading the front page of the *Umtali Post* which my father was holding—he was reading the back page, the sports page—and was drawn to the headline: 'CECIL KOP DESTROYED BY FIRE'. Cecil Kop, I knew, was the impressive mountain at the head of Christmas Pass, coincidentally, near where we'd broken down, and was something of a shrine to the residents of Umtali; it even had a giant cross on the summit, underlining the fact that it was a white man—Kingsley Fairbridge, founder of the Society for the Furtherance of Child Emigration to the Colonies—who had brought Western civilization and Christianity to this corner of Africa. Not only was Cecil Kop revered by white

Umtalians, but it was also part of a nature reserve that straddled the mountains surrounding the town, and here was the *Umtali Post* reporting that an estimated 5,000 acres had been burned out, some 5,000 acres of pristine bush that was home to several species of rare antelope and more than a dozen varieties of aloe that occurred only in the Cecil Kop reserve area. The chief of the fire brigade described it as "a natural disaster", the words 'environmental' and 'ecological' still several years off.

My father was more interested in the MCC* cricket tour that was planned for 1964: "Look, Bets. The paper says Ted Dexter will be the captain."

"Oh."

"Knew him at Radley. Excellent racquets player."

"Oh." My mother was preoccupied with trying to get a spoon of Shreddies into Caroline's recalcitrant mouth.

Another subsequent disaster occurred a few days later at Zimbabwe Ruins, not on the scale of the scorched Cecil Kop but on a more personal level. I was unaware at the time that a great debate was raging in the halls of academia as to the origins of Great Zimbabwe—as this breath-taking wonder of the world is called today—with the Bantuphiles claiming it had been built by the local Shona, specifically the Karanga, a powerful Shona clan, and the Europhiles prognosticating that there was simply no way that a backward people like the Shona could have even begun to contemplate a project of such magnitude and beauty and therefore it could only have been constructed by the Phoenicians. Even thirty or forty years later—despite the overwhelming evidence to the contrary that Great Zimbabwe was the hub of a vast Karanga kingdom (as well as its forerunner, Mapungubwe, and its successor, the Monomatapa empire)— white laymen around the *braai* were still saying, "I'm telling you, these lazy *munts* could never in a million years build anything that complex."

The Zimbabwe Ruins Motel had a large, thatched dining room with open sides, airy and spacious. At breakfast one morning, my father asked me to nip back to the room, a thatched rondavel,† and retrieve his pen so that he could do the crossword puzzle in the newspaper. Entrusted with the keys to the room, it was an important mission that I embraced with a sense of responsibility and, feeling all grown up, decided to test out my father's shaving razor—types safety—in the bathroom of the rondavel. I'd often watched my father shaving and was intrigued. Dispensing with the idea of shaving foam and a mirror, I flamboyantly slid the Wilkinson blade over my face, across the top lip, under the

---

*Marylebone Cricket Club
†a traditional circular African dwelling with a conical thatched roof (Afrikaans)

line of the jaw and down my throat, repeating the exercise several times until I was satisfied that I now knew how to shave.

The thatched dining room went silent as I made my entrance, the muted hush sounding like an inverse H-bomb detonation. Something clearly wasn't right. It wasn't: my whole face was awash with blood, it appeared as if I'd just had my throat slit.

"My God!" shrieked my mother. "He's been attacked by natives!"

"Christopher!" my father hissed under his breath. "What … did … you … do?"

I touched my face, and my hand came away bloody-red. "I … I … was trying out your razor …"

"Jesus Christ! You bloody little fool!"

"I'm sorry, daddy."

"Bets! Get him out of here … to the room. And get him fixed up. Now!"

As my mother bustled me out, picking our way among the tables of diners—some concerned, others bemused—my father called out after us: "And where's my pen?"

If this little contretemps wasn't embarrassing enough, returning to the dining room some fifteen minutes later—with my face padded with cotton wool orange from the lashings of mercurochrome that my mother had applied—was the ultimate indignity as I tried vainly to sidle in unnoticed. Previously concerned and bemused diners sniggered over their poached eggs and my sisters giggled unabashedly, singing, "Here comes Father Christmas, here comes Father Christmas," while my father silently immersed himself in the crossword.

This episode marked the end of the holiday and by the time we reached Salisbury—back via the circuitous route of Car Mart Umtali to pick up the Austin complete with brand-new camshaft—the lacerations on my face and neck had not yet healed completely.

"Teddy's arriving in a couple of days," said my father as we turned into Midvale Road.

"Yes, and she's going to have an absolute fit when she sees Christopher's face," my mother responded, stating the obvious.

Granma Teddy was coming! She would blame my father for the facial butchery—"Mike, you should jolly well know better than to leave razors lying around within reach of the children!"—and she had promised she would take us to the pictures to see *The Incredible Journey* at The Palace.

★

"KENNEDY'S BEEN SHOT!"

I sat up in bed with a jolt. There was a ruckus in the passage.

"KENNEDY'S JUST BEEN SHOT! BETS, MIKE!"

I jumped out of bed and in the darkness stumbled to the door. Peering out, I caught the tail end of Granma Teddy in her nightgown hurrying to the sitting room, the reverie of *The Incredible Journey* that we'd seen that afternoon at The Palace dissipating in an instant. Clandestinely, I followed her to the sitting room and took up my traditional listening post just round the corner at the top of the split-level steps.

"What? Jack?" I heard my mother ask, dully.

From the clinking of crystal glasses, I suspected both my parents were on the Teacher's. My father had come home late after an extended nets session and had dipped straight into the whisky, something he always did after the battery of Lion lagers at Sports Club, and my mother invariably joined him, out of a sense of conjugal duty more than anything else.

"Yes! John. JFK. Shot! Assassinated in Dallas," Granma Teddy said breathlessly, all a-thither. "It's just been on the BBC."

"Bets, turn the wireless on," my father instructed with the trace of a slur.

I heard the crackle of the airwaves as my mother tuned in to the Southern Rhodesian Broadcasting Corporation.

"Why isn't that bloody thing tuned?" snapped my father.

"Not sure, Mike. I think Caroline's been playing with the knobs again."

I could sense Granma Teddy's exasperation. She'd just heard the shocking news on the BBC on her transistor radio, now here these two were fannying about as if absolute, final confirmation was needed from the SRBC. To deal with her exasperation, I heard the sounds of ice tinkling as she poured herself a Teacher's; neat it would be.

"He's just died in hospital. Shot in the head," she added.

This was simply too much: John F. Kennedy dead? I struggled to comprehend. John Kennedy, Jack Kennedy—it had taken me some time to realize that they were one and the same—was dead? I felt the knot in my stomach tighten and I thought I might be sick. JFK was my idol: war hero, young, handsome and clean-cut, he was my embodiment of the future, not only for the United States but for the world (even though he was a Catholic). Now what?

"I suppose they'll swear in Lyndon Johnson now," said my father, apparently unimpressed by the enormity of it all.

"He's a bloody dead loss," added my mother insightfully.

"It's all too terrible," said Granma Teddy. "Just too appalling. Get me another drink, will you, Mike."

Two days later a similar scenario played itself out.

"OSWALD'S BEEN SHOT!"

I sat up in bed with a jolt. There was a ruckus in the passage.

"LEE HARVEY OSWALD HAS JUST BEEN SHOT! BETS, MIKE!"

I jumped out of bed and in the darkness stumbled to the door. Peering out, I caught the tail end of Granma Teddy in her nightgown hurrying to the sitting room with the astounding news that JFK's killer had himself just been shot.

"What?" my father was perplexed.

"Yes, shot at point-blank range by Jack Ruby."

"Jack who?"

(Another Jack, very confusing.)

"Ruby. Owns a nightclub."

"What a dreadful bore," stated my mother. It was all bit much for her, as it indeed was for me. I mean, what sort of society allows its president to get shot and then, worse, allows the president's executioner to get killed himself, before justice can even be served? Had the world gone mad? The pictures in the next edition of *LIFE* confirmed that it had as I studied for many hours the photo of Ruby shooting Oswald. The set determination, almost glee, on Ruby's porky face as he pulled the trigger, the open-mouthed grimace from Lee Harvey Oswald as he took the bullet: it was all so surreal, a split-second watershed of the twentieth century captured on film for eternity. And what made it infinitely more incomprehensible was that Oswald was an ex-Marine and Marines weren't murderers, were they.

In the following edition of *LIFE*, as the curtain came down on 1963, Lyndon B. Johnson announced to the world that America now had some 15,000 military advisers in Vietnam, South Vietnam specifically. I didn't calculate the ratios, but I knew this was patently untrue, that one cannot possibly need 15,000 American soldiers to advise South Vietnamese soldiers, not unless South Vietnam had in excess of a million troops who needed advising. But maybe they did? What I did know, with a hint of foreboding, was that war between the Free World and the Communists was inevitable. And it was equally inevitable that the United States would win it. This much I knew.

Almost as an irrelevant postscript, the Federation of Rhodesia and Nyasaland was dissolved and Southern Rhodesia sought independence based upon the 1961 Constitution but this was rejected by the United Kingdom.

★

It was time for the annual December treat: the visit to Stanley Avenue in town to watch the two trumpeters, Life Guards from the Household Cavalry, in action, one positioned on the balcony of Greatermans department store and the other across the road on the Barbours department store balcony. Quite how they managed to see each other from under the rims of their plumed helmets rammed down onto their noses was a mystery, but like the traffic that came to a reverential standstill, their martial music had me enthralled. With their glittering silver *cuirassier* breastplates, gleaming-black thigh-high jackboots and music as haunting as the cry of a fish eagle, they were to me the utter encapsulation of the British Empire and my chest swelled with pride.

Salisbury, a spotlessly clean city—well, the centre of town at least—was laid out in a relatively simple grid system. The CBD (central business district) was bounded by Manica Road to the south (which, heading east, eventually became the Umtali road) and Jameson Avenue to the north. In between, from the south, were Speke, Stanley, Gordon, Baker and Union avenues (the sequence in the ditty we learned went, "Manica, Speak to Stanley Gordon about the Bakers' Union with Jameson"). From west to east, starting at Causeway, ran Inez Terrace, Angwa Street, First, Second, Third and Fourth streets (the streets continued up to Tenth but after Fourth became residential, the area known as The Avenues).

It was in this area of some forty or fifty city blocks—'Town'—that my parents and Granma Teddy did all their special shopping: clothes and perfume from the upmarket department stores of Meikles, Greatermans, Barbours and Sanders (with its plush tea lounge, The Bird Cage, where Granma Teddy always ordered anchovy toast), school uniforms from McCullagh & Bothwell, Kingstons the stationers where I would redeem my Christmas and birthday gift vouchers buying books, comics and, later, records, The Palace and Rainbow cinemas (the latter being where we watched the 1964 blockbuster, *Mary Poppins*) and, above all, what would shortly become the centre of the universe—The Southern Cross Hobby Shop, or simply The Hobby Shop, in Angwa Arcade on Angwa Street.

Although Cecil Rhodes's 1890 pioneers had raised the Union Flag in what became the jacaranda-lined Cecil Square (between Second and Third streets and Stanley and Union avenues), the town itself began life around the area of The Kopje, a very small hill—more a pimple—west of what was the low-lying swamp that ultimately became Causeway and Kingsway. As the town grew, it spread commercially and residentially east- and northward and industrially southward and The Kopje was left behind, relegated to hill-starts for driving examiners and the sentinel for the red-light district, the main thoroughfare for which was Pioneer Street where mulatto street-walkers—most certainly not of the Christine Keeler ilk—plied their trade (black prostitutes were excluded from the red-light district until the late sixties and early seventies). The area between The Kopje and Causeway was unkindly known as the Cow's Guts, but a thriving conglomeration of Indian bazaars, panel-beaters, low-grade butcheries, taverns and snooker saloons it was.

The family doctor, Dr Kantor, and family dentist, Dr Carter, both kept their rooms in the CBD and both conveniently in Anlaby House, a sterile-smelling, modernistic, nutria-brick-brown, linoleum-tiled four-storey-plus-mezzanine edifice on the corner of Angwa and Baker that attracted the medical profession, accountants, lawyers and employment agents. Dr Carter wasn't there too long as he quickly earned enough money to build himself a state-of-the art dental surgery, all chrome and glass, on the Enterprise Road next door to the Presbyterian church. A pleasant, ginger-haired man with freckles, he always had tomato sandwiches for lunch, something I knew because I inevitably seemed to get the 2 o'clock appointment and Dr Carter inevitably had a wayward tomato pip on his chin which I was too circumspect to point out. Dr Kantor, however, wasn't to follow the medical-profession trend of relocating to the suburbs for nearly three decades, settled as she was in Anlaby House and content as she was with the plethora of house calls that she made in her stately black Rover. A handsome Jewish woman, her dark hair streaked with steel grey, Fay Kantor had been the family GP since 1956 and had in fact brought me and my sisters into the world. Too professional to ever be regarded as a family friend, she was nevertheless the reassuring health bedrock of the family, and I would like to believe that our fondness for her was reciprocal.

★

On 13 April 1964 Ian Smith became prime minister, replacing Winston Field who did not support unilateral independence. ZANU held its annual congress in Gwelo, described by Ndabaningi Sithole as the famous 'Clarion for War'. ZANU and the PCC were promptly banned. Nkomo, Sithole, Mugabe and other nationalist leaders were detained. On 4 July 1964, a five-man ZANU guerrilla gang, the Tanzania-trained and Sithole-inspired 'Crocodile Gang', paved the way for the Second *Chimurenga*—the war of liberation, the First *Chimurenga* being the 1896 Shona uprising—with the murder of Pieter Johannes Andries Oberholzer in the mountainous Chimanimani region on the border with Mozambique. It would become a watershed moment.

As Uncle Pat had predicted, on 11 June 1964 Nelson Mandela was sentenced to life imprisonment. It was also the day the Dr Kantor made a house call, diagnosing the twins with mumps.

"For God's sake Betty! Get him out of here," shouted Granma Teddy. "If Christopher catches it, he'll be sterile."

"Come on, Christopher. You're not allowed in here. You ... will ... get ... very ... very ... sick. And you'll never have babies," said my mother, shepherding me out the twins' room.

I had no idea what anyone was talking about, and the thought of babies wasn't particularly appealing anyway: my sisters had been a challenge ever since I could remember. Maybe they would die: it sounded that serious, though I did dare hope.

I heard the strains of 'Baby Love' on the wireless and scuttled off to listen, terrified I might miss a few bars. As soon as The Supremes had exploded onto the music scene, Skeeter Davis was promptly relegated. I simply couldn't get enough of them and would sit transfixed for the three minutes that it took for the song to play itself out, wishing it would never end. The baby-doll voices, the infectious beat that *LIFE* magazine called Motown and the three divine women—Diana Ross, Mary Wilson and Florence Ballard—who made up the group, combined to transform my world into something approaching heaven. Perhaps even surpassing The Supremes was The Ronettes, made up of Veronica Bennett (or Ronnie Spector), her older sister Estelle Bennett and their cousin Nedra Talley. 'Baby I Love You', 'Be My Baby' and 'Walking in the Rain' were their smash hits of 1963 and 1964, driven by that Phil Spector 'Wall of Sound'—a phrase I only discovered years later—that more than any sound or any event or anything of the era became *the* definitive soundtrack of the early sixties and which embedded itself holistically into my psyche forever. That these six women were black—negresses—seemed only to enhance their appeal, but I did vaguely wonder why the SRBC didn't exclude them. Perhaps because they *looked* like whites, with their straight hair and fine facial features, unlike our stereotypical local natives with their frizzy hair and clumsy English. I never heard any Rhodesian blacks singing on the SRBC* but occasionally South African natives, like Miriam Makeba with her monumental international hit 'Pata Pata', would compete for airplay with the more popular white fare of The Bachelors, Peter and Gordon, and The Seekers.

The twins were quarantined in their room for a week, and I relished the

---

*This of course the 'white' SRBC. The Africans had their own 'black' SRBC station that operated out of Highfields, a township just the other side of The Kopje.

break from their badgering, particularly at breakfast time: Theresa, Pluto, Sam and occasionally Giah were all I needed. I was also still smarting from the turd-in-the bath incident where I'd been wrongly accused of being the perpetrator—even my mother believed it to be true—when I knew without doubt that the offensive chipolata-type floater had clearly emanated from Sarah's bottom. So, from time to time, I would poke my head round the door of their room and return some harassment, well-crafted abuse such as, "Bullfrogs, bullfrogs, bullfrogs, nah, nah, na, nah, na."

★

On 24 October 1964 Northern Rhodesia became the independent nation of Zambia under the leadership of the fly-whisk-and-kerchief-waving Dr Kenneth Kaunda who, embarrassingly, would shed the occasional tear in public. This was worthy of notice: not only had the wind of change swept south down the continent, but it was also now whispering on our very doorstep, the mighty Zambezi River, and as much as a physical obstacle that that was, I somehow felt vulnerable: the old order was changing, with phrases like majority rule and one-man-one-vote omnipresent. There was a quiet inevitability about it all and although I could not absolutely identify the feeling—not quite a foreboding—I just knew that our time would come. In what form, in what manner or when, I had no idea, but the visceral angst of The Animals' 'The House of the Rising Sun' did seem to capture the essence of the remaining white bastions of Southern Rhodesia, South West Africa, Angola, Mozambique and South Africa. Surely nothing would change with the omnipotent South Africa as the foundation of the subcontinent? I took some comfort from this. Yet even with Rhodesia dropping its 'Southern' prefix—now irrelevant as the Northern was no longer extant—a peculiar feeling, akin to a kind of lonely emasculation, appeared to blanket the country (well, the white bits at least) now that we had lost our brothers across the Zambezi to the embryonic ravages of black rule.

John Sandys-Thomas said: "Well, we'll bloody well make Rhodesia work. We'll damned well show 'em. Ian Smith's on the right track. No caving in to the bloody British."

My father was more circumspect and I could sense an underlying nervousness: "I'm not so sure, Sandy. Maybe Graham White was right. That the writing *is* on the wall."

"Piffle, Mike! Don't be such a bloomin' Jonah."

"You heard about Teddy's brother?" Di Edmunds added. "Had to flee the country overnight, hidden in the back of a bloody Biddulph's removals van.

Seems like he'd pissed off Kaunda and his UNIP cronies who wanted to lock him up the day they got independence."

"Damned fool. Lost everything."

Eavesdropping from my traditional listening post at the top of the split-level steps, I was unaccountably agitated, my alarm levels rising. This was my great-uncle they were talking about, Granma Teddy's brother, our kin, and if he could lose everything then what was there to prevent us from losing everything? Would we then be the damned fools?*

But the 24th of October proved more auspicious than one African country's independence from Great Britain: it was the first day of the four-day match against the touring MCC, Rhodesia versus the Marylebone Cricket Club, and it was happening at the Police Ground and, what's more, we were going to watch. My excitement knew no bounds. Of course, I supported Rhodesia—the batting class of the Pithey brothers, Tony and David, the wily leg spinner Jack du Preez, the mercurial Colin Bland who was fast turning fielding into a beautiful art form, the sublime bowlers Goofy Lawrence and Joe Partridge—but the MCC was the stuff of legend and here it was, right on my doorstep at the BSAP Morris Depot, barely a stone's throw from the Enterprise Road in The Avenues.

I'd had a taste of the legend a couple of days earlier when Ted Dexter and Ken Barrington had popped round to the house for a drink. Ted Dexter, some six foot six of him, banged his head on the frame of the French door leading from the patio into the dining room. I winced, embarrassed and overawed, and scurried away to relative safety behind the settee whence I could view two of my all-time heroes in real life without getting in the way or being trampled on.

"Don't stare, Christopher! It's rude," chided my mother.

But Lord Ted simply smiled and ruffled my hair. I liked him.

Cramming camping chairs and a cooler bag into the Austin Cambridge, my father and I set off for the Police Ground, my mother and the twins sitting this one out. Looking at the programme, I was devastated to see that Ted Dexter wasn't playing. Still, Barrington was, which was a consolation. Finding a spot on the long leg boundary, not too far from the rickety sight screen—not ideal but all the good spots at cover and mid-wicket had been taken—we unfolded our chairs and prepared for the day's play, my father dipping into the cooler bag for his first Lion lager of the day. I was given a sixpence to buy an ice-cream and so off I went in search of the Lyons Maid man, weaving in and out of the sea of umbrellas, the carnival atmosphere pervasive. With his floppy hat pulled down

---

*Another of Granma Teddy's brothers had not too long before been murdered by the Mau Mau on his gold mine near Lake Victoria.

over his forehead, his shirt half untucked from his shorts and his long socks beginning to sag, my father seemed relaxed, even happy.

Rhodesia won the toss and chose to bat. Tony Pithey made 65 and Colin Bland a cavalier 66 in Rhodesia's first innings of 281 all out. The MCC replied with 298 all out, with Parfitt scoring 82 and the classy Barrington seventy-four. It was close-fought contest from which the MCC ultimately emerged victorious on the final day, winning by five wickets. My father and I watched all four days' play, with him making considerable inroads into the Lion lager stocks in the cooler bag—it was, after all, October, the hottest month of the year—and me being fed a liberal flow of tickies and sixpences to support the Lyons Maid and Dairibord ice-cream vendors, the latter being Washington—a sort of early Denzel—who was just starting out on his legendary ice-cream-selling career which would span decades.

As the sun was setting behind the clocktower, dipping in and out of the tall cypresses at the back of the clubhouse and casting shadows that lengthened across the field, now empty of cricketers, umpires and stumps but filled with rampant children armed with cricket bats and tennis balls, my father zipped up the cooler bag, the empty bottles clinking dully in the melted-ice water.

"Come on, young man. We'd better get a move on. Those women will be waiting for us at home."

I grinned at the conspiratorial 'us and them' allusion. It had been a good four days, an epic, and at times like these I truly loved my father.

3
Don't Let Me Be Misunderstood— The Animals, 1965

So it was that during the war my father and his younger sister Sally were shunted from pillar to post, from father to mother, from air base to air-raid shelter, until finally the siblings settled in the small seaside hamlet of Lamorna Cove in Cornwall where their mother Esmé was managing the local hotel. It was here that my father's love of the sea was spawned, culminating in an epic solo voyage in his small sailing skiff from Lamorna on the English Channel, round Land's End and to St Ives on the Bristol Channel—no mean feat for a 12-year-old boy.

After the war and the time in New Mexico, my father was sent to Radley College, a fine English public school. This fortunate coup was engineered by his uncle, Theo Cocks, a man of letters and a teacher at Radley. Theo was clearly something of an institution at the school and was therefore able to pull the necessary strings to get his itinerant nephew admitted—presumably at reduced fees. My father repaid his benefactor by studying diligently and excelled in Latin, Greek and Maths. On the sports field he played 1st XI cricket and hockey and was an accomplished racquets player. He finished his schooling at Radley in 1950, but because of his parents' unhappy circumstances was denied the opportunity of attending university despite his excellent academic results. He attempted to join the Merchant Navy but failed the medical, being told he had 'a bad back'. Uncle Theo again stepped into the breach, made a few calls, and found my father a position as an articled clerk with a firm of insurance brokers in London.

★

"*Dominus Pastor* … the Lord is my shepherd."
I glanced at the boy next to me who had uttered these words of wisdom. We

were standing at the school gate, our first day of prep school,* looking up at the imposing stonework and the sign embedded therein, the same sign as the badges on the pockets of our emerald-green blazers (my blazer, threadbare in places, was less than bright emerald green because it had been bought from the school's second-hand shop—"No point in wasting bloody money on new stuff," my father had said. "Before you know it, he'll have grown out it."): ST. JOHN'S PREPATORY SCHOOL above a shield with the image of a sheep and a crook, with DOMINUS PASTOR in the scroll below it.

I was slightly disappointed: it was all a bit pacifist. I'd been hoping for a crusader, ideally Richard the Lionheart, with the tip of his broadsword resting lightly on Saladin's corpse.

"Hello," I said shyly.

"Oh, hello, old chap," the boy turned. "The name's Dudley."

"Dudley who?"

"No, silly fellow. Dudley's my surname. What's yours?"

"Cocks."

"Pleased to meet you, Cocks. What's your first name?"

"Christopher."

"Well, blistering barnacles! So's mine! You shall be Cockso, then."

"Well …," I stumbled, searching for a suitable riposte, "you shall be Duddo!"

"Splendid! Cockso and Duddo it is, then!"

Shorter than me, with dark hair, a pale complexion—his nose, longer than most, was continually red, as if he'd been out in the snow too long or had a cold—and spindly legs with knock knees, I liked Christopher Richard Knox Dudley immediately and instinctively. I liked his *joie de vivre*, I liked his attitude, his lack of fear and I liked his very proper English accent. For the first time I paid attention to my own and was less than pleased when I noticed more than a hint of a colonial Rhodesian twang, something I might need to deal with in the future.

A continuous stream of cars was pulling in from Fisher Avenue, Rolf Valley, to disgorge other, older boys in the drop-off carpark outside the gate and a continuous stream of boys was bustling past us, bumping and shoving in their haste to claim their new desks in their new classes.

"Bandits at twelve o'clock, Cockso. Look sharp, old boy," warned Duddo, minding out the way of the hoard of older boys. (Duddo's father, I was to discover later, was a former Spitfire pilot, with Duddo the splitting image of his

*a very English thing, preparing a boy for senior school

father but without the RAF fighter-pilot moustache and with both sharing the same faint amusement with life.)

"Where do we go?"

"Mama told me to look for the Standard 1 classroom, or ask for our teacher, Mrs Lewis."

"Right."

"Tally ho!" cried Duddo

Following the throng through the gate and down the paved pathway, my new friend and I tried to keep on an even keel and at the same time establish where we were going, the leather satchels on our backs bouncing and slipping in the mêlée. My cap was knocked off my head and bending to retrieve it, I bumped into an immovable object. It was a woman.

"Ah, what have here? New boys, are we?"

"Yes, ma'am," replied Duddo, doffing his cap.

So that's how it was done. Duddo had obviously been prepped.

I looked up at the woman, clearly a teacher—I could tell by the dowdy, calf-length frock and the tousled hair, *sans* style—and although she appeared quite formidable, what with the trace of a moustache and a large black mole on her chin with hairs sticking out, something a witch might envy, there was an air of benevolent authority about her.

"And what might your names be?"

"Dudley, ma'am." I noticed Duddo had now removed his cap entirely.

"And yours?"

"Cocks … ma'am," I replied, but without a cap to doff.

"I am Mrs Scrase, the Standard 2 teacher. I shall have the dubious pleasure of your company next year, but for now you need to go to Mrs Lewis's classroom."

I noticed two other new boys behind Mrs Scrase's frock, both red-haired, the one tall and gangly with a round face, the other my height with a pleasant face and spectacles. I would soon learn that the tall, gangly one was Mark Bushnell and the shorter one was Graeme Fleming—Busho and Flemo as they'd shortly become.

"Right then! Follow me."

So off we followed, across the central quadrangle with its lone plane tree in the middle, to the Standard 1 classroom in a prefabricated block that also housed Standards 2, 3 and 4, the staff room and the school office.

Duddo, Busho, Flemo and me, Cockso, were to become firm friends and in time the nucleus of the Colts XI and later the 1st XI cricket teams with Duddo a devious off-spinner and our opening bat, Busho our opening bowler in the mould of Harold Larwood, Flemo a cunning left-arm leg-spinner and the other opening bat and me, because I was never much of a bowler, the wicketkeeper and a useful but erratic lower-middle-order bat.

Mrs Scrase ushered us through the door into the classroom. "Here are some more little rabbits for you Mrs Lewis."

"Thank you, Mary."

"Assembly in ten minutes. Your monkeys to all be in the front."

"Right-e-oh."

Mrs Lewis, an elderly woman with a slight stoop and a dowdy, lower-than-calf-length frock that had perhaps once boasted a floral print, smiled kindly at the four of us. "Your lockers are over there with your names on. Put your satchels in them and then find your desk with your name tag on it."

The class, as silent as death, was almost full. Under the baleful stares of the other boys, we shuffled to the back of the room where the lockers were situated and deposited our satchels. I sat at my desk, intrigued by the lift-up lid, the ink-stained porcelain ink-well and the crude lettering that had been chiselled into the desktop by pupils past. I opened the lid to peek inside: empty.

A bell went, the naval brass bell from HMS *Snoopy* next to the tuckshop, signalling assembly. We stood up and followed Mrs Lewis in single file, across the quadrangle again, to the prefabricated Standard 5 and 6 classrooms that doubled as the hall for assemblies and school plays, with a concertina-type partition that could be opened and closed. (A new hall was to be built later that year, a more durable prefab-cement structure.) The third side of the quadrangle, a red face-brick building, housed the tuckshop, the kitchen and the ablution block. The fourth side was open, facing onto the Fisher Avenue carpark. There were two playing fields, the Little Field behind the ablution block and the Big Field behind the Standards 5 and 6 block, separated by a line of plane trees that shed hairy little seed pods which were to prove useful in an adversary's underpants.

That was St John's: six classes of thirty-odd boys each, two playing fields with gum-pole rugby posts dug in after the athletics season and then pulled out again before the cricket season—the fielder at deep extra cover and the 440-yard athlete in lane three needed to step carefully to avoid spraining an ankle in the indentations—and two wire-mesh cricket nets on a cement floor. Oh, and the swimming pool. As small as the school was, my parents had chosen St John's because it was a private school, and therefore multiracial, and because Latin and French were taught (to my father's enduring disappointment, Greek was not: "Well, if I had to bloody learn it, I don't see why he should get away with it."). Most of my Highlands Kindergarten friends, including Dean Wood, had carried on to Highlands Junior School. Simon Brewer had been dispatched to Ruzawi, a posh private boarding school out beyond Marandellas on the Umtali road—which served him right—and I secretly suspected that Jimmy Scott had been cannibalized by Oliver Grey as I never heard of him again.

Assembly was conducted by the headmaster, Mr Hickman, a dapper, no-nonsense, little man with a toothbrush moustache, thinning, swept-back hair and a twinkle in his eye, who led off with the hymn, 'Onward Christian Soldiers'—this was more like it, sterner stuff, martial stuff—with the Standard 5 teacher, the rotund Mrs Law, playing the piano with some gusto. Along with Mrs Scrase and Mrs Lewis off to the side singing lustily were the Standard 3 teacher, Mr Gardiner, a younger man with a close-cropped beard and a leer, and the Standard 4 teacher, Mr Stansbury, a tall, rosy-faced man with curly hair.

The school secretary, Mrs Dickinson—no relation, I don't think, to Vernon from T&D Motors—did not attend assembly, what with answering the phone, dealing with school fees, and drinking tea. The final staff member, Alfred Hickman, was also excused assembly, being too busy preparing the staff teas and the tuckshop in time for the 10 o'clock breaktime rush, stacking his shelves with packets of Willards crisps, doughnuts, apricots, packets of sherbet and licorice sticks and his freezer with Lyons Maid and Dairibord ice lollies and penny-cools, as well as ensuring the urn was filled with (free) suitably watered-down Mazoe orange juice. Being black, Alfred didn't have a surname—if he had it wasn't publicized—but pigmentation apart, he was the mirror image of Peter Hickman, small and dapper with a toothbrush moustache and thus his surname might well have been Hickman.

★

On 21 February 1965 civil rights leader Malcolm X was shot to death at a rally in the Audubon Ballroom in Manhattan by three Nation of Islam radicals, X having repudiated that organization before founding Muslim Mosque, Inc. and the Organization of Afro-American Unity. The killers, using a sawn-off shotgun and semi-automatic pistols, were identified as Talmadge Hayer, Norman 3X Butler and Thomas 15X Johnson. Apart from the preposterous idea that Americans could roam the streets with such arsenals—our BSAP policemen did not carry arms aside from truncheons—I struggled with all the X-names, but the 30,000 mourners at the funeral in Harlem, including Andrew Young, were proof enough of his stature. I wondered whether Martin Luther King was there.

Nine days later, on 2 March, President Johnson, or specifically Defense

Secretary Robert McNamara, announced the commencement of Operation *Rolling Thunder*—which, half a century later, still clinches the number-one spot on the Military Operations Nomenclature charts ahead of *Barbarossa* and *Desert Storm*—as squadrons of F-105 Thunderchiefs and B-52 Stratofortresses took to the skies over Hanoi to bomb North Vietnam into submission at worst and from the face of the earth at best. Now this was more like it and although I didn't like LBJ—too old, too jowly and without any of JFK's charisma—as a 7-year-old hawk, I supported the idea that the sheer power of the American war machine, something beautiful to behold, would clearly finish the job of annihilating the evils of communism in South-East Asia once and for all.

But then, barely a week later, on 10 March, Barry McGuire released 'Eve of Destruction' which, overnight, became an international hit, though not in Southern Rhodesia where the song was given little airplay, if any : protest songs that spoke out against the white mores of Western civilization and Christianity combatting the Yellow Communist Peril—switch to *Swart Gevaar* or Black Danger* for southern Africa—were regarded by the board of the SRBC as tantamount to treason, too close to home, and so, although not banned per se, they were simply ignored. Yet it was too powerful a song to ignore—Granma Teddy described it as "one of those ghastly Beatnik songs"—combining as it did McGuire's pounding acoustic guitar and his migraine-raspy voice shouting angrily at the world.

Perversely though, and it was not lost on me, it would have made an excellent soundtrack to the footage on ITN's *Roving Report*, viewed on Sunday nights at the Davies's after Palmer, Nicklaus and Player (and now Trevino) had dropped their final putts of the day, of B-52s dropping their sticks of bombs in the stratosphere over Hanoi. Twenty-nine-year-old McGuire, according to *LIFE*, was a folk singer who had emerged from the Beat Generation, initially with a duo called, wait for it, Barry and Barry, and then with the New Christy Minstrels based in Hollywood, with San Francisco still a year of two away from the hippy invasion. My father was 32 and thus only three years older than McGuire, something I completely failed to reconcile : I simply could not imagine my insurance-broking father with long, blond hair belting out a protest song. It was all very muddling : 'Eve of Destruction' was a song with the equivalent power of a Stratofortress and yet it was diametrically opposed to everything those B-52s were doing over North Vietnam, treasonably so, surely? On the one hand I could understand the wariness of the SRBC board of governors but

*Alternatively, *Rooi Gevaar* or Red Danger, as in Communism

on the other I admired and liked the power of this new protest music and how it could, and did, speak for a generation. There was something romantic about being anti-establishment but for the moment my loyalties lay with the status quo and things military: after all the British Empire would simply not have happened with the regiments of pacifists who would in a short space of time explode under the mantle of Flower Power.

In May 1965, the first armed ZAPU guerrillas entered Rhodesia from Zambia across the Zambezi and the government declared a state of emergency (that fifty-eight years later is still in place). I had no idea what a state of emergency was: I imagined the country's fleet of police cars, ambulances and fire engines zooming around with sirens blaring.

I was, however, preparing for my own little version of ferment: I was about to start violin lessons. For the first term I had learned the piano, taught by Mrs Patricia Gooch in her cottage across the *vlei* that bordered the Little Field. However, with no piano at home on which to practise—pianos were beyond my parents' means—Mrs Gooch wisely suggested that I learn a smaller, cheaper, more portable instrument. It so happened that she was also a violin teacher, with the additional boon that she had a spare three-quarter-size violin for sale at a reasonable price and which would suit me admirably. And so, once a week at 5 p.m. on a Wednesday, I took violin lessons where I grappled with the intricacies of perhaps the most difficult instrument in the entire range of orchestral instruments. Only Grade 1, it was impossibly hard going: the chin rest cut into my left clavicle, I developed a crick in my neck from trying to grip and balance the instrument with my chin and the tips of the fingers on my left hand were lacerated (almost) by the garrote-like strings.

Equally excruciating was just getting there. It was perhaps a 400-yard walk from Mrs Lewis's classroom to Mrs Gooch's cottage, but with a treacherous barbed-wire fence and a malignant *vlei* between the two locations. In summer, the *vlei* was in places a foot deep in water and my feet rarely escaped a soaking. I would arrive at Mrs Gooch's and take off my sodden shoes and socks before I went into the house with Mrs Gooch thin-lipped and peering over the rim of her spectacles, wordless. In winter, dark by 5 p.m., the *vlei* turned to ice which rarely melted because of the aspect of the slope.

Disaster occurred one evening on my way there when I got tangled up in the barbed-wire fence and in the process of trying to prevent the violin and my school satchel from tumbling into the water, I somehow ended up almost upside down, the barbs clawing at my uniform, and watched in slow motion as two dozen precious marbles fell out from my blazer pocket into the murky depths.

It was marble craze at school I had had a good season, accruing some rather special grannies, cat's eyes, smokies and goons, none of which now remained in my pocket. Gone.

Disaster occurred again that year when Mrs Gooch told me that I would be doing a violin solo—'The Bluebells of Scotland'—for parents' evening in the new hall. It was a terrifying experience. I was shaking with nerves and couldn't tune the violin properly, coupled with the bow going rogue and sliding uncontrollably over the strings (my block of rosin had inexplicably shattered, and I'd been unable to rosin up the bow). It undoubtedly sounded like the proverbial cats' chorus and was the longest three minutes of my brief life, peppered with the sniggers of some oafish parents. The applause at the end, rather the death, was desultorily dutiful. I crept out the back of the hall, packed my violin and bow away in the case and cried.

★

Our rose deliveries were scheduled for Tuesday afternoons after school and Saturday mornings, 'our' being my mother and me. Although arduous work, I was an integral cog in a well-oiled machine and was proud of the crucial role I played: the success of the deliveries hinged on me. Prior to setting off from the house, I would do a quick inspection of the Opel station wagon to establish how many tins of roses had been loaded by Peter and George, and therefore the level of intensity of the delivery schedule. The bench seat at the back had been folded forward to expand the boot space, with newspaper laid to absorb water spillage. The rose tins were fashioned from old one-gallon paint tins painted yellow for easy identification, with COCKS roughly stencilled on in slightly smudged black: my mother's corporate colours, I suppose. For carriage a piece of wire was used in the manner of a bucket handle. With each tin holding some two dozen roses wrapped in newspaper and filled with water, the wire handle was an instrument of torture in my hands.

"Twelve tins today, Christopher," my mother called out, fastening her *doek* and slipping on her Ray-Bans as she got into the car. "Better get a bit of a move on. Don't want to hit the bloody rush hour."

"Where first, mummy?"

"I think we start with The Elizabeth. Only got two tins today. Get it out the way before the traffic starts."

The Hotel Elizabeth, an unprepossessing three-storey building that looked more like a block of flats struggling to avoid inner-city stigma, was situated on the corner of Manica Road and Causeway, the wrong side of Causeway which zoned it as Cow's Guts, just. Despite its location and its mediocre two-star rating—once upon a time it had had three—it was still regarded salubrious enough to be frequented by white people, not the oiks or the navvies but middle-class whites, particularly Gallic, as the hotel was owned by a Belgian refugee from the Congo and attracted a colourful francophone clientele. Parking was never too much of a problem at the Hotel Elizabeth and even if the yellow-lined loading zone was occupied, my mother was confident enough to double-park, motor running, while I grabbed two tins of roses from the back, got them balanced in each hand and staggered in to the foyer, timing my run so that I wouldn't need to stop to massage the wire-induced welts on the palms of my hands before plonking the tins on the worn carpeting in front of the reception desk.

Hercule Poirot leaned over the counter and peered down at me, flashing two fingers: "*Ah, Christoph, mon fils! Duex aujourd'hui, n'est-ce pas?*"

I nodded, breathless.

"*Bon.* Say 'ello to your *belle maman.*"

I smiled weakly and nodded again.

"Hokay. *À bientôt.*"

My mother was looking anxiously in the rear-view mirror as I clambered in. She had spotted a courtesy officer—a bizarre appellation—still several cars off, studying the parking meters along the pavement. Courtesy cops would issue a ticket for a meter less than a minute expired. In fact, they'd linger by a meter about to expire, counting down the seconds, biro poised, for the red EXPIRED flag to *ka-ching* into middle of the glass screen. Entrapment this would later be known as. Double-parking was as equally heinous an infringement with the courtesy cops brooking no argument before writing up a ticket. Ruthless, cold-hearted people, they were the enemy. But my mother was adamant: she saw no earthly reason to waste a tickey or a sixpence in a meter for a short-term sojourn, preferring to double-park for ease of quick getaway. "Bloody tickey thieves," she called them.

"Who did you see?" she asked, pulling out. "The owner?"

"Yes. He said I must say hello."

"Oh, did he just? The randy little Walloon!"

Next stop, after a frenetic dash down Manica Road and left into Second Street, the Ambassador Hotel on the corner of Union Avenue and Second Street, opposite the Union Avenue Post Office. Also seemingly like an innocuous apartment block from the outside, the Ambassador was a star above the Hotel Elizabeth and what a difference that star made. Tastefully modern in the glass-

and-chrome style, airy and with a professional ambience, the hotel had taken its name from the governmental precinct that ran from Second Street to Fourth, housing the high court, Parliament and the prime minister's office, among a host of other judicial and civil service departments. The concierge, a tall, cadaverous black man with a red fez and a red coat and tails, controlled his door with an iron rod—he had seen service with the Rhodesian African Rifles in the Burma campaign and later Malaya—and would suffer no nonsense from rowdy guests, drunken passers-by trying to gain access or street touts. His 'door' also extended to the street, specifically the loading zone which, rightly, was only for loading and unloading into and out of his hotel. No double-parking interlopers for him either. I didn't know his name as we never spoke, exchanging only the briefest nod of recognition or greeting. He would ensure that our delivery was seamless, guiding the Opel into the loading zone and holding the back door open while I unloaded the rose tins that I would carry through the double plate-glass doors, leaving them unobtrusively to the side, careful to avoid spilling any water. He would take them from there: delivery boys, even a white delivery boy doing what was ostensibly a black man's job, were *personæ non grata* in the hotel foyer.

There was no proof of delivery, no signing or issue of receipt at any of the three hotels. If the hotel's order was four tins, then four tins were delivered and that was that.

"Six down, six to go," said my mother, swinging back out into Second Street.

I groaned inwardly: six tins to Meikle's, the toughest assignment of all. That meant three round trips from the car to the hotel kitchens. With parking being what it was—impossible: columns of double-parkers and even triple-parkers hogging the inside lanes—it sometimes meant we'd need to do a hit-and-run. My mother would double- or triple-park alongside the ranks of gleaming Mercedes Benzes, Rovers and Bentleys, opposite the sweeping entrance to the hotel and I'd leap out, frantically dodging harassed drivers and angry courtesy cops, open the back of the car and grab two tins as my mother inched out into the traffic to drive round the block. Then the hundred yards or so to the hotel kitchens, past the pair of monumental, sphinxlike lions, past the doorman dressed like a tinpot African dictator with his military peaked cap and a dazzling array of medals covering every inch of his barrel-like chest, through the imposing arches and into the foyer the size of a football pitch. It was here that I'd draw breath, surreptitiously placing the tins on the football-pitch-sized Persian carpet to avoid the glares of sundry front-of-house and food-and-beverage managers who were more concerned that the delivery urchin was not spotted by the teeming throng of tobacco farmers—or tobacco growers as they styled themselves—in the adjoining lounge celebrating yet another bumper sale of their crop on the world-famous tobacco auction floors. The din, embracing the entire ground floor of Salisbury's grand dame of hotels, Rhodesia's Raffles and the epitome of colonial taste, was punctuated, like machine-gun fire, by monstrous guffaws, snorts *à la* Uncle Pat—in fact I'm sure I caught a glimpse of him—and laughs so explosive that they could not possibly have originated from within a human frame. Taking a final peek at the sea of tweed and safari suits, and a deep breath, I gathered up my tins for the last leg to the chromed double swing doors where one final challenge awaited: to ensure I didn't get bowled over by a waiter bursting through from the other side. The kitchen, as cavernous as the lounge and equally *fortissimo*, was a bustling hive of chefs, sous-chefs, cleaners and waiters, none of whom paid me the slightest attention as I found my spot, dumped the two tins on the floor and snatched a few empties from the previous delivery before the withdrawal back on to Stanley Avenue to start the whole cycle over again, this assuming I could find the Opel. Scanning the traffic over the road to Cecil Square, round the corner up past Kingstons on Second Street, across the Stanley Avenue traffic lights toward Greatermans, it was nowhere to be seen. Then, cruising alongside the double-parkers at little more than an idle, appeared the Opel infiltrator, my mother and I making eye contact as she slithered to a gentle halt, and I dashed once more into the breach for round two.

★

It was a hot August evening, still not spring but the worst of the winter cold more or less done with, although nights might yet produce a black frost. I didn't like Augusts. With the summer rains a good three months off, days were dry, hot and dusty, the sky opaque and brown from the smoke of a thousand bushfires that burned across the country, leaving the veld charred and lifeless. An uncomfortable wind blew continually, irascibly, buffeting karma and temper alike to subside only at night when the last of the winter cold would creep in, insidiously, and in the morning a frost would blanket the blackened veld.

Like the veld fires of southern Africa, mid-August saw the eruption of the Watts riots in Los Angeles which left thirty-four people dead, a thousand injured and four thousand arrested. I struggled to come to terms with the pictures in *LIFE*, trying vainly to reconcile them with our own township riots that seemed paltry by comparison. Thirty-four dead against a backdrop of 'I Got You Babe' by Sonny and Cher and Petula Clark's smash hit 'Downtown'.

At times I thought music was only there to soften the ugliness of the world's reality, and perhaps it was.

We were having sundowners at Di and Joy's house at 4 Borrowdale Lane, a functional fifties house with a peculiar entrance, a curved, white wall encircling the porch like a billowing sail and the front door with a porthole window above a brass Horatio Nelson knocker. I suspect that a generation of architects had seen war service with the Royal Navy. (In fact, they had, as witnessed by Granma Teddy's architect friends Herbert and Albert, ex-Royal Navy and ex-Kriegsmarine respectively who lived in a grand house called The Poop that overlooked Swartkops River which emptied into Bluewater Bay, Port Elizabeth.)

Having been duly encouraged by Di to "fuck off and play outside", my sisters and I soon tired of the unimposing garden laced with garden gnomes and tractor tyres that served as sleeping quarters for the pair of listless Rhodesian Ridgebacks, and quietly weaseled our way back into the sitting room to scrounge another Coke from Joy who tended to spoil us.

"Oh, do leave them be, Betty," coughed Joy through a cloud of cigarette smoke. "One more Coke can't do any harm."

The adult talk was on Uncle Pat who had recently given up farming to pursue a career in radio broadcasting.

"Bloody fool," quipped Di. "Went bust."

"Poor old Cottontail," clucked my mother, shaking her head in an attempt at sadness.

"Not so sure about the 'poor old', Betty," added Joy. "It was just a matter of time. First the Land Bank repossessed the Cessna. Then the fancy car and then the farm."

"What happened with the onions?" asked my father. "Patrick convinced everyone that he'd make his millions from onions."

"Compost … like his tobacco," replied Di. "Just shows you, doesn't it."

"What?"

"What'll happen to you if you're an idle bloody swine and razz it up all the time."

I felt a pang of guilt: I still hadn't done my weekend prep. Did that mean I was in danger of becoming an idle bloody swine?

"So, what's he going to do now?" asked my father.

"He wants to write radio plays," ventured my mother, knowing full well that the very idea was preposterous.

"Hah!" snorted Di derisively. "Who for? The SRBC?"

"Probably."

Di laughed dismissively into her whisky and soda. "Well, good luck to the bugger. Just so long as he doesn't pitch up on our doorstep asking for a bed."

"We could always give him Brutus's tractor tyre," suggested Joy.

"No bloody ways. What about Brutus?"

I wasn't sure I was as quite amused as the adults. After all, I liked Uncle Pat and had enjoyed the trips to his farm out in Sipolilo.

"So, Cottontail's planning a career in radio," stated my father. "A bard in the making."

Di looked askance at my father, as if his contribution was somehow irrelevant.

"He'll become the bumbling bard of bollocks!" beamed my father, rather pleased with his witty alliteration.

No one laughed.

My mother hurriedly changed the subject. "So, how's the business going, Di?"

"P&R Transport? Marvellously. What with all these rumours of UDI flying around, the oil companies are spending millions on new storage facilities." "And not only do we get to transport the fuel tanks on our trucks, we get to install them as well," added Joy smugly.

Business: more my father's comfort zone. "So you have contracts for all this work?"

"Absolutely," said Di. "With Shell, BP, Mobil, Total …"

"And what's entailed in installing the tanks?"

"Bugger all, really, said Joy, "Roll them off the trucks and build stands for them. Throw a concrete base, weld a few lengths of angle iron together and hoick the tank on top."

"The only downside is the travel. Most of the work is out in the bush at rural fuel depots. *Dorps** like Mtoko, Mount Darwin, Umvukwes, Centenary," said Di.

"This UDI talk," inquired my father, suddenly serious. "Is there any substance to it or is it just talk?"

"Damned right there's substance behind it, Mike," replied Di, equally seriously. "All the farmers are talking about it. And they should know; they're the backbone of the Rhodesian Front."

"But surely Smith wouldn't do anything so stupid?"

"Don't bet on it, Mike. Boss Lilford's stirring the right-wing pot, all the

*villages (Afrikaans)

77

good old boys like Harper and Lardner-Burke. Mark my word, it'll happen."

"They're all ghastly bloody right-wingers," my mother contributed, now well over the Teacher's threshold.

And then I saw it. I had to do a double take to ensure it was what I thought it was. Hesitantly edging closer to Joy who was at the gramophone about to put a record on the turntable, I saw the record sleeve in her hand. It was the new Françoise Hardy album, the one with her hit 'All over the World'. I'd recognize the classic beauty of that face anywhere: the full, sensual lips, the sculpted cheekbones, the tumbling hair always a shade awry, the languid eyes. My heart skipped a beat, The Supremes now promptly relegated and forgotten.

"Please can I see it, Joy?" I asked, tugging at the record sleeve.

"Christopher's in love with Françoise Hardy," said Caroline.

"Yes ... and he wants to marry her," mimicked Sarah in a singsong tone.

Joy laughed, that hacking laugh. "Well, she's certainly a beauty, isn't she? Wouldn't mind marrying her myself."

But before I had time to become intimate with the record sleeve it was time to go. Night had fallen and tomorrow was a big day. We were entertaining. A meet-the-parents braai, or barbecue, and invited were the Dudleys, the Bushnells and the Flemings, all identified by my parents as potential friends.

It was too much to take in: Duddo, Busho, Flemo and Françoise Hardy, all in one August weekend.

★

"*Errrppp!*"

I sat bolt upright in bed. Had the crows gone rabid?

"*Errrppp!*"

There it was again. Then I heard my father's voice outside my bedroom window, the back way up from the kitchen to the servants' *khayas*.

"Theresa! Where're the boys?"

"I don't know, *mustah*."

"Well, that's no bloody use, is it? We've got guests coming for lunch and Peter needs to get the fire going for the braai."

"Yes, *mustah*."

Silence.

"*Errrppp!*"

I heard panting as Peter came running, Pluto and Sam snapping irritatingly at his heels.

"Peter! Where on earth have you been?"

78

"Toilet, *mustah*. Do shit."

"Delightful, thank you. Have you got the braai ready?"

"Yes, *mustah*. I cut more wood now."

"Good. What wood are you using" The poplars from the river?

"Yes, *mustah*."

"A bit too wet probably, but I'm not buying bloody charcoal."

Silence, the logic lost on Peter.

"Well, come on now, let's get a move on," instructed my father.

Silence again as the impromptu meeting adjourned, Peter grabbing an axe from the storeroom to hack down more wet poplar wood and Theresa back to the kitchen to prepare the couscous and potato salads.

The braai, positioned on the front lawn next to the tickey-creepered wall by the Pride of India, was testimony to my father's paucity of engineering skills. I remembered when it had been made six months before: an old forty-four-gallon drum that my father had scrounged from P&R Transport cut in half, lengthways, by Peter using a chisel and a four-pound hammer—no fancy angle-grinder for him, let alone a hacksaw—with jagged edges capable of snaring a cook's arm, brutally. The building-sand sieve, with equally ferocious edges at adult-groin height, doubled as the grill. The entire half-drum arrangement—the other half had been converted into a flowerbox positioned at the one end of the patio with a fine stand of geraniums in it—was mounted precariously on some old breeze blocks that my father had found in the Umwindsi River. On a previous occasion this super-structure had collapsed and the Pride of India had caught fire. What a brouhaha that was.

Within an hour a damp fire was spewing forth thick white smoke that permeated and enveloped the whole house. I could hear the wet poplar wood hissing and squeaking angrily.

"Mike! For God's sake!" shrieked my mother. "Do something about that bloody smoke. It's ruining my couscous salad!"

I could sense a crisis looming and dashed outside to assist my father who was trying to wave away the smoke with the *Sunday Mail* as Theresa—the appointed barbecuer for the day—huddled by the braai with her *doek* over her face in an effort to keep the smoke at bay in a manner not unlike a British Tommy avoiding a mustard-gas attack at Ypres.

"Christopher!" yelled my father. "Bring the hosepipe!"

That was it. The good fight was lost and my father would shortly be rushing up to the Caltex garage at Chisipite to buy a bag of charcoal.

The guests all arrived at the same time, almost in convoy. I wondered whether it was coincidence or had they rendezvoused at the corner of Midvale and Enterprise prior to making their grand entrance? This was it. I took a deep breath. With my hair smartly combed from the not-quite-straight parting over the niggly cow's lick and across my head, my shirt tucked into my shorts and my socks pulled up, I was as ready as I'd ever be.

First out were the Dudleys, Richard, Fay and Christopher. Duddo's elder sister Susan was not present as she was staying the weekend with a friend which, Duddo had advised beforehand, was a good thing. Fay, or Faysie as my parents referred to her, was a tall, vivacious woman with a beautiful complexion and a smile that could light up a room. I fell in love with her in an instant as I'm told had every Spitfire pilot in Fighter Command.

"So you must be Cockso!"

I nodded dumbly, smitten.

"Well, you're a pretty little chap, aren't you?"

I gulped dumbly, smitten some more.

"Richard, this is Cockso," Fay said to her husband. "The one Chris won't stop talking about."

The informality, the friendliness of it all had me blushing in delight.

Richard Dudley smiled at me, like I was already part of the family. "Oh, hello Cockso, old chap," he said, shaking my hand. "You like fly-fishing?"

"You mean trout?" I asked.

"Absolutely. We've taken the cottage at Inyanga* for a week during the hols. Love to have you along."

I gasped and looked at my mother whose frown indicated that it was a fair idea but that there were many factors to consider before leaping in with a yes.

"We'll chat to your mama about it," said Richard with a wink.

I liked Richard instinctively. Not quite as tall as his willowy wife, his hair was combed across a slightly thinning pate and below the fighter-pilot moustache his mouth was perpetually fixed with the hint of smirk as if he found life marginally and continually droll, though I suspected it was rather a smug "I got Fay ahead of the entire Fighter Command".

On the other hand, the Bushnells, Audrey and Derek, were the antithesis of the Dudleys: serious about life, though nevertheless likeable under the veneer of formality. Audrey, or Dahling Audrey as my parents called her behind her back, ruled the roost with an iron rod and although Derek, an urbane and ingenuous North Countryman, was more or less impervious to her social rigidity, their

---

*Nyanga today

only child Mark wasn't and his life was an embarrassing hell because of it. So much so that Audrey would bring Mark his freshly prepared packed lunch to school every day five minutes before the 1 o'clock lunchtime bell, while the rest of us made do with Marmite sandwiches made the night before, the crusts hard and curled, along with a blackening banana and perhaps three or four soggy samoosas, all wrapped in second-hand grease-paper or tinfoil that smelled of old cooking oil. And she would pick Mark out for the slightest behavioural misdemeanor: he had to be perfect—at school, socially and domestically. She called him 'Mork', an indication of the elocution lessons she'd probably taken in an earlier life to rid herself of a vexatious North Country accent that ostensibly came across as vulgar and inappropriate, especially for the wife of a gifted corporate businessman like Derek who, incidentally, had no such pretensions and wore his accent unashamedly. Audrey was, however, as hard on herself as she was on her son. Always dressed impeccably in a pastel-coloured gabardine suit with the skirt just below the knees, with white nylon stockings and high-heeled shoes (not too high), she wore her hair frugally in a bob, always immaculately styled and that framed an attractive face with too much foundation. That said, Audrey was in fact a darling and was extremely fond of her son's friends and as proud of their achievements as she was of her own son's. In time she even began to call me Cockso.

Les and Sheila Fleming were Scottish, or Scotch as my father said, and middle of the road 'twixt the Dudleys and the Bushnells. The entire family, parents and four children (including Graeme's younger sister Alison), was red headed. Mr Fleming, a dapper man with a sharp wit and half-moon spectacles on a string round his neck, was in finance and reminded me of Robert Louis Stevenson's Mr Rankeillor in *Kidnapped*.

However, I sensed trouble. From behind my mother's skirts the twins had spotted Graeme who, with his fine features and wavy russet hair, was clearly the catch of the day as indicated by their giggles and glances. "Little tykes," Fay had called them. She was right and I wasn't about to let them monopolize my friends, so I marshalled them all to embark on a voyage of exploration to the jungles of the bamboo stand, pretending not to hear Audrey's admonishment of "You can't go down there, Mork! There'll be poisonous snakes in there."

With one eye out for his mother, Busho nevertheless got fully involved in our game of Anglo-Saxons versus Celtic brigands, with him and Flemo being the Celts—because of their red hair, naturally—and Duddo and me the Anglo-Saxons. Armed with bamboo poles, the object of the game was for the Celts to seek refuge in the bamboos, or in the poplars down by the river, and attempt to ambush the Anglo-Saxons, whereupon a short, sharp conflict would ensue with Anglo-Saxon bamboo pole attempting to destroy Celtic bamboo pole. In one such battle, with Flemo out of action because he'd lost his spectacles and sustained a minor head wound—a shard of bamboo leaf had gone into his eye—Duddo and I had Busho cornered up against a clump of young bamboos and were busy finishing him off with some well-aimed thrusts to the torso when Audrey appeared from nowhere.

"WHAT ON EARTH IS GOING ON HERE? MORK!"

Dropping our poles in alarm and leaving our 'kill' to the ravages of his mother, Duddo and I promptly fled, side-stepping a crouching Flemo who was clutching his one eye, to our temporary HQ behind the large compost heap. At the same time Busho, clearly combat-weary, lost his balance and managed to collapse, bottom-first, onto a large emerging bamboo shoot, ripping his trousers and causing himself considerable pain from the subsequent impalement.

An uncanny silence descended upon the bamboo glade as Duddo and I peeked round the corner of the compost heap. Empty: no Audrey, no Busho, no Flemo. It was obvious that the Celts had been medevaced to the dressing station that doubled as my parents' bathroom to have their wounds attended to, Flemo with some eyedrops and Busho with some rectally applied Savlon.

Stepping out into the glade, Duddo and I gathered up our cudgels and stashed them carefully in a clump of bamboos in case of further Celtic dissent.

"Well, Cockso," stated Duddo, surveying the battleground like a general, "I'd say the field is ours."

"Rather, Duddo, rather," I acknowledged. I'd been working on my accent.

The game was done, so we made our way back to the house but not unobtrusively enough to avoid the glare of censure from Audrey. Busho and Flemo, both patched up, were sitting quietly in my bedroom under instruction from Audrey. Flemo had an eyepatch on which elicited an "Ahoy me heartie!" from Duddo and a tactless "Anglo-Saxons forever!" from me.

I went outside and joined Theresa, Sam and Pluto at the braai where the pork sausages and lamb chops were sizzling merrily, if only to take in Theresa's comforting aroma. I loved her smell, the earthiness of the Lifebuoy soap, her musky femininity. I stood next to her and took her hand. She smiled at me, the smile of an angel, and she squeezed my hand.

I glanced over at the adults on the patio, awash in Lion lagers and pink gins, and even from the distance of the braai I could ascertain my father flirting with Fay. I felt a pang of jealousy. Flemo and Busho had been let out and joined us for lunch. With plates on our laps, sitting on the lawn, I was happy.

The day sadly ended when Pluto, his nose wet and greasy from the helpings of lamb-chop bones he'd been tossed, decided to thrust it into Audrey's gabardine crotch area which left an embarrassing and unsightly stain. I thought Audrey was about to have apoplexy, but she managed it well, helped in part by my mother's mortified flapping and mutterings of "Salt, that'll do it." But it was the signal for the Bushnell departure and like dominoes the rest followed, despite my father's lingering flirtation with Fay.

★

November 1965 was not a good month for me, in spite of my birthday, *The Sound of Music* and *That Darn Cat* which starred Hayley Mills and Dean Martin. Not only did our prime minister do the unthinkable and break with the Crown but to add to my misery I was diagnosed with flat feet.

"Well, I'm not surprised," my father had said. "Look at *your* feet, Bets. That's where he gets them from: your Short genes."

So began a decade-long attempt at therapy under the orthopedic and family friend Bill James who, queerly, was known as Mr James and not Dr James, which in my eyes confirmed he was not qualified. The therapy entailed endless hours of foot exercises to strengthen my arches: picking up marbles and pencils with my toes and pointing them like a ballet dancer, accompanied by my sisters' jibes that I was "a spastic". Worse, however, was the reconstruction needed for every pair of new shoes: a built-in lump, supposedly orthopedic, had to be installed by Mr James to physically force my non-existent arches to arch, something that never happened and only ever caused me undue pain in the manner I could imagine of Chinese foot binding.

Also that November began a ritual that was to become an annual trial of torturous proportions: the Christmas card production line. I knew there was trouble brewing when I overheard my parents talking one evening over their Teacher's.

"Bloody Christmas cards are costing us a fortune, Bets." "I know they are, Mike, but we can't *not* send to everyone. After all, everyone sends them to us and it's rude not to do the same."

This much was true as witnessed by the dozens and dozens, no, hundreds and hundreds, of Christmas cards that adorned the house every festive season, strung out on lengths of string across every conceivable stretch of blank interior wall.

"I mean, what does a Christmas card cost?" asked my father.

"About sixpence. I get bargain packs from the SPCA."

"Still … work it out. Multiply by a couple of hundred, even three hundred, more."

"Hmm …"

"That's a good ten quid … nor more."

"Hmm …"

"That's a lot of money."

"Hmm …"

"We need to cut back, Bets. During the war when there was no money and no cardboard for Christmas cards, we had to make our own."

I wondered out of what? Bark? Alarmed, I could see where this was heading and head that way it indeed did as a few days later my sisters and I found ourselves forcibly ensconced at the dining-room table with an array of crayons designing and making Christmas cards, each and every one customized and personalized.

"Besides," my father had said, "it'll be good for the children. Make 'em appreciate Christmas."

It didn't.

From Meg and Forbes down the road to Grandfather Cocks in England, Grandma Esmé in Toronto and dozens and dozens of unknown aunts, uncles and cousins from New Zealand to New Mexico, my sisters and I serviced them all. But with the improvement in our geography came a corresponding bitterness at the faceless hordes of family and friends, none of whom were our friends but my parents', some even old school friends like Ted Dexter. And every card was quality-checked by my mother.

"Sloppy, Caroline. That doesn't look like a Christmas tree at all. Do it again and stop rushing it."

And then the final inscription: "Dear Ted and family. Happy Christmas. Lots of love from Michael, Betty, Christopher, Sarah and Caroline" with abbreviations such as Xmas, Mike and Chris strictly forbidden.

It truly rankled but money was money.

The Household Cavalry trumpeters didn't come that Christmas. In fact, they never came again. We were the pariah state of Rhodesia and I was forced to content myself with Pete Seeger's ballad 'Turn! Turn! Turn!' made famous by The Byrds.

Life would never quite be the same again.

My great-great-great-great-grandmother Mrs George (Elizabeth) Edmunds, the daughter of Solomon and Betty Burchall, was baptized at St Andrew's Church, West Tarring, on 18 September 1776. She married George Edmunds at West Tarring on 19 July 1796. They had twelve children, all of whom attained adult life: Eliza, illegible, Charles (Admiral), Richard, Sarah, Harriett, Emily (Mrs Waugh), Walter, Alfred, John, Edward and Anna (Mrs Pagden). George Edmunds died at West Tarring on 16 January 1837 aged 64. Elizabeth died aged 92 at West Tarring in November 1868.

Hugh Fraser Sandeman (1799–1882), my great-great-great-grandfather.

Married to Hugh Sandeman was Julia Burnand (1803–92) from Alsace–Lorraine.

'A Victorian lady'. This might be my great-grandmother Maud Lamond (née Sandeman) c. 1890.

This is 'Aunt Lizzie', a formidable woman. I'm unsure whether she was a Lamond or a Sandeman.

My great-grandfather Guy Edmunds and oldest son Robert (Bob or 'Boy'), c. 1908.

My great-grandmother Beatrice Louise (née Hayden) with sons Charles (left) and Robert, c. 1910.

My great-grandfather Guy Edmunds as a major during the Great War.

Adrian Cocks, my grandfather, flying an RAF Airco DH.9A over the rugged Sind desert, near Karachi, in 1928.

My grandfather's notes to this photo read: "The chap in the back seat had his goggles 'down'. We pilots couldn't be bothered with the things! Over Karachi Sind desert below. Guess who? Khaki shorts, cotton shirt, flying topee. Happy days! 1928. Taken from a chum's aircraft flying alongside. Pity he just clipped my rudder and elevator."

My paternal grandmother Esmé Lamond on her wedding day.

My maternal grandmother Teddy (née Edmunds)

My maternal grandfather Clifton Max Short who died in 1935 aged only 37.

Esmé Lamond.

Granma Teddy at Nutcombe Farm in Addo, Eastern Cape, c. 1961.

Roy Matthews, Granma Teddy's second husband, in the uniform of a brigadier, Indian Army, 1961.

My paternal grandparents Esmé and Adrian Cocks prior to their divorce. The body language and their almost artistic positioning say it all.

My mother Betty Short as a debutante, London, 1952.

My father Michael Cocks, c. 1952.

My mother's cousin Di Edmunds (and young friend), Johannesburg, c. 1950.

My parents in Salisbury, c. 1958. Presumably Tessa the boxer is on the other end of the lead.

My mother and me (with the large, misshapen head), Midvale Road, 1957.

In jolly spirits is John Sandys-Thomas ('Sandy') with an unidentified pretty woman on his right and my mother on his left, c. 1960.

My father and my sisters at Uncle Pat Matthews' farm in Sipolilo, c. 1963.

My mother, Granma Teddy, the twins and me, c. 1961. Looking down towards the Umwindsi River, the area behind us was soon all planted to roses.

The author with Fred the tractor driver, Nutcombe Farm, Addo, c. 1961.

My sixth birthday, 1963, with me slouching in the foreground. Theresa is standing (with tray). Evadne Sandys-Thomas (with sunglasses) is kneeling at right. My sisters are at the back (one is standing). My first love Shona is kneeling in front of Theresa. Her sister Sally-Anne is on Evadne's right. Simon Brewer is the boy on the right; the other boy, on the left, is Alistair Hatrick. The scruffy straw fence behind is the boundary with the Whites' house. The 'table' for the occasion was the door that my father used under his mattress, to stiffen it because of his bad back.

With Father Christmas at Greatermans, 1963. Caroline is in the middle and Sarah is at right.

Sitting on my father's Austin Cambridge, with Granma Teddy, 1965.

The Short family homestead, Crofthouse, at Salem in the Eastern Cape. Originally built by the Croft family, it was bought by Joseph Short in 1836. (The Shorts had previously lived at Shortlands.) My mother's cousin, Jarrett Short, bought the property in the 1970s. Jarrett is wearing shorts here.

Day 1, Standard 1, St. John's Preparatory School, January 1965.

The Davies' pool at 3 Midvale Road, c. 1964. From left: Forbes Davies, Caroline (dressed, so no swimming for her), me, Sarah and my father, in the pool.

Now in Standard 2, with my mother's Opel station wagon parked in the drive, 1966.

Me as Peter Pan in the Highlands Kindergarten 1964 stage production. It was the green tights and the lipstick that attracted the homophobic comments.

On holiday, with my mother and the twins, King's Beach, Port Elizabeth.

The St Johns staff, c. 1968. Standing from left: Mr Gardiner, Peter Stansbury, Peter Hickman (headmaster); front from left: Mrs Law ('Ma' Law), Mary Scrase, Mrs Dickinson (secretary), Mrs Lewis and Mrs Wrathall (not present: Alfred).

As a St Mary's choirboy, I was finally awarded my surplice in 1967, shortly after the raid on the Délice Bakery.

Troutbeck, one of the many reservoirs in Inyanga. (Farai A. Chindiya CC BY-SA 4.0)

Lizzie Mutasa.

Granma Teddy and the Austin Westminster, Bluewater Bay, Port Elizabeth.

Granma Teddy at Polo Cottage.

Riding Happy, 1968.

The donkey cart at the Willowtree stables, pulled alternately by Two Pounds and Two Rand.

With my sisters on the verandah of Jean Butter's house at Willowtree. Sarah is at left and Caroline right. Jean was a pioneer in South Africa importing Jack Russells.

The Lord Chamberlain is
commanded by Her Majesty to invite

Mrs Betty Short

to an Afternoon Party in the Garden of Buckingham Palace
on Thursday 17th July, 1952 from 4 to 6 o'clock.
(Weather Permitting)

Morning Dress, or Uniform or Lounge Suit.

The invitation to an Afternoon Party at Buckingham Palace.

Patron: HER MAJESTY THE QUEEN
President: HER MAJESTY QUEEN ELIZABETH THE QUEEN MOTHER

THE ASSOCIATED BOARD OF

The ROYAL SCHOOLS of MUSIC

Royal Academy of Music   Royal College of Music

Royal Manchester College of Music   Royal Scottish Academy of Music

This is to certify that

CHRISTOPHER M. COCKS.

was examined in   VIOLIN   **playing &**

passed with merit in

Grade   I (Primary)   in   1967

The holder of this Certificate was presented for examination by

Mrs. Patricia Gooch

William Cole

Secretary to the Board

Grade 1 violin certificate, 1967.

4
We'll Sing in the Sunshine—Gale Garnett, 1966

My paternal grandmother, the feisty Esmé, was born a Lamond, in Rangoon, Burma. According to Robert Bain in *The Clans and Tartans of Scotland* (Collins, 1976) the Clan Lamond, or Lamont, is one of the most ancient of all the Highland clans and hails from Argyllshire on the Kyle of Bute. In 1456, John Lamont became the Bailie of Cowal; in 1539, Johyn Lamont of Inveryne was knighted and moved the clan's principal seat to Toward Castle where Mary Queen of Scots was his guest in 1563. During the Civil War of 1646, the fiendish Campbells swept through from the north, ravaging the countryside, destroying the Lamont castles of Toward and Ascog and treacherously massacred over 200 Lamonts at Dunoon. (The Marquess of Argyll was executed in 1661 for this.) The chief's seat was later established at Ardlamont. In 1809, John Lamont, the nineteenth chief, commanded the Gordon Highlanders at Corunna. Whether I can trace any direct ancestry to any of these esteemed people is debatable, but I do know the Lamonds were well connected. For example, my grandmother was a direct descendant of Robert Peel (as am I, presumably). Her mother, Maud, was a Sandeman—the Sandeman Port family from Perth—and like any well-to-do nineteenth-century Scottish family, all the Sandeman men saw military service in India, before going into the family Port or stock-broking businesses. Looking at the Sandeman family tree there are any number of Colonel Sandemans in the Indian Army. One, Sir Robert, even had a fort named after him.

★

Socially, New Year's Day 1966 elevenses at the Cockses was a more subdued affair than in previous years. Politically, it was not.

Forbes Davies was shaking his head in extreme annoyance. I'd never seen him so animated. "This damnable UDI!" he spluttered. "It's *the* most foolish thing I've ever heard of. Absolutely preposterous!" finishing off with a "Really!" that came out as a snort.

"Come now, Forbes," said Bruce Thoms, slugging on a bottle of Lion lager, "it's not the end of the world. There'll be lots of opportunities."

"For what! For war?" snapped Forbes. "Because that's what it'll come to, you mark my words."

"Oh, don't exaggerate, Forbes," added Bruce. "Your boss, Tiny Rowland, wouldn't be in such a hurry to do business with the Zambians if he thought there was going to be a war."

"Lonrho are pragmatists," explained Forbes. "We're an African company and we do business in Africa … black, white, independent, colony … doesn't matter."

"Well, at least Tiny'll be on the northern bank of the Zambezi when the Parachute Regiment invades Rhodesia," quipped Di Edmunds, "so he won't get shot like the rest of us."

"Or bombed by the RAF," added Joy helpfully. "I hear their Vulcan bombers are being deployed to Lusaka."

"There's no ways the Brits would invade," said John Sandys-Thomas in that deadpan tone of his. "We're kith and kin."

"Means nothing as far as Harold Wilson is concerned. The Labour government has a pathological hatred of Ian Smith and white Rhodesians," said Di.

"They're all ghastly bloody right-wingers. Wish the RAF would bomb them all to smithereens." I'd never seen my mother so animated either.

"But how would the British army invade?" asked Sandy rhetorically and not a bit self-righteously. "There's only one bridge across the Zambezi and that's at Chirundu. We could stop them in their tracks with one Ferret armoured car."

Joy laughed huskily: "We've only got two Ferrets and one's got a puncture."

Di laughed too: "That's why they've mobilized the Parachute Regiment. They're not going to *drive* into Rhodesia in Land Rovers, they're going to come the airborne route and parachute onto the Borrowdale racecourse."

"With only steely-eyed Mike and his police reservists between them and the prime minister's residence," chortled Joy.

"Who'll beat the buggers to death with the soggy end of his truncheon."

Di, Joy and Bruce erupted into raucous laughter, Forbes snortled, Sandy chuckled quietly to himself—Evadne was not present as she was dealing with Peter's head wound in my parents' bathroom, a result of the eldest son Michael discovering my father's police reserve truncheon under the bed and employing it with vigour on his brother's skull, something the twins had witnessed and who were now peering round the bathroom door, viewing the carnage like alarmed monkeys—and, to give my father his due, he was smiling, rather pleased with the attention, as negative as it was. (I had recently noticed that my father never laughed, at least not a proper gut-wrenching laugh but a quiet snigger; though, more usually, an enigmatic half-smile.)

Apart from Meg who was paying absolutely no attention to any of the proceedings, my mother was the only person not smiling. She didn't think the image of her husband armed only with a truncheon and, if he was lucky, a German shepherd, trying to apprehend a platoon of British Paras in the slightest bit funny.

Nor did I. Not at all. The very idea of fighting the British army, *my* British army, turned my stomach. It was simply too much to contemplate and at that moment I hated Ian Smith with every fibre of my being for having manipulated us into such a dreadful predicament.

"*Bibamus, moriendum est.*"

I looked up. It was Meg and I smiled at her. I loved Meg and she loved me.

"Chris ... ta ... fah! I ... need ... another ... pink ... gin."

"What does that mean, Meg?"

"It means, 'Let us drink, for we must die', which is Mr Seneca's way of saying, 'Chris ... ta ... fah! I ... need ... another ... pink ... gin.'"

I saw my mother looking at us. She knew exactly what was going on. Shaking her head, she crossed the patio to refill Meg's drink, if only to ensure that the tot did not exceed two fingers.

The sound of a car pulling into the driveway, accompanied by Pluto and Sam's welcoming chorus, announced the arrival of our final guest.

"That must be Cottontail," said my father.

Uncle Pat! I rushed out onto the driveway to meet him and there he was, trying to extricate his great frame from a Mini-Minor. Gone was the silver Jaguar and I immediately felt sorry for him. I could see he found it demeaning, but he carried it off with nonchalant exuberance.

"Christofaah! My dear boy." How delightful to see you!" He wrapped me in his bulk and gave me a big hug. He smelled of cigar smoke but it was a pleasant smell, homely.

"I'm sorry they took your farm away, Uncle Pat."

He knelt down in front of me, his gapped teeth stained a slightly darker yellow, and took me by the shoulders. "You know what, Christofaah? I'm *not* sorry. In fact, they've done me a favour. I was never much of a tobacco farmer and now I'm doing something that *I* want to do and something I think I'm good at."

I nodded thoughtfully. His words stayed with me forever.

I knew Uncle Pat now had to make his entrance and I was nervous for him. No one had seen him since the foreclosure. That there was a stigma to it all was undoubted, a taint, a slightly bad smell that would never fully disappear, but again, he carried it off with poise and grace as if the whole affair was really neither here nor there.

Bruce Thoms was first to break the ice: "Soooo, Patrick, you're doing something with the RBC?"*

"I am indeed, dear boy. I have a sound test next week as a newsreader, which is looking rather promising."

"Well, you've certainly got a face for radio," said Joy.

They all laughed, including Pat, the ice properly broken.

"And," he continued, "they've actually decided to buy my first radio play."

"Good heavens!" explained Di. "We must listen out for it. What's it called?"

"I've called it *The Onion Grower and the Jaguar*," and with that everyone burst out laughing.

Perhaps 1966 wouldn't be so bad after all.

But it was.

A week later the Commonwealth Conference was held in Lagos, the first time outside of the United Kingdom, to address the illegitimate Smith regime. Britain was under pressure to sort out the Rhodesia problem. On 8 January, Operation *Crimp* was launched outside Cu Chi in the Binh Duong Province north of Saigon, the first divisional-strength operation of the war in South Vietnam. Under the command of the US 1st Infantry Division, 8,000 troops from the US 3rd Infantry Brigade and the US 173rd Airborne Brigade, including the 1st Battalion, Royal Australian Regiment, and supported by artillery, targeted a major underground Viet Cong headquarters that included a network of 200 miles of tunnels. Heavy fighting took place and although the allies killed over 300 Viet Cong and captured ninety-two, the tunnel network was only partially destroyed. Allied casualties amounted to twenty-two killed and over a hundred wounded. Referred to as the battle of Ho Bo Woods in *LIFE* and on *Roving Report*—which we could watch on the Davies's TV in the luxury of our own house as they were taking their six-week overseas holiday after New Year—I was stunned to see, for the first time, images of dead and wounded GIs, drawn as I was in macabre manner to the graphic visuals. How could this be? American soldiers weren't meant to die? And this dreadful business of having to go into the VC tunnels? I could envisage nothing more terrifying.

---

*They'd dropped the S.

Then, two months later, on 9 March, four battalions of the North Vietnamese Army's 325th Division attacked a Special Forces camp in the A Shau valley, thirty miles southwest of Hué and adjacent to the Ho Chi Minh trail, the crucial supply route for the in-country NVA and the Viet Cong. Although supported by some 400-odd South Vietnamese irregulars, the Green Berets were hopelessly outnumbered, and the camp was overrun the next day. Again, I was stunned by the fact that the might of the United States meant nothing to the hordes of 'yellow' men in pyjamas and pith helmets. Surely it was only a temporary hiccup, and that General Westmoreland would get things back on track? Surely the results of Operation *Rolling Thunder* would start kicking in? But the feelings of unease did not go away, and I knew that the whole affair was going to take a few weeks, or months, longer than expected.

★

By the end of January, I was well ensconced in Mrs Scrace's Standard 2 class learning French and Britain formally ceased all trade with Rhodesia. Worse, the Mother Country had applied sanctions and, worse still, at the insistence of the OAU, the Organization of African Unity, had also gone to the United Nations urging the world to do the same, which, apart from South Africa and Portugal, it did. I thought this a low blow and a very un-British thing to do and could only put it down to the fact that it was instigated by Labour.

The effect of sanctions in my life was hard, far-reaching and instant. Consumables, such as foodstuffs, were the first to disappear from the shelves of my mother's supermarket, Macey's, down in Newlands where no amount of owner Sam Levy's green stamps could compensate for empty shelves. Breakfast cereals in particular were regarded as 'non-essential' and overnight brands like Kellogg's were gone. Post Toasties (corn flakes), Shreddies, All-Bran flakes, Weet-Bix, Coco Pops, Rice Krispies and Quaker Oats were replaced by locally produced cardboard in the form of Puffed Wheat, Honey Krunchees and Cocoa Puffs, none with much snap, crackle or pop. The only truly superior replacement was ProNutro, a light and wholesome wheat and soya cereal that, in time, came in a variety of flavours such as banana and chocolate and which essentially became our staple diet. Gone too were Nestlé and Cadbury with Peppermint Crisp, Jelly Tots and Smarties replaced by locally made cardboard brands such as Arenel and Sharon's. Ribena was gone but we still had Mazoe Orange Juice.

Alcohol also took a nosedive, with real Scotch taking pole position on the burgeoning black market. Ersatz alternatives promptly sprang up with local varieties of whiskey, gin, brandy, cane, rum and vodka all deriving from cane spirit and all smelling, and apparently tasting, of petrol. Imported wines gave way to vinegar masquerading as Chenin Blanc, coffee turned into chicory, Marmite into Fray Bentos and Anchovette Paste vanished entirely.

Fish, both fresh and canned, evaporated, my father bemoaning for decades the loss of his beloved herrings and kippers. Prawns, crayfish, sole and cod were superseded by bream, a local tilapia that tasted muddy, rare imports of chambo from Malawi and a tiny sardine called kapenta that thrived in the recently built Kariba dam and which proved a useful protein alternative for impoverished peasants and cats.

Lamb too disappeared. Being locally produced, chicken and pork were unaffected, though beef was, despite the fact that Rhodesian beef boasted an international reputation on a par with Argentinian. The shortages were because all the best cuts—rump, sirloin, fillet and T-bone—were exported, clandestinely by piratical sanctions-busters in unmarked DC-7s. A visit to my mother's butcher in Newlands became a depressing event that not even the sawdusted floor could enliven. Not that the family could afford the prime cuts anyway—we had rolled roast beef once a week, on Saturday nights, with Yorkshire pudding, roast potatoes and parsnips accompanied by broccoli or cauliflower in a white sauce—with oxtail, tongue, livers, kidneys and ox brains fried in breadcrumbs being the standard weekday fare. My parents, nostalgically revisiting the shortages of 1939–45 and beyond, also had a penchant, though perhaps rather the budget, for tripe, pig's trotters, Welsh rarebit, kedgeree and bubble and squeak, most of which my sisters and I loathed.

Strangely, imported books and magazines limped on for several months and in some cases a few years, and for the time being my parents' subscription to *LIFE* magazine and mine—through my mother and the good offices of Kingstons—to *Beezer* and *Treasure* continued apace until such time as the hubristic Rhodesian Front phenomenon of 'belt-tightening' came into effect, coupled with a downturn in the family budget. (This happened around the time when my mother reduced our lavatory-paper quota from four to two squares per person per sitting.) Even my favourite Ladybird books seemed immune from Mr Wilson's malignity and for the time being I was able to savour the likes of Alfred the Great, Robert the Bruce, Horatio Nelson, Walter Raleigh, Captain James Cook, Henry V and Julius Caesar and Roman Britian. I read how Captain Scott was pipped to the South Pole by Norwegian Road Amundsen and perished for his trouble. I read of the Iceni warrior queen Boudicea* and how she and her hordes of Britons revolted against the Roman occupiers and nearly caused an upset against the run of play.

The cruellest blow at my level was the devastating impact that sanctions had on The Hobby Shop, the Mecca of Toys south of the Congo River and north of the Limpopo. With each visit the shelves became more and more barren until my favourite Britains toy soldiers and Airfix models—I wasn't interested in anything else, not the model railways, not the Scalextric, nor the kites, the roller skates, or the boxing gloves—disappeared completely and the husband-and-wife owners sold up and moved 'down south' to Durban.

American and British motor cars no longer came in, although the French, the Japanese and, to some extent, the Germans, weren't quite so fussy about sanctions, with several makes and models—Mazda, Datsun, Renault, Citroën and BMW—assembled locally.

Music, however, remained unbowed, thanks primarily to international record labels for whom sanctions were immaterial and local record manufacturers. It was the time of the British Invasion, when British musicians were taking America—with The Beatles and The Rolling Stones in the van—and the rest of the world, including the colonies, by storm.

Coinciding with the British Invasion was the endowment of my father's 1950 Bush Bakelite wireless set—he'd splashed out on a fancy Sony transistor radio—that took pride of place on my recently acquired desk, which the man at the Treasure Trove had told my mother was "in good nick, love". The beige wireless, about a cubic foot all told, included shortwave (SW) and medium wave (MW) which I learned was the same as AM, sort of, the amplitude modulated wavelength. Not being technically gifted, I nevertheless made it my life mission to understand the intricacies of wavelengths and tuning, crucial aspects in the ongoing search for good music. Although I could occasionally find LM Radio on shortwave—depending on the height and angle of the homemade wire aerial affixed to the wall with Sellotape—SW proved a fickle wavelength and inevitably I returned to the new local station Radio Jacaranda that the RBC had recently launched as a pop-music-only station to cater for younger tastes and which was driven by trendy DJs like Martin Locke, Jeremy Dawes and Ian Warren with whom I could relate: "All very mod," Granma Teddy had said. Now I could listen to music in *my* time and *all* the time if I wanted to, which I did. And unlike the RBC that only aired the Hit Parade at 10 o'clock on

*Pronounced Bow-da-seeya; however, somewhere along the line someone has changed it to Boudicca, pronounced Boo-dikka.

Saturday mornings, Radio Jacaranda had its own hit parade every day at 6 p.m. for half an hour which proved fortuitous in terms of timings: school sports and afternoon prep were done with, and supper was an hour off.

The first two months of 1966 saw Nancy Sinatra and Chris Montez hitting the charts with 'These Boots Are Made for Walking' and 'The More I See You' respectively. A few weeks later Nancy Sinatra's father, Frank, had a monster hit with 'Strangers in the Night', "a smoochy song" as my father called it and the ultimate weapon in Bruce Thoms's *arsenal d'amour*. The British Invasion contributed 'My Love' and 'A Groovy Kind of Love' by, respectively, Petula Clark and The Mindbenders *sans* Wayne Fontana who had only recently stomped off stage in a huff. Petula Clark had already stolen my heart with her 1964 hit 'Downtown' but with 'My Love' she imprinted in me indelibly and for life, her class, her style, her timeless beauty and her towering voice. That beauty spot on the left of her chin, the auburn beehive hairdo a mite unkempt and the hint of buck teeth, all combined with the lyrics and melodies of her long-time songwriting partner, the sublime Tony Hatch, to create something exceedingly special that would endure for over half a century.

Written by Carole Bayer Sager and Toni Wine, The Mindbenders' one and only hit 'A Groovy Kind of Love' reached number 2 in both the UK and US charts and sold over a million copies globally, although the album of the same name flopped. Nowhere near the class and verve of Petula Clark, the song did however stimulate some robust arguments between me and my sisters who were adamant that the lines 'Wouldn't you agree? / Baby, you and me' were actually 'Wouldn't you agree? / Betty, you and me' and that the song had been specifically written for our mother. No amount of "LISTEN!" could convince them otherwise and in screaming, hair-tearing frustration I considered applying my cricket bat to their stupid heads.

The other topic of discussion was the etymology of the word 'groovy', a new word that had entered our Midvale Road lexicon. To me it was patently obvious that it originated from the grooves in a record that directed the stylus, the pickup needle, but to my sisters it wasn't, convinced as they were that the word was made up and meaningless.

"It could have been grovey," said Caroline, snickering.

"Or gravy," said Sarah, giggling.

"You're both BFs!" I retorted angrily to their gasps of horror.

Again, the cricket bat option presented itself, but instead I decided I'd test 'groovy' out, along with that other new word 'cool', on Mrs Scrace, as my sisters raced off to tell my mother that I'd called them bloody fools.

Learning poetry by heart was hard work but something that Mrs Scrace drilled into us. Liking the poem helped and I was fortunate that I'd been given *Tarantella* by Hilaire Belloc. I enjoyed the story-telling, the meter, the rhythm:

Do you remember an Inn, Miranda?
Do you remember an Inn?
And the tedding and the spreading
Of the straw for a bedding,
And the fleas that tease in the High Pyrenees,
And the wine that tasted of tar?
And the cheers and the jeers of the young muleteers
(Under the vine of the dark verandah)?

Not only did we have to recite our appointed poem to the rest of the class, but we then had to give a brief précis on its meaning and how it had affected us.

"So, Christopher, what are your thoughts on *Tarantella*?" asked Mrs Scrace.

"I think it's pretty groovy, ma'am."

There was a sharp pause and a raised, bushy eyebrow. "You think it's *what*, Christopher?"

"Groovy, Mrs Scrace. I think it's pretty cool."

The other bushy eyebrow lifted. "Groovy *and* cool!"

"Yes, ma'am ... both."

"Groovy as in tongue-and-groove woodworking?"

"Ermm ..."

"And cool as in Fahrenheit?"

"Ermm ..."

The class was hushed: they knew I'd been cornered, like a rat, and the killer blow was about to fall.

"Well, Christopher. I tell you what. If you can recite *Matilda* by Hilaire Belloc by tomorrow, I might consider overlooking your wholly inappropriate use of English."

I gulped and the class gasped: *Matilda* was an epic. "Ermm ... both verses, ma'am?"

"Oh, *pourquoi pas*. That'll be groovy *and* cool." The bushy eyebrows subsided slowly, first the one then the other.

What most certainly wasn't groovy or cool was petrol rationing. Within weeks of UDI, the Royal Navy had set up what became known as the Beira Blockade, with a clutch of frigates and destroyers, and occasionally an aircraft carrier, roaming offshore in the Mozambique Channel to intercept and turn about any Beira-bound vessel carrying oil destined for Rhodesia's oil refinery at Feruka in Umtali. In April white Rhodesians watched enrapt as the *Joanna V*, a Greek-registered tanker, successfully ran the blockade with a large element of bravura, only to be stymied at the final hurdle when the British government pressurized its Portuguese counterpart into refusing to unload the cargo. Again, very un-British and just not cricket. The country became increasingly reliant on South Africa for its fuel imports as petrol rationing was swiftly and ruthlessly introduced.

My mother, being a housewife, was classified as 'type private/ non-essential' and was issued five units a month, or five gallons, and on the first of every month she would queue at the Highlands TMB to receive her five coupons. I was alarmed. I knew five gallons was a pittance. Had we been reduced to this? It was dire and I knew the ramifications were momentous.

"Bets," said my father one evening. "We need to discuss your car."

"What about it?"

"Well, five units isn't very much. We're going to have to look at some cuts."

"What sort of cuts? And why can't you give me some of your business allowance?"

"You know I'm not allowed to do that. It's an offence."

"Oh."

There was a pause with ice tinkling in crystal glasses the only the sound to be heard.

"What's your fuel consumption, Bets?" my father asked firmly.

"I've no idea, Mike. I just go to T&D and tell them to fill up."

"Well, it's got to stop. We have to be extremely careful now. I imagine the Opel's consumption is around thirty miles to the gallon. Five gallons gives you a hundred and fifty miles a month."

"Really? That's not very much."

"It's five miles a day, Bets … only."

"Oh … that's rather a nuisance."

"It means you're going to have to monitor your trips extremely carefully, Bets. No more nipping up to Délice for cigarettes or popping down to Newlands because you forgot to get the dogs' bones."

There was another pause, a longer one this time and I suspected I knew what was coming.

"And Christopher's going to have to ride to school. I measured the distance last week: it's two miles, so four miles a day there and back."

"He can't ride to school, Mike. He's too small!"

"No choice, Bets. You still have to take the twins to Highlands KG, which is a lot closer, but you simply cannot do both. Take Christopher down to Jowett's tomorrow and get him a decent second-hand bicycle. And we need to think about getting rid of the Opel and getting something smaller."

And so it was the following day that my mother took me down to Jowett's in Newlands where an irascible Mr Jowett sold us a sturdy 20-inch Raleigh with drop handlebars and a three-speed for £20; well, he assured us it was a Raleigh as the whole bike frame, including the branding, had been hand-painted in bright-red enamel, which I didn't think at all groovy or cool.

"Bring i' baahk in coupla yeers en' ah'll swop i' aaht fer a twenty-four inch."

"Thank you, Mr Jowett," my mother replied formally, having grudgingly parted with twenty pounds.

"'Eer, aah'll ge' the boy ter wheel 'i aaht fer yer."

"Christopher can manage, Mr Jowett, thank you very much. Good day to you."

For the next four years I cycled to school, four miles a day, twenty miles a week, come rain or shine and I came to know the route intimately: down the path to the Umwindsi River and up through the veld on the other side to Steppes Road (past some massive boulders where Granma Teddy had said lions lurked), turn right onto meandering Willowmead Lane after a steep climb, right again onto Rolf Avenue, down the dip and then left into Fisher Avenue at the BP garage on the corner—where we'd spend our pocket-money pennies, tickeys and sixpences on crisps and gobstoppers at the garage shop—for the final 200 yards to the *Dominus Pastor* sign.

The elemental challenges occurred in the low-lying areas, principally the Umwindsi valley where in summer flash floods were liable to render the return passage impassable, forcing me to turn back onto Steppes Road and take the long way round via Drew Road and onto Enterprise, appending a further mile to my journey. Occasionally, too weary and too drenched to contemplate the additional round trip, I would brave the river and push my bike through the muddy torrent, at times waist- or chest-high in floodwater.

Winters were bitter and when the hoar frost came the valley was a carpet of whiteness, with icicles suspended from the stubbly, burned veld and the leafless poplars, sentinels to the stark and lifeless landscape. School rules always dictated that we had to wear our caps when cycling, so balaclavas were precluded, as were track suits which were not official school uniform. There was no winter uniform, so the grey shirt, shorts and socks so amenable in summer became our icy nemesis, barely alleviated by the tenuous mittens and earmuffs that my mother had knitted.

I managed to hook up with fellow cyclist Dan Winch, a new boy in my class who had recently arrived in the area with his divorcee mother and younger brother Nicholas and who were living in a small cottage on Kent Road. As Midvale Road was on his route, Dan, with precise, almost pretty features and an English complexion, became my riding mate and friend for the duration of my prep-school years.

★

The shrill blast of a whistle interrupted my afternoon prep. Barking dogs and urgent shouting announced quite clearly that some sort of fracas was in progress, apparently coming from the top of the drive, on Midvale Road. I rushed outside, disregarding my mother's alarmed "Christopher! Stay inside!" which only piqued my curiosity.

A grey police Land Rover was parked on the road and standing in front of it was a white policeman trying to restrain a rampant, snarling, slavering German shepherd. Behind the vehicle I caught a glimpse of George fleeing down the road, hotly pursued by two black constables.

"Stop that man!" the white patrol officer shouted, followed by another blast of his whistle.

I arrived at the top of the drive to see a constable rugby-tackling George and bowling him into the base of a bauhinia tree in a cloud of dust, his police headgear—a sort of khaki pith helmet affair with the top cut off like a boiled egg—bouncing onto the road. The second constable, portlier, arrived directly, surveyed the writhing bodies at his feet and drew his truncheon with which he started belaying George about the torso.

"*Iwe!* Blarr'fukkensheet, *skelm*," he shouted, each syllable perfectly synchronized with a blow of the truncheon, which impressed me. I wasn't too sure what he was saying but was able to hazard a guess at "Hey you! Bloody fucking shit, you rascal."

My mother arrived, cigarette dangling, "What on earth ..." but her question was drowned out by George's screaming, "*Maiwe! Maiwe!* Surrender ..." ("My word! My word! Surrender ...")

The two constables, breathless and sweating, heaved a battered George to his feet before the second constable handcuffed him, giving him a final clout about the ribs with his truncheon for good measure.

"Blarr'fukkensheet ... *Sattaan!*" ("Bloody fucking shit ... Satan!")

The young white patrol officer, with an Adolf Hitler moustache and a peaked khaki cap instead of a cut-off pith helmet, had stuffed the German shepherd into the front of the Land Rover, where it was incandescent, frothing and salivating over the passenger window.

"Mrs Cocks?"

"Yes?"

"Ma'am, you're going to have to get yourself a new garden boy. We're arresting this man for the illegal production of *skokiaan. Kachasu.*"*

"*Skokiaan*? Good heavens!"

"Yes, ma'am. Plain-clothes CID have been tailing him for several months now. He's been producing it round the back of his *khaya*—over there, in a forty-four-gallon drum—and he's been selling it at the shebeen behind the Lewisam garage."

"*Skokiaan*? Good heavens!"

"Yes, ma'am, and a particularly lethal brew it is too. He's been using battery acid, fertilizer and even a couple of dead rats."

"Fertilizer? My mother queried. "Not my roses' ammonium nitrate?"

"'Fraid so, ma'am."

Struggling impotently, George was hustled by the two black policemen to the back of the Land Rover and bundled inside, the grey steel door with the steel-mesh window slamming shut behind him and padlocked. As the vehicle started up, I caught a glimpse of George staring at me through the mesh. Etched on his face was a look of undiluted hatred, his eyes boring into me like hot coals. I shivered and instinctively went to my mother as Pluto and Sam came bounding up the drive wondering what all the fuss was about.

Disturbed by George's look, I struggled to sleep that night. That he hated me was obvious, but why? What had I ever done to upset him? I scoured my mind, wracking my brain, but could think of nothing until, eventually, the conclusion that I had not wanted to draw came to me: he hated me because I was white.

Our staff woes were by no means over. Two days later, at breakfast, I saw Theresa crying over a bubbling pot of Maltabella porridge on the stove.

"What's the matter, Theresa?" I tugged at her apron.

She shook her head, as if to affirm that nothing was the matter. "It's okay, *Mustah* Christopher."

But I knew it wasn't okay and rushed through to the dining room where my

---

*The same thing, skokiaan is South African, kachasu is Shona.

mother had just finished seeing my father off to work.

"Mummy, mummy, why is Theresa crying? What's wrong?" I knew innately that there was something seriously wrong. I just felt it, an overwhelming feeling of uneasiness.

"You wouldn't understand, Christopher," my mother said. "You're just too young."

That's when I knew it, that Theresa was leaving. "Understand WHAT!" I shouted, the panic rising. "I WILL understand it, mummy. I will, I will, I WILL!"

I could see that my mother was equally distressed but putting on a brave face, masking it: she hadn't even censured me for my cheek. My sisters, the ice maidens, were upset, too. I went back to the kitchen and found Theresa sitting on the back step, head bowed in her hands, sobbing quietly. I sat down next to her, felt the warmth of her body and attempted to put my arm around her waist. She lifted her face, that soft, beautiful, tear-stained face, and smiled at me. She put her arms around me and hugged me tightly.

That was the last time I saw Theresa. By lunch she was gone. I suspected this was my father's final instruction before he had left for work that morning. I studied him when he came back for lunch, and it was as if nothing untoward had happened. There was no mention of Theresa, none; it was if she had not existed.

My mother, naturally, was forced to stand in for Theresa, rushing around waiting on my father at the table and I think it was at that moment, for the first time in my life, that I despised my father. I never did discover why Theresa left. To even mention her name was anathema. All I knew was that there was an emptiness, a hole in our lives that would take some fixing, if ever.

Of course, with George now 'in the stokkies'* and Theresa banished to who knows where, my mother was left with something of a staff crisis, in that Peter was now expected to cover for them while word went out to the reserves that we now needed two servants. As Peter was strictly an 'outside boy', he would need some spot training for inside duties. Granma Teddy was of a mind that Peter had never seen the inside of a house—a cave or a hut, yes—so my mother gave up a couple of days to train him how to wash dishes, sweep and polish the floors, do the dusting, do the ironing and, most importantly, polish the array of shoes left outside our bedrooms overnight for a first-light polish, every day. (It always intrigued me that I'd leave a selection of dirty, muddy shoes outside my

---

*in the stocks, i.e. in gaol

door at night and, lo and behold! when I woke up in the morning, there they were, clean and shiny.) My mother would handle the laundry—except "the bloody ironing"—and the cooking. My sisters and I were expected to continue making our beds.

Weeks went by and, according to my father, the arrangement was "working just fine … not sure why we need so many bloody servants", oblivious of the black bags under my mother's eyes and the garden that had gone on the rampage.

It was one Saturday morning when I noticed two Africans up at the top of the drive, where a gate and fence should have been. I rushed to tell my mother: "Mummy, there are two Africans on the road, a man and a woman."

"Oh, thank goodness. That'll be the new staff, Elizabeth and Francis. Be a good boy and tell them to come down."

I dashed up the drive to meet them. "*Mangawani. Makadi?* I inquired, showing off my few words of Shona—Good morning, how are you?—and extended my hand in greeting.

Elizabeth laughed, more of an appreciative side-chuckle, and took my hand in the African-style greeting of grasp–upward-clasp–grasp, three smooth, easy movements before replying in a torrent of Shona which was meaningless to me, other than the word 'Christopher'. I smiled awkwardly. She noticed my embarrassment and in almost-passable English asked if I was Christopher.

"*Ehe*," I nodded.

She then indicated her companion: "This one Francis … garden boy."

Francis was a slightly built, verging-on-skinny, malnourished twenty-something. He appeared to have no hips, his longs prevented from falling down by an old leather belt that had several new holes punched inside to accommodate his hips which had to be somewhere. His eyes were downcast, as if afraid to make eye contact. (He never made eye contact in all the time I knew him.) I shook his hand African style, noticing the limpness of the handshake, very much a Shona thing. He smiled, a gentle smile that became his trademark, that and a grubby roll-up fag between his lips.

I took them down to meet the *medem*.

Elizabeth Mutasa, or more properly, Princess Elizabeth Mutasa, was—unlike Francis—not from Mtoko but hailed from the Inyanga district on the country's eastern border which was Mutasa clan territory. She was closely related to Chief Mutasa, hence the title. Somewhere in her late thirties, with piercing brown eyes, unkempt hair—feral more accurately —and a hair-spouting mole-slash-wart on her chin, I soon found out she had a side hustle going as a *nanga* ('witchdoctor' is misleading, 'traditional healer' is nearer the mark). She always wore a shawl, normally a blanket, and black horn-rimmed spectacles which lived on the edge of her nose.

But to us she was Lizzie.

Within two days she'd taken control of the 'inside' duties, with Peter reverting to some inside and some outside duties, as had been George's remit. Francis was strictly outside and became my father's sidekick on his interminable building projects, the latest being terrace work outside the kitchen at the back of the house where the slope was quickly eroding. Francis was soon inducted into the realm of my father's *errpps*, something he endured without complaint. My father later came up with a nickname for Francis, quite bizarrely, Tar Baby, a local up-and-coming heavyweight boxer. Where this came from was anyone's guess, but neither I nor my sisters bought into it: I just didn't see the humour.

★

On 28 April 1966, seven ZANU nationalist guerrillas were killed by security forces near the town of Sinoia, some seventy miles northwest of Salisbury. This was the first so-called major 'contact' of what was becoming a burgeoning bush war. It would later be immortalized, grandly so, by the nationalists as the Battle of Chinhoyi. Security forces was a new term to me, which I soon learned included anyone in uniform on the government side, including Police Reservist M. G. Cocks. In this instance, at the contact site on the Hunyani River, just outside the mining town of Sinoia, the security forces comprised a mixed bag of policemen, both regulars and reservists, sundry territorial army soldiers and an Alouette III helicopter with a machine gun. I was to hear that the security forces were all on different radio channels and unable to communicate with one another and that the helicopter had to land to issue instructions.

A fortnight later, just north of Hartley, a farming town some fifty miles west of Salisbury, Johannes Viljoen and his wife were shot dead at their farmstead by ZANU guerrillas (called terrorists by the government). The children were spared but I found this whole episode alarming. Did this mean that the terrorists would be coming into Salisbury? Hartley wasn't that far away.

I felt that precautions were needed and summoned my sisters for an *indaba* up by the massive Natal fig tree in the top corner of the property next to the fancy house in which the Saunders family had recently taken up residence. (The eldest son Gary was a year my junior and had just started Standard 1 at St John's).

My sisters, sitting cross-legged under the tree, were suitably solemn. This had to be serious. I explained 'the Viljoen incident', as it had become known.

They listened, wide-eyed.

"So, the children have got no mummy and daddy?" asked Caroline.

"Uh uh."

"Who will look after them?" asked Sarah.

"I don't know, but we have to be ready if the terrorists come here. What we must do is dig a tunnel so if they come, we can run and hide."

The twins nodded sagely. This made sense.

"Where?"

"Right here. Under the tree. We will start the tunnel here then dig under the fence so we can escape to the Saunders."

So began The Great Tunnel, a project that was to endure sporadically for several years and achieve a final underground distance of around five or six feet, not too bad considering the stream of obstacles that was constantly thrown in the path of our feverishly intermittent picking and shovelling. To start with, digging directly under a 100-year-plus-old tree with roots boasting girths the size of a large child's torso, was something I had not considered in the planning stage. Second, the hole—it took some time to evolve into a tunnel—was more of a crater and was regularly infested with vile-smelling Matabele ants, some an inch long with evil mandibles that could, and did, inflict an excruciatingly painful bite. And last, when it rained, the crater filled up with water, Somme-style, rendering further digging impossible until the sludge eventually seeped away, probably into the Matabele ants' nest in the bowels of the earth.

Sarah and Caroline, disappointingly, started flagging after a few months, their labour of five or six hours a week dwindling to three or four, then to one or two, then nothing. Undaunted, I continued, occasionally assisted by Dan Winch. but he too lost interest and stopped coming round for fear of being shanghaied into tunnelling duties. Ultimately, I too gave up the unequal struggle and diversified into treehouse and go-kart construction instead.

★

In May that year, Stokely Carmichael, a black activist and widely considered Malcolm X's successor, coined the term 'black power' when speaking to journalists in Atlanta. I was curious: was black power, which soon became Black Power, in any way related to the aspirations of the ZANU terrorists? It was vaguely unsettling. What did impress me was his name: Stokely Carmichael just had to be *the* coolest name around and I would have given anything to have.

Equally cool that month was the Rolling Stones' powerhouse number 1 hit 'Paint It Black' which literally exploded onto the charts and was played *ad nauseam* on Radio Jacaranda, fortunately. With a Hammond organ, castanets and Brian Jones distinctive on sitar, it was revolutionary in musical terms and in a short space of time became the unofficial anthem for the Vietnam War and would remain so forever. The Troggs' 'Wild Thing' at number 2 was light years behind it.

Also in May 1966, Mary Quant—who should have been awarded a Nobel Prize—was recognized as the inventor of the miniskirt, something male-kind and some female-kind would be forever grateful for. I certainly was and relished the visits by some of my parents' trendier female friends to the house—Di George, with her astonishing sculpted bronzed legs, being top of the list. Sadly, Fay Dudley never got to wear a miniskirt.

Talking of Mrs Dudley, Duddo and I got to see the 1942 MGM black-and-white movie *Mrs Minerva* at The Palace, starring Greer Garson (another very cool name) and Walter Pidgeon (not cool). The film, a Battle of Britain-type war film, had a profound impact on me, not least because the gorgeous Greer Garson could quite easily have been Fay Dudley's twin. It was to be a double-header fantasy for several weeks. The excitement of the movie was however marred by a very grumpy woman in the row in front of us who objected to our incessant chatter and turned round and gave both of us a good, sharp slap. It was degrading which Duddo and I felt was wholly unwarranted. *And* she chain-smoked!

On 30 July 1966 England beat West Germany 4–2 to win the World Cup. And rightly so, in my opinion: the planets were in alignment. The mutterings of the third, controversial, English goal not crossing the line was just sour grapes by the West Germans. And as for the Latin Americans—Brazil, Uruguay and Argentina in particular—repeatedly complaining that they had been victimized by strongly biased European refereeing and brutally and literally shin-kicked out of the competition; well, that was just typical of those dago types, as some were saying. (It struck me that Spiro at Délice Bakery might be one of these dago types.)

A year later, while on holiday at Granma Teddy's at Addo in the Sundays River Valley, I happened to accompany her when she was taking her Hillman Minx to the garage for a service. I had particularly wanted to go because the garage owner-cum-mechanic was a Hans Wiedemann who had been Rommel's personal mechanic in the Afrika Korps. Of course, I got stage fright and clammed up in front of the very nice man with blue, blue eyes and a big, big smile but what I did pick up on though was the discussion Granma Teddy and Hans were having … about the World Cup. Granma Teddy was almost crying laughing when Hans stated that "*Ja,* zer *kleine Engländer* zink zat *Fußball* has been coming home, *ja?* Zey don't comprehend zat zis vas a short visit to say *auf wiedersehen* and zat ze new home for *Fußball* is going to be Bonn and zen one day Berlin. *Ja, ja*, maybe also Buenos Aires and Rio de Janeiro, maybe even Montevideo and Rome. But Engländ? *Nein, nein, nein.* Like ze *Englisch* autos … *kaput!*" He laughed, a deep belly laugh, and winked at me. I couldn't help but smile despite the blasphemy.

A few days after the World Cup Final, Peter was hit by a bus.

Lizzie came rushing into the kitchen, all a-tither, fanning herself with her greasy apron which hadn't been washed since her arrival, bearing the bad news. In between bouts of hyperventilation, it came out, or bits did.

"Mm …. mm … mm … *Maiwe! Maiwe!*"

"Breathe Lizzie," said my mother. "Where did it happen?"

"Mm … mm … at the bus stop, there by Lewisam. Peter, he was going to his home, to Mtoko. *Maiwe!* Too terrible. Jesus is my witness. This is too bad. Too terrible."

Francis had by now appeared, shaking his head, clearly distraught. He had been there and seen it all.

My father too had appeared. "What happened, Tar Baby?"

"*Mustah*, Peter walked in front of the bus. It was the Matambanadzo bus. And *BAM!* The bus hit Peter. In the head, *BAM!* and Peter falled down and drive him over. Fucked."

I was aghast, my sisters were crying, my mother was shaking and Lizzie was emitting the opening refrain of an anguished wail.

"That's enough, all of you," said my father a little too brusquely. "We all need to calm down … and what happened then, Tar Baby?"

"The polisi come and they call the ambulance. Then the ambulance come and take Peter."

"So, he was not dead?"

"I don't know, *mustah. Kabanga* … maybe."

"Well, I imagine they wouldn't have called an ambulance if he was dead," quipped my father, more to himself than anyone. "Bets, get on the phone to Harari Central and ask for Casualty. That's where they would have taken him."

Lizzie had by now sat herself down at the kitchen table. I thought a cup of tea might be a good idea for her and Francis, so I put the kettle on, heaped several big spoons of tea leaves into the once-silver, battle-scarred teapot and filled it up with boiling water. Then found two big mugs, half-filled them with milk, added six teaspoons of sugar to each and poured the tea, unstrained, into each mug. Africans like their tea milky and sweet.

"*Maswita*, Christopher," sniffled Lizzie.

"Thank you, *mustah*," added Francis.

I heard my mother on the phone in the sitting room. She tended to speak slowly and loudly on the phone to black people. "Yes, today … at about three o'clock … Peter … Peter Mushonga [ironically, Shona for medicine] … Yes … he was in an accident … with a bus … Lewisam Garage … Yes, that's it … Okay, I'll hold."

Silence.

For several minutes.

Then, "Hello? … Yes, I'm still here … Hmm … hmm … yes, I understand … Hmm, okay, that's fine … Thank you very much … Goodbye."

The sound of the handpiece clicking in the cradle. And Talleyrand falling off the wall.

I had barely breathed for the duration of the call. Sarah and Caroline had retreated to their bedroom to grieve, and my father was sitting at the kitchen table with Lizzie and Francis, with Pluto and Sam under the table wondering where their dinner was.

Then the sound of my mother lighting a cigarette, an extravagant exhale as she came back into the kitchen. "Well … he's not dead. He's unconscious. They have just operated, and he has just come out of theatre. It seems his skull was split open, most of his ribs are broken, both his collarbones are dislocated, and he has a fractured pelvis. But he seems to be stable. They were worried about his lungs, but his breathing is okay. The nurse says I can phone tomorrow morning."

"Jesus is my witness," Lizzie repeated.

My father stood up. "Time for a Teacher's, Bets."

★

It was an icy winter's day, a black frost had ravaged the Umwindsi valley and Dan and I were on our way to school, trying to get through the *vlei* as fast as we could before the earmuffs and mittens iced up. We smelled it then but gave it no more than a passing thought. It was only when we'd cleared the valley and stopped up the opposite slope to draw breath that we talked about it.

"Did you smell that, Dan?"

He nodded. "Of course. Stinks. Probably a dead dog or something."

"*Ja*, probably."

Winter gave way to spring, the dry, dusty middle season of nothingness. It had been a few weeks and we'd long since forgotten that smell, but it came back, fresher, sweeter, more rancid, more pervasive—and it was clearly more than one dead dog. Now it was a race to get through the *vlei* to escape it. Like it had become some sort of living-dead.

Then one day on our morning school run, the path down to the river was blocked. By a police Land Rover that straddled it. A black constable appeared from behind the vehicle with his right hand raised.

"Halt!"

We stopped.

"You cannot pass. You must go back."

This was potentially a massive inconvenience: we'd have to take the long route via Drew Road which would surely make us late for school.

I tried to make the point but the flurry of a German shepherd barking hysterically and a babble of excited voices in the bush toward the river interrupted my objection. A voice called out. It was a European: "Got another one here, inspector."

"Jesus Christ!" Presumably it was the inspector. "That's number six."

The other European responded, "Correct, sir. Where the fuck is Constable Moyo! Moyo ... GET HERE NOW! And bring another body bag."

The constable blocking our path was indeed Constable Moyo. Schoolboys forgotten, he turned abruptly and plunged into the back of the Land Rover to emerge a minute later with a big black plastic bag and scurried into the bush near the dry riverbed.

Dan and I watched, glued to the spectacle unfolding in front of us. Two constables appeared out of the bush with another black plastic bag that had something floppy and viscous inside. You could tell by the way the bag was lolling around and how the policemen were struggling to gain any purchase. They plonked the black bag beside the path, about twenty yards beyond the Land Rover, alongside several other black bags, maybe three or four. As the bag fell, something inside slithered out. It looked like it had once been a leg, but apart from what was most obviously rotting flesh, the vilest of odours assailed our senses and we started retching.

That's when the white patrol officer saw us. Even at a distance of twenty yards or so, his fury was palpable. "You two! WHAT THE FUCK ARE YOU DOING HERE!"

We knew we were in a whole pile of trouble. Deep, deep trouble. We did what our instincts were screaming at us to do: we jumped on our bikes and turned tail, peddling for our life's worth back up the path toward Midvale Road. The white policeman did not follow. He had bigger fish to fry.

We were late for school. Mrs Scrase did not believe us. Mr Hickman did not believe us, but we got off with a warning. When I got home, I breathlessly told my mother. She was only half listening, and I don't think she believed me either.

"Christopher, I had a call from Mr Hickman today. Said you were late. That it's most unlike you. And that you fibbed and told him some made-up story about you and Dan being stopped by the police."

"But mummy … it's true. There were bodies. I promise you …"

But she wasn't listening. She had dinner instructions for Lizzie.

The next day at breakfast I got hold of *The Rhodesia Herald* before my father. I scoured it, clumsily trying to flip the large pages. Nothing. The next day nothing. Then in the Friday edition on page five, near the bottom of the page, a small article no more than two or three column inches screamed out at me:

SERIAL KILLER ON THE LOOSE
Following the gruesome discovery on Tuesday this week of eight corpses near the Umwindsi River in Highlands, Police are appealing to the Public for any information that will lead to the arrest of the perpetrator of this heinous crime. BSAP Inspector Seamus O'Reilly made the request following the discovery of the bodies, all in various stages of decomposition.
"The modus operandi is the same," said O'Reilly. "All the victims are native women in their early twenties. They were all strangled, raped and then hacked to death, probably with a small axe or a panga."
A thorough search of the area for clues and the murder weapon has turned up empty.
The investigation is ongoing.

So, there it was! I knew it! Lizzie came into the dining room with my father's herrings. I gagged instinctively. How could he eat that vile stuff?

"Lizzie! Look here!" I thrust the bottom of page five between her gaze and the herrings.

She peered over the horn rims, scanning the article quickly before *mustah* made his grand, business-like entrance.

"Hah!" she gasped. She looked directly at me, a look of profound concern. "Christopher [she never referred to me as *mustah*], you come to my house after school, and I give you *mushonga*. To give you protection. This is very bad." She clicked and tut-tutted before shuffling back into the kitchen.

I duly popped into Lizzie's *khaya* that evening after school. It comprised one room, a big room, which was furnished with two easy chairs, a small table with two dining-room chairs and a double bed behind a screen of large, coloured prints draped from the ceiling. A large, well-worn Persian rug covered the concrete floor. I liked Lizzie's room. It smelled nice. Different but nice. Lifebuoy-soap different.

Like a co-conspirator, Lizzie closed the door behind me, pulled something from her apron pocket and thrust it into the palm of my hand. I looked at it. It was a two-inch cutting of a twig. Sensing my confusion, she took the twig and rubbed the one end against her teeth.

"Christopher. Like this. Rub like this. Every day before you sleep. *Wazinzwa?*"

I nodded. "Yes, I understand."

"It will make you strong so bad people no take your heart." She patted her chest then squeezed my hand.

From that day forth I was 'addicted' to Lizzie's vile, bitter concoctions, an arrangement that would last for over two decades. (Another favourite was grinding up a type of root and sprinkling it in the bath.) I vaguely knew that one day compensation would be required—it was only right, after all—but quite when and in what form has yet to manifest itself. It was enough to know that I was, for now, protected by Lizzie's armour that had in all certainty emanated from the two-inch cutting. And just as well too for three weeks later another small article in *The Rhodesia Herald* jumped off page two—promoted up the batting order from page five:

SERIAL KILLER NABBED

In a dramatic turn of events, Police yesterday arrested the alleged killer who hacked eight women to death. Their decomposing bodies were discovered in August near the Umwindsi River in Highlands. Acting on a tip-off, Police had surrounded an illicit shebeen in the Lewisham Shopping Centre before swooping to nab the suspect who was clearly under the influence of skokiaan. He had been acting in a suspicious manner, threatening the owner of the shebeen, a Mrs Florence Ngwenya, with a hatchet.

★

"VERWOERD'S BEEN STABBED!"

I sat up in bed with a jolt. There was a ruckus in the passage.

"VERWOERD'S JUST BEEN STABBED! BETS, MIKE!"

I jumped out of bed and in the darkness stumbled to the door. Peering out, I caught the tail end of Granma Teddy in her nightgown hurrying to the sitting room, the reverie of Elsa the lioness in *Born Free* that we'd seen that afternoon at The Palace dissipating in an instant. Clandestinely, I followed her to the sitting room and took up my traditional listening post just round the corner at the top of the split-level steps.

"What? Dr HF?" I heard my mother ask, dully.

From the clinking of crystal glasses, I suspected both my parents were on the Teacher's.

"Yes! Hendrik Verwoerd. Stabbed! Assassinated in the House of Assembly in Cape Town," Granma Teddy said breathlessly, all a-thither. "It's just been on the BBC."

"Bets, turn the wireless on," my father instructed with the trace of a slur.

My mother, flustered, grabbed the transistor radio from the mantelpiece and fiddled clumsily with the knobs. Even I could see she was clueless about the intricacies of FM, SW, AM and MW. Then, suddenly, above the crackling and the static, like the sonic boom of an ICBM, The Supremes invaded the room on volume ten with 'You Can't Hurry Love'.

"JESUS! BETS! TURN THAT DOWN!"

"I'm trying, Mike. Give me a second, will you."

I could see Granma Teddy shaking her head. I couldn't make out if was to do with my father or Dr Verwoerd's demise.

My mother gave up on the Sony and switched it off, thrusting the wretched thing at my father. He could do no better, his senses dulled by a Teacher's too far.

"Well, as I was saying," said Granma Teddy, "the BBC said he was stabbed by a demented Greek called Dimitri Tsafendas or something."

"What's a demented Greek doing in Parliament?" my mother asked.

"Apparently, he works there. Some kind of messenger or something."

"Well, Verwoerd's a nasty piece of work. He deserves it," said my mother with a hint of defiance.

"Betty, really! What have you done with this bloody thing?" My father was also about to give up on the transistor.

"He went to school here. Did you know that?" interjected my grandmother.

"What!"

"Yes, Milton in Bulawayo … the bad news of course is that that dreadful

Vorster will take over as PM."

"Oh him!" my mother said. "Bloody Nazi."

"Yes, got locked up in the war. By Eric Pagden. Poor Eric had to go into hiding after the Nats came to power in forty-eight." I'd heard Granma Teddy talk about Eric Pagden before. They were good friends.

"Milton Shmilton …" added my father, several stanzas behind it all. "Isn't that where all the Yids go to school?" Shock tactics.

"Oh Mike, do shut up," snapped Granma Teddy. "You're nothing but a damned Nazi yourself."

I could make out my father mimicking my grandmother, a bit like some of the boys did when Mrs Scrase wasn't looking.

The 6th of September might have been a bad day for Dr Hendrik Frensch Verwoerd, but the 7th of September was an equally bad day for Christopher Michael Cocks. I, however, lived to tell the tale. That evening, after my homework, I was called in to the sitting room by my parents. I acceded to the request but not without some niggling reservations. This was not a lone parent mentioning something *en passant*: it was a deputation of two parents. The big guns.

"Christopher," my father glanced up from *The Herald* crossword. "Your mother has something to tell you."

I was intrigued by *The Herald* crossword. It was apparently 'cryptic' so it was several levels above thicko ability. My father was quite good at it and often he'd finish it, barring one or two stubborn clues. (A few years later, I found I'd inherited my father's knack of crosswords and would irritate him beyond reason by filling in his missing clues.)

"Christopher," my mother began. "Your father and I have decided it would be appropriate if you were to become a choirboy at Saint Mary's."

"What!" I was stunned. And what was it with that stupid, meaningless word 'appropriate'?

"Christopher! Don't answer your mother back!" snapped my father.

"But … but, mummy! I can't. I just can't …"

"Why not!" challenged my father.

"It's Father Neahum. He's very scary. I think he's THE DEVIL."

"Oh, what nonsense!"

"Now, Christopher. I had a meeting today with Father Neahum and he would *love* to have you as a new choirboy. The Joughin boys are choirboys there, so you'd know somebody at least. It will be good for you. And you know Mrs Gillespie, don't you? She's in the choir too. Her son, Ian, is also a choirboy."

The Joughin boys went to Highlands Junior School, and I didn't like them.

"You would have choir practice every Thursday evening at 7 o'clock and then the Sunday service at 9 o'clock … and maybe the occasional wedding on Saturday afternoons."

I could feel the hysteria rising. I was cornered. "But, how will I get there?"

"I'm sorry, darling, but you'll have to go on your bike. I just don't have enough petrol coupons to take you."

"But you take the twins to ballet," I blurted out, almost in tears. This was not right. It was so unfair.

"Christopher, your mother has spoken and that's that," said my father bluntly.

I looked at him in anger. I wanted to challenge him. After all, he had only recently stopped going to church altogether. Completely. Every Sunday had become maybe one or two Sundays a month, then a Sunday every couple of months, then Christmas and Easter only … and now nothing. No pretence whatsoever. At least my mother still made an effort at Christmas and Easter. And here I was, the sacrificial lamb of expedience to the slaughter. I was seething inside. It was two and a half miles from Midvale Road to St. Mary's on the corner of Enterprise Road and Glenara Avenue, diagonally opposite Governor's Lodge The thought of the five-mile round trip twice, sometimes three times, a week was just too much to contemplate. My life was about to be wholly consumed by THE CHURCH and the terrifying figure of Father Beelzebub.

★

On 13 September 1966, security forces announced the commencement of Operation *Yodel*, to kill or capture a group of fifteen ZANU terrorists who had crossed the Zambezi River near Chirundu with the intent of killing civilians and committing acts of sabotage. A week later a security forces communiqué—a brilliant word, I thought—announced the completion of the operation with the accounting of all fifteen terrorists: fourteen killed and one captured. Security forces suffered one wounded, which I thought a good return. However, I was extremely disappointed by the choice of the name of the operation. Who on earth came up with a name like *Yodel*? Surely not a military man, it must have been a faceless civil servant with a penchant for *The Sound of Music*. If our security forces were to be taken seriously, they would have to up their game and come up with names more martial, in line with *Overlord* or *Barbarossa*. I had recently started dabbling in books on the Second World War—*The Great Escape* and *The Tunnel Escape* (*The Wooden Horse*) being my first two—and the Germans had any number of superb military operations such as *Zitadelle*, *Panzerfaust*, *Wiking* and even *Werewolf*. Could we not follow their lead and have something like *Hyena* or *Jackal* or *Matabele Ant*—why not?

Shortly after Operation *Yodel*, the third and last term of the 1966 school year opened with the astounding news that Douglas Bader was coming to the school to give a talk; apparently, he was a good friend of Mr Hickman's. The entire school was a-buzz with excitement, and I decided I needed to brush up on my Second World War vocabulary just in case we had an opportunity to ask questions of this famous RAF fighter pilot with tin legs. Fortunately, I'd learned quite a lot from Duddo's father, words and phrases like 'tally ho', 'roger', 'bandits 12 o'clock high' and 'bag a Jerry kite'. I also felt it appropriate to be able to drop in a few Luftwaffe words too, to add to the authenticity, words like *Abschuss* (a shootdown) and *Jäger* (fighter pilot). But my ultimate *coup de main* had to be a sentence I'd picked up in one of the escape books when an escaped RAF flyer ('in mufti') had boarded the ferry at Kiel bound for neutral Sweden. On the deck with him, gazing at the receding coastline of Germany, was an off-duty German officer, who turned to the RAF chap and said: "*Da drüben liegt die Heimat.*" My heart was in my mouth in case the English flyer blundered and said something stupid that would compromise him. As it was, the German officer had simply said "Over there lies the homeland" and the studied response of "*Ja*" ensured a narrow escape. I spent many hours memorizing the expression. I was convinced that one day it would come in handy.

The big day came, and the entire school was ushered into the hall. The junior classes (us) sat on the floor as there weren't enough chairs to go round. Mr Hickman, with a copy of *Reach for the Sky* tucked under his arm, then came in with the great man, the only sound to be heard above the reverential hush being the squeaking of leather and tin legs. Reaching the front of the assembly, he turned, smiled at us all and then proceeded to light his pipe, popping the used matchsticks into the pocket of his tweed jacket; disappointingly, he had come 'in mufti' and not his dashing RAF uniform.

Duddo nudged me, whispering: "Squadron Leader 242 Squadron, mainly Canadians. Got a DFC and bar and DSO and bar."

"Roger that," I whispered in return.

With a mischievous grin and a puff on the pipe, the first words Douglas Bader spoke were: "Why are you all staring at my legs?"

We were awestruck but laughed nervously, a bit embarrassed. He was exactly like the photographs, with a broad, crinkly brow, wavy hair swept back and parted on the left, a kind, open face and a twinkle in his eye. He chatted easily, relating some of his wartime experiences, being shot down over France, meeting the Luftwaffe ace Adolf Galland, and his three long years as a POW in Colditz Castle.

At the end of his talk, Mr Hickman said there was only time for two or three questions. I was about to put my hand up when a senior boy preempted me. It was a wasted question—"Sir, which aircraft is faster, a Spitfire or a Messerschmitt?"—as Duddo shook his head in disbelief: anyone worth his Battle of Britain salt knew the Bf 109 was faster but that the Spitfire was better in the turn. Then Mr Gardiner asked a question about living with tin legs and that was it. With a "Tally ho, lads", the legendary fighter pilot was gone.

On 10 October, a new Beach Boys song obliterated the Radio Jacaranda airwaves: 'Good Vibrations'. In much the same way that 'Paint It Black' had done a few months earlier, 'Good Vibrations' was revolutionary in its almost-orchestral composition, sonic use of synthesizers and the trademark complex Beach Boys harmonies, used properly this time and not in silly surfing songs. Referred to as a "pocket symphony" by the record label, Capitol, 'Good Vibrations' instantly topped the charts in the United States and the United Kingdom. I was mesmerized and hurried home after school every day to ensure I got my homework done quickly so I could listen to the Jacaranda hit parade in the evening.

Eleven days later, on 21 October, the Aberfan disaster occurred in the Taff Valley* after a colliery spoil tip collapsed above the Welsh mining town and like volcanic magma engulfed a primary school and several houses, killing 144 people, including 28 adults and 116 children, mainly schoolchildren. Looking at the images in the newspaper, I was horrified. These were children my age, the teachers killed could have been my teachers, and in an instant 'Good Vibrations' lost some of its gloss, unwittingly becoming, in my mind, a soundtrack for tragedy and death.

Life went on at 4 Chiromo, Midvale Road but by the close of October, I found myself facing the hiding of my life. Dan Winch was round and we—my sisters included—were playing cricket on the lawn, but with a proper cricket ball and not a tennis ball as suggested by my mother; her consistent warnings were ignored. It was Dan and me against the two girls and we were leading by an innings and several hundred runs. Sarah was bowling the last ball of her over which I dispatched to square leg with gusto. Unfortunately, square leg was aligned with the French doors on to the patio, and, sure enough, like a

*Coincidentally, fifty-seven years later, I found myself living in Brynmawr, fifteen miles and two valleys east of Aberfan.

rocket, the cricket ball smashed into the bottom pane of glass (the largest too). The sounds of shattered glass tinkled jarringly as Dan Winch fled—jumped on his bike and was gone—and my sisters were doing that stupid "Ooh wa, ooh wa" thing flicking their fingers downward in a poor but quite clear cane-on-a-bottom imitation.

My mother came storming out. "Christopher! GET TO YOUR ROOM! THIS MINUTE! YOUR FATHER WILL BE HOME SOON AND BY GOD YOU CAN EXPECT THE HIDING OF YOUR LIFE!"

I got the message and skulked off to await my fate. It was like waiting for an execution but without the last meal and the priest. I felt like vomiting and tried to force it—a dry run—wishing my father would hurry up and get home so we could be done with the torture. The house was eerily quiet, the twins hiding somewhere, probably in the crater/ tunnel up by the fig tree, out of the way of any fallout. Sure enough, around 5.30 p.m., the sounds of a car coming down the drive could be heard. Yes, it was my father's new company car, a fancy Citroën DS 19. I heard the engine being switched off, a car door closing and my mother's muted tones as she came inside with my father. There was a pause as he inspected the crime scene, the paneless area now taped up with cardboard that Francis had attended to. More muted voices. Then the sounds of footsteps up the passage, male footsteps.

I was shaking as my father came into the bedroom, a leather slipper in his hand. I tried not to show my fear. There were no preliminaries, no how-do-you-plead?, no pronouncement of sentence.

"Christopher, stand up, pull your pants down and bend over."

Whack … whack … whack … whack … whack … whack. Six times. I tried not to wince as the leather struck flesh. I was convinced there was blood.

Without a word, my father turned and left the room.

Frustrated anger welled inside me, not from the extraordinary pain but from the feeling of helplessness, the indignity of it all. I let out a loud, visceral "*Aaaarggghhh!*", picked up a Clarks school shoe and hurled it with all my might across the room at the drawn curtains.

The door burst open and my father, now incandescent with rage, shouted: "HOW DARE YOU! NOW BEND OVER … AGAIN." He grabbed me by my neck and forced me into the bend-over position.

Whack … whack … whack … whack … whack … whack. Six times.

This time, I collapsed onto the bed and cried—more of a simper, really—as I heard my father in the sitting room: "Bets, get me a Teacher's … the little bastard. Next time it'll be a hosepipe, mark my words."

Tinkling of crystal glasses and ice.

But it wasn't over yet. Like a Greek tragedy, I lifted myself from the bed and washed my face in the mini washbasin. It was when I went to retrieve the shoe that I noticed some broken glass on the floor. Tentatively pulling back the corner of the curtain, I saw that a windowpane was broken, one of the smaller ones, with glass littering the windowsill. Clearly the curtains had been inadequate in cushioning the force of the Clarks projectile. It was the Midvale Road *Kristallnacht*.

I sat down on the bed, breathing deeply. Think. What now? Think. Coming clean was clearly not an option: my bum was not ready for a hosepipe. I was fairly sure I could hide the crime from my parents: by keeping that one side of the curtain slightly closed during the day would do it if they ever came in the room, not that they often did. The area of concern was from the outside as the path down from the servants' *khayas* to the kitchen went directly past my window. A broken windowpane with jagged glass would soon be spotted and the game would be up. I had to get rid of the evidence, the bits of broken glass still putty-embedded: without close inspection, a clean, paneless window could ostensibly be mistaken for a healthy windowpane. My father was making inroads into the Teacher's while I sneaked into their bedroom to access his toolbox in the corner. I was ruthlessly focused: secure hammer and chisel, return to bedroom, gently tap out the putty, scoop up all the bits of putty and glass into a plastic bag, return hammer and chisel to toolbox and *voilà!*, all done. The plastic bag of evidence was stashed under the bed to be disposed of in the morning.

Surprisingly, the plan worked and several months went by. I knew it couldn't last forever: winter would come, and the hole had to be closed up. Eventually, I decided that the only way to deal with the problem was to come clean, well sort of clean, of a fashion. I waited until my father was away on a three-day business trip to Umtali before approaching my mother.

"Mummy, there's a broken window in my bedroom." Boldly said.

"Whaaat! How did it happen?"

I showed her the crime scene. "It was an accident, mummy. Yesterday I was playing on the bed with Dan Winch, and he accidentally kicked the window and it broke … and I even cleaned up the broken bits and the putty and everything."

"Oh well," she sighed. "Accidents happen. I'll get a new pane and some putty from Brain Brothers tomorrow and Francis can get it put in before daddy gets back."

★

There was another bout of trouble. One of the games my sisters and I had developed was a game we called 'Berlin Wall', which I thought quite topical. We divided the property into two, East and West, with the dividing line, the tickey-creeper-covered wall with the full-stop Pride of India at the one end, being the Berlin Wall. Two of us played East Berliners whose challenge was to get past the wall undetected into West Berlin (the rose garden and down to the river) while the third person played an East German border guard whose job it was to stop them. The border guard was armed with an AK-47 disguised as a truncheon and wore a Warsaw Pact helmet disguised as a white Police Reserve helmet. I happened to be the East German border guard in this instance and had very clearly shot the two escaping *Ossies* who had been hiding under the Pride of India. The problem arose when the two East Berliners declined to accept that they had been shot.

Very rapidly the situation escalated and got personal. Caroline, sensing the danger, managed to weasel her way behind some rose bushes (in the West), convinced she had made good her escape. Sarah, on the other hand, stood her ground, determined to prove her point, and win it—she was like that. Phrases like "you and your stupid game" and "I hope you die" only served to exacerbate matters.

I don't know what made me do it, but I lost my temper and in a white rage blindly picked up the nearest missile to hand, in this case one of Pluto's dried-out old dog's bones and hurled it as hard as I could at Sarah, whose back was momentarily turned. Aimed only in the general direction of Sarah's being, she happened to turn at the precisely the wrong (or right) moment and the bone, probably the weight of a cricket ball, and larger, made contact with her right temple. She screamed out and fell to ground, poleaxed, blood gushing forth as it tends to do with head wounds.

Caroline, not realizing what had happened, hearing only the scream, came bursting out of the cover of the rose bushes to see her sister prostrate, holding her head, hands bloodied and moaning softly in what was clearly some form of death rattle. She then screamed and ran inside to find my mother. I meanwhile was frozen to the spot, quite unsure of what to do and how to react. Sarah's moaning had stopped, her body lifeless. One thing was certain: sororicide would be frowned upon and regardless that I was still a minor, the best I could hope for would be some sort of boys' home. I'd heard there was a particularly brutal one in Bulawayo. Besides, the Australian Cricket XI had just arrived in Salisbury for their first match on their southern African tour and my father had managed to get tickets. (I had temporarily put the acrimony of the hidings behind us, a sort of unilateral truce on my part, magnanimously so.)

Interrupted from my ponderings by my mother's "Oh my god! What happened?", I looked up to see her and Lizzie lifting the limp form of my sister—moaning again, a good sign, or at least proof of life—and hoiking her inside to a bedroom where she'd be Dettolled and bandaged.

I sat down on the grass, nonplussed. Pluto had rediscovered his old bone and was happily gnawing at it, his tail *thwacking* the ground. I was for it now. Just had to be. There was no getting out of this one. I resigned myself to a fate unknown. As Doris Day had sung, *que sera, sera*. The Australian cricket match would surely be first privilege to go.

Presently, my mother, Lizzie and Caroline came outside, like a deputation, a posse.

"What happened, Christopher?"

Then, in the manner of some sort of divine intervention, either that or a form of malignant possession, the explanation came tumbling out of my mouth. It was so utterly implausible that I couldn't quite believe they were my words. "I don't know exactly, mummy. We were playing Berlin Wall and Sarah was standing there." I indicated where X marked the spot, putting on my most desperately earnest, I-promise-you-I'm-not-lying face. "Then all of a sudden, this thing, I think it was that dog's bone, came flying over the roof from the Saunders' garden and hit Sarah. Out of the blue. Just like that." I took a deep breath. "It must have missed me by inches," I added for good measure.

"Goodness!" exclaimed my mother, as she, Lizzie and Caroline all turned and looked up at the roof. "How odd!"

Lizzie was tut-tutting, shaking her head. She knew those Saunders boys were bad news.

And with that they all turned and went back inside. Fortunately, my father was late back from Sports Club that evening: after-nets drinks had gone on a bit.

That Saturday, the bone-incident forgotten and Sarah's bandaged head aside, my father and I packed up the cooler box and the deck chairs into the Citroën and tootled off to the Police Ground, nice and early to get better seats this time round: we did, squeezing in next to some farmers at the mid-wicket/cover boundary. Washington was still Dairibord's boots on the ground and kept me well supplied with ice lollies for the duration, which unfortunately did not stretch to the full four days because of a Rhodesian batting collapse in the first innings.

Rhodesia batted first and could only manage 149 all out, with only Rob Ullyet at number 3 making anything presentable, a gritty 60, before being caught by Veivers off Hawke's bowling. Martin was the pick of the bowlers, taking 5 for 26.

Things appeared to be looking up for the Rhodesians when Aussie captain and opening bat (before the days of batters) Bobby Simpson was caught behind off the bowling of Parker for 8, the wicketkeeper being the towering Howie Gardiner. It was short-lived and the tourists consolidated with the other opener, Ian Redpath, carrying his bat for an undefeated 139, for the Australians to reach 307 all out. Leg spinner Jack du Preez took 6 for 98 in 32 overs, with 8 maidens.

On Day 3, at lunch, I happened to spot the Joughin boys playing cricket on the field, as were hundreds of boys, with normally a cooler box or beer crate as the wickets (and tennis balls, not proper cricket balls). I kept a low profile. I knew they'd ask me to join in, but I knew I wouldn't get a look-in with a bat, let alone a bowl, and would likely end up as a fielder out in the deep, relegated to vainly chasing monster sixes.

The Rhodesians' second innings was an improvement over their first, a more respectable 265 all out. Opener Nick Frangos made 49, captain Tony Pithey 67 and Howie Gardiner came in with a swashbuckling 81. Ian Chappell was the pick of the bowlers with 5 for 53 from 34 overs with 14 maidens (all overarm too). The Australian second innings was a formality as the tourists cruised past their target of 108 with 8 wickets to spare and Bobby Simpson unbeaten on 44.

We arrived home that evening to be met with much frivolity and ululations (from Lizzie; men didn't ululate). My mother came out to the car to meet us, smiling broadly.

"Peter's back."

"What?"

"Peter? Our Peter?" asked my father.

"Yes, he's recovered."

"Good heavens! Where is he?"

"In the kitchen. Can't you hear?"

I dashed inside and sure enough, there was Peter, that booming gut-laugh the same as ever as he greeted me fondly. Lizzie and Francis were grinning from ear to ear, the twins were skipping about merrily with Sarah's bandage coming adrift and Pluto's tail *thwacking* anything and everything in sight, convinced that the gaiety was on his account. I studied Peter, curious how one could be hit by a bus and survive to tell the tale. Apart from his speech which was noticeably slower—and the inch-wide by half-inch-deep scar which ran from the bridge of his nose up over his forehead, across the top of his skull and down to the nape of his neck—there was little different from the 'old' Peter.

141

★

Depressingly, in December 1966, the United Nations expanded the raft of sanctions against Rhodesia. Harold Wilson and Ian Smith met on HMS *Tiger* off Gibraltar to find a solution to the impasse. Even I knew it was a waste of time and was proved right when the British prime minister affirmed, "No independence before majority rule." Smith didn't seem to care; it was infuriating. Couldn't he see what was happening?

Then petrol rationing was tightened, and my mother's allocation was reduced to two units a month … two gallons. In one fell swoop this decided the fate of the Opel, which was traded in at Car Mart for a more fuel-efficient second-hand Mini-Minor, a white one, "1962 model, love, only seventy-four thousand miles on the clock … genuine …"

It also decided the fate of my mother's rose business. Without a station wagon in which to transport the roses and without adequate fuel, it was doomed. No amount of free-wheeling downhill would make a difference. One afternoon, after a thunderstorm, I noticed my mother on the front lawn looking at the roses. There was a good flush in the offing: they'd need cutting soon. She was smoking, her shoulders slumped. I went up to her. She had been crying. I held her hand.

"Oh, hello darling," she sniffed. "What are you up to? Haven't you got choir practice this afternoon?"

"Yes, just now … I'm sorry about your roses, mummy."

She looked down at me, her makeup smudged and runny. She looked so forlorn as she squeezed my hand. "So'm I darling … so'm I."

After some time, she took a deep breath. "Come on, love, you've got to get off to your choir practice and I've got to get dinner organized. Oh, you must also do some violin practice when you get back."

Choir at St Mary's had, as I knew it would, become all-consuming. From the Thursday evening practice to a very-likely wedding on Saturday afternoon (for which we were paid a shilling), to the big Sunday-morning service, it was all-in Christian—Protestant, mind you—intensity. With two hymns for the wedding and five for the Sunday service, that was seven new, rather freshly recycled, hymns that we had to practise a week. Not to mention the three round trips on my bike, in all weather, which amounted to fifteen miles a week … just to salve my parents' conscience. (Add the twenty for the school run, that was a grand total of thirty-five miles a week, almost the distance from Salisbury to Marandellas, and that excluding any leisure cycling.)

The choir was made up of around twenty adults—mainly middle-aged women and perhaps half a dozen men, including Mr Joughin as lead chorister—and some fifteen choirboys ranging in age from 12 down to 8-ish. There were no choirgirls, which I found odd. Nor were there any blacks: they worshipped in the *vlei* behind Lewisam Garage, next to the riding school paddocks. I saw them on Saturday afternoons and Sundays, several groups of them dotted around the *vlei*, perhaps twenty or so white-robed women, mainly, per group.

Before my first Sunday service, Mrs Gillespie took me round the back of the church to the vestry to try on some cassocks, red ones.

"Did you know, Cristopher, that the word 'cassock' comes from the Middle French *casaque*, meaning a long coat?"

I didn't know this but would be sure to remember it, if only to impress Mrs Scrace.

We found one my size, but I noticed I wasn't given a surplice, the loose white cotton tunic worn over the cassock that the older choirboys (and of course all the adults) wore. Mrs Gillespie called it a 'liturgical vestment'.

"No, Christopher, you only get presented your surplice after a year as a choirboy. You also have to learn 'The Apostles' Creed' off by heart."

I sighed inwardly. The Creed, as I knew it, was extraordinarily long; three times longer than The Lord's Prayer.

This galled as both the Joughin boys and Ian Gillespie had their surplices, and they were younger than me. I felt that a red cassock served only to mark one out as a beginner, which it did. It was marginally demeaning.

I'd arrive at choir practice around ten minutes beforehand to find the boys engaged in a lively game of stingers in the carpark. (Stingers was a simple game: whoever was 'on' had to throw the tennis ball as hard as he could at those who were not 'on'. If he struck/ stung anyone with the ball, then that person would be 'on'.) Choir practice was conducted 'in mufti' in the choir stalls at the front of the church, near the altar. The men took up the back row of the stalls, the women the middle rows and the choirboys the front two rows, with the surplice-free newbies, like me, right in the front. Mrs Joughin played the organ, a very big one with gargantuan pipes, which was positioned behind the choir pews and Father Neahum conducted the choir practice, neck a-quiver. In each pew, at each chorister position, was a neat pile of three small books: a hymnal, a psalter and *The Book of Common Prayer*, which became a part of my life, as much as *Swallows and Amazons* and *Reach for the Sky*.

I didn't mind the hymns; in fact, I found several quite stirring. Charles Wesley's 'Love Divine, All Loves Excelling' seemed to be in Father Neahum's Top 10, even though it was a Methodist hymn ("dreadful bloody bores" according to my mother) as was John Wesley's 'O God, Our Help in Ages Past'. 'Dear Lord and Father of Mankind', 'For Those in Peril on The Sea' and 'Guide Me, O Thou Great Redeemer' were my favourites. Of course, many were seasonal specialties, used only at Easters and Christmases. (My father's favourite hymn was 'Abide with Me', but he'd lost the franchise as he'd defected to the ranks of the atheists.)

Christmas 1966 was a biggie. Not only was it a Holy Communion service—with a full house, Communion could sometimes take up to half an hour—but there had been hymnal creep: I looked up at the board, whilst we, the procession, assembled outside the vast church doors, and saw, somehow, we now had seven to get through. Hopefully one would take place during Holy Communion, otherwise we were looking at a two-hour epic. We shuffled into our positions behind the multi-roled, multi-talented Mr Joughin who, as head server, head deacon and head chorister, would lead the procession off, holding the twelve-foot-high cross (*sans* Jesus). Following were the two assistant servers and in file behind them the choirboys, juniors first, each holding a candle—lit by Mrs Gillespie once we'd shuffled into rank—and then the adult choristers. Last around ten paces behind this impressive phalanx was God's representative for Highlands, Father Neahum, in his finest vestments of cassock, surplice, chasuble, stole and cincture, which I'd learned the rope belt was called.

Mrs Joughin had pulled out all the stops as the opening chords of Bach's 'Jesu, Joy of Man's Desiring' (hymn number 1) consumed the interior of the church and our bosoms. Her husband stepped off, chin forward, leading the procession at a suitably reverential pace down the aisle. I noticed my mother and sisters in one of the pews near the back; the twins were snickering and pointing at me as I drew level. Once we arrived at the stalls, we took our positions in the pews, putting our candles in special candle holders on the bench to our front. Everyone, apart from the front row, blew out their candles: there'd recently been an incident when a surplice had caught fire.

It was after Communion, which I couldn't take as I had not been confirmed, when we were into the third verse of hymn number 4, more properly a carol, 'Once in Royal David's City', that I heard a bit of a kerfuffle in the pew behind me. I turned to see one of the older boys having some sort of paroxysm. His face was flushed and he was emitting a series of hushed, primeval grunts. His right hand was nowhere to be seen, but I did notice what appeared to be a series of rapid wrist movements under his cassock, at around groin height, either that or a frantic mongoose was trying to escape. I was fascinated, as repugnant as it seemed: what *was* that? A pay-attention jab in the ribs from the choirboy next to me had me focused on the final verse despite the suffocated groans in the pew behind.

And then those magical words that signified the end of the proceedings: "May the grace of our Lord Jesus Christ, and the love of God, and the fellowship of the Holy Spirit be with us all, now … [dramatic pasue] … and evermore. Amen."

"AMEN!" in response, *fortissimo*.

After the service, waiting for my mother and sisters, I saw the older choirboys fooling around in the carpark with the boy who had clearly recovered from his paroxysm the target for much schoolboy abuse, vaguely audible above the hustle of the congregation coming out the church.

I spotted my mother and sisters and we bundled into the Mini, twins in the back, to get home to begin the big Christmas ceremony of opening presents. I was still wearing my cassock, an obvious target for my sisters.

"Mummy, why is Christopher wearing a dress?" asked the one, innocence personified. The other one was sniggering.

I turned and glared at them, to no effect.

"That's enough, both of you!" snapped my mother, inserting the key into the ignition.

"Christopher's a homo, Christopher's a homo," they chanted in that incredibly irritating singsong voice.

My mother turned round, leaned over into the back and attempted to give them both a good clout on the legs, but it was an awkward angle, and she merely clipped her fingers on the heel of Sarah's shoe. "Ouch! GODDAMMIT! THAT'S ENOUGH! I never want to hear you using that word again. DO … YOU … UNDERSTAND!"

The twins nodded vigorously, unable to quite hide their smirks.

Climbing into the car next to ours was the Joughin clan. With the driver's window down, Mrs Joughin had clearly caught the gist of the commotion in the Mini; horrified, she was unsure which was worse: my mother's blasphemy, my sisters' vulgarity, or my mother's inability to control my sisters' vulgarity.

The trip home was tense, sniggers in the back barely suppressed as my mother slipped the gearstick into neutral to free-wheel the last mile downhill to the Midvale Road turnoff.

It probably wasn't the appropriate time, but I asked nevertheless: "Mummy, what does 'wanking for Jesus' mean?"

I ducked to avoid the unChristmassy clout, unleashed wildly as we were turning the corner.

The Mini rolled down the drive to be met by my father, tapping his watch. "Heavens, Bets! Where've you been?"

My mother, still flustered from the 'wanking for Jesus' comment, was trying to get out the car—Minis are very low, only a few inches' freeboard above ground—at the same time as trying to light a cigarette. "Where d'you think we've been, Mike? At bloody church, that's where!"

"There were seven hymns, daddy. Long ones too … and Communion," I added helpfully.

"Almost as bad as the Catholics," my father muttered. "Well, let's get a bit of a move on. The servants have been waiting for ages."

"Well blame bloody Father bloody Neahum," said my mother, *sotto voce*, through a cloud of cigarette smoke.

My sisters and I were champing at the bit to get the presents presentation under way. I dashed to my bedroom, stripped off my cassock and flung on a shirt and some shorts. We took up our usual positions near the Christmas tree in the sitting room, with the mountain of presents beneath. The tree, a genuine fir tree or fir tree offcut that had been lopped off one of the firs on the boundary with the Saunders, was a good ten to twelve feet tall, so tall that it was bent against the ceiling at the top, unceremoniously squashing the magnificent star that I had made in Mrs Hess's KG2 class all those years ago. In fact, apart from a few baubles and the tinsel, most of the decorations were courtesy of me and my sisters, manufactured in tandem with the Christmas card production line.

"Alright Lizzie!" announced my father grandly. "Let's get on with it!"

"*Mustah.*"

To the strains of the RBC's live broadcast from the Anglican Cathedral in Salisbury,[*] 'Silent Night' it was, Lizzie, Peter and Francis shuffled in in single file and took up their traditional positions to receive their 'Clismass', an abbreviation of Christmas box, from my father who was this year's present dispenser. My mother went to a lot of trouble with the staff's Christmas boxes, which included bottles of beer (or Cokes), tinned food, rice, tea, sweets, sugar and a shirt (not too gay). Lizzie received another shawl. And of course, the all-important envelope in each box with the cash—the *bonsella*, the Clismass bonus.

With much handclapping and *Tatenda mustahs*, they shuffled out again.

"Don't spend it all at once, Tar Baby!" shouted my father after them.

"*Mustah,*" sheepishly mumbled by Francis.

Then it was our turn and in anticipation we opened our presents—with

---

[*]Boney M's Christmas songs album was still fifteen years off.

some care as the paper was to be recycled for Christmas 1967—mine being a platoon of Britains soldiers (Eighth Army in desert attire), an Airfix model (a Messerschmitt Bf 109), a *Dandy* annual, a Parker fountain pen (from Granma Teddy) and a few white envelopes with ten-shilling notes inside, from the likes of Meg and Forbes who were on holiday in a place called Las Palmas—we'd had some prime black-and-white TV viewing since they'd been gone: *The Lone Ranger*, *Roy Rogers* and *The Forest Rangers*—and Godmother Joy in Port Elizabeth. Ten shillings was a lot of money for us, considering our pocket money was only sixpence a week. Well, because I was older, I always got more than the twins who were still languishing in the tickey bracket. This would change in a week's time when 1967 would see my pocket money increase to a shilling and the twins to sixpence.

Pluto and Sam were not neglected and were given large, fresh bones. As they were hauling them outside to begin the gnawing process, from nowhere a thought popped into my head, almost distractedly, that they were preparing future ordnance for me to employ against my sisters' foreheads.

Then began the cleaning-up process, mainly all the salvageable Christmas paper to be neatly folded, after which the remaining unopened presents were consolidated into a smaller pile under the tree. These were for the latecomers and absentees (like Meg and Forbes), the latecomers being the milkman, the postman, the newspaper boy and the rubbish boys who would all get their Christmas boxes during the course of the following week when their services resumed.

Then it was stand down till suppertime, the big Christmas dinner, with my mother's divine brandy snaps and brandy butter and the Christmas pudding jammed full of tickeys and sixpences. I was happy reading my *Dandy* in the sitting room, the twins went scurrying off to their bedroom to play with their new Barbie Dolls, Pluto and Sam were outside on their bones, my mother plunged herself into the kitchen to start thinking about dinner and my father resumed his position on the patio to finish clipping his toenails and preparing the latest vegetable garden harvest of beetroot and rhubarb for cooking (in winter, he'd be shelling peas). Rhubarb, like herrings, was another of those 1939–45 delicacies that my father was passionate about. In due course, Pluto would be coaxed away from his bone to come and lick up all the toenail clippings—he had a thing about them; perhaps it was the calcium—well, those which had avoided the two big cooking pots of rhubarb and beetroot.

1966 was to become a memorable year for southern African black nationalists. Apart from the Battle of Sinoia (Chinhoyi) that formally signalled the start of Chimurenga II—the 'bush war' if you were white—in Rhodesia, things were happening in the UN-mandated-to-South Africa territory of South West Africa to our west. The country was technically a neighbour because of the geographical oddity of the Caprivi Strip extending eastward from South West Africa proper to 'touch' Rhodesia, Zambia and Bechuanaland (Botswana) at a cartographic dot in the middle of the Zambezi River. In September 1965 seven PLAN guerrillas had infiltrated South West Africa from Angola and established a base at Ongulumbashe on the border. (Proving that liberation nomenclature is a minefield of acronyms, PLAN = People's Liberation Army of Namibia, the armed wing of SWAPO, the South West Africa People's Organization.) It took the white South Africans a year to respond. On 26 August 1966, a combined force of forty-two SADF paratroopers and SAP policemen (South African Defence Force and South African Police respectively) was ferried in by helicopter to strike the camp in what the South Africans called Operation *Blouwildebees* (Blue Wildebeest). In the ensuing fight, of the seventeen guerrillas in camp at the time, two were killed, one was wounded and eight were captured, leaving six to scarper into the hinterland of Owamboland. This action—the Battle of Ongulumbashe—signalled the commencement of what the South Africans called the 'Border War'. For SWAPO, the date would become a national holiday in an independent Namibia: Heroes' Day.

5
San Francisco (Flowers in Your Hair)—
Scott MacKenzie, 1967

The Short family, progenitors of my grandfather Clifton Short, were West Country settlers who arrived in Algoa Bay in 1820 aboard the good ship *Aurora*, together with the Sephton party. Along with his wife Mary, from Kempsford, Gloucestershire, Joseph Short, 'a gardener' by trade, from Bath, had applied for the passage, along with thousands of other would-be hopefuls desperate for a new start in life following the political upheavals and economic ravages of a post-Napoleonic-Wars Britain. Being a gardener—presumably a market gardener (rather than a mere garden boy who mows the lawn and scoffles the flowerbeds)—was obviously enough for the selection committee to give the Short family the nod.

The 1820 settlers found that their new life wasn't quite as glamorous as the advertising brochures had made out. Literally abandoned on the sands of what are today's Port Elizabeth tourist havens of King's and Pollock beaches, with the women swooning in the scorching heat despite their parasols, these now-less-than-intrepid adventurers were expected by His newly minted Majesty King George IV, to venture into the interior—in an easterly and northeasterly direction only—and carve for themselves farms and livelihoods out the of the forbidding, rancid countryside. What His Majesty had neglected to mention were the thousands of hostile Xhosa warriors sharpening their assegais on the eastern bank of the Great Fish River in preparation for the attempted *umlungu*[*] occupation. In fact, His Majesty's prime minister, Lord Liverpool, hadn't been entirely honest with the King's émigrés, omitting to advise them of the true raison d'être of the expedition: to create a buffer zone on the Cape Colony's eastern extremity to prevent Bantu seepage into British territory. (Interestingly, Lord Liverpool was at the time revamping his Tory cabinet, importing younger, middle-class blood into the ranks, among whom was Robert Peel.)

Many settlers, gazing helplessly to the horizon, over miles and miles of flat,

---

[*]white man (Xhosa and Zulu); *murungu* in Shona

featureless, impenetrable bush, threw in their *lappies** there and then and sneaked off across the Summerstrand to the burgeoning settlement of Port Elizabeth with its rough-and-ready semblance of civilization.

However, Joseph Short was hewn of sterner stuff and made his way northeast, across the mighty Bushman's River to his allocated property, to be called Shortlands, near what was to become the village of Salem, a hundred miles from Port Elizabeth as the seagull flies and some twelve miles south of Grahamstown. The first few years were hard. The soil in the area is sandy, saline and unfit for most crops—except pineapples (it took a century to discover this)—and annual rainfall is poor and potable water scarce. Livestock, though, appeared to thrive and it wasn't too long before the restless Bantu across the Fish were eyeing the white man's cattle, sheep and goats with envy.

Inevitably, trouble ensued and there followed for the next six decades a series of bloody conflicts which were known at the time as the Kaffir Wars and more recently and less offensively as the Frontier Wars, with the native hordes sweeping westward across the Fish, plundering, killing and stealing cattle. The English settlers, together with local Boer farmers and sundry British army platoons, would in turn retaliate, form commandos and sweep eastward across the Fish, plundering, killing and stealing cattle.

The Shorts were in the thick of things with several of the menfolk being killed in battle. "Slain by a kaffir spear" occurs more than once in the family tree and on the gravestones in the Salem graveyard that are testimony to the savagery of the times. My mother's late cousin, Jarrett Short, retired to the village of Salem in the 1980s and acquired Upper Croft, the original Croft family homestead built in 1836. Declared a national monument, the house is a solid stone structure with much unchanged in its 187-year existence. The kitchen, which faces east—and therefore the threat of the black hordes—still has its rifle-slit windows with appropriately sited fields of fire. I was fortunate to visit Jarrett in his twilight years and, with a wealth of family knowledge, he entertained me for hours with stories of the past.

"Joseph's one son was a bloody fool," he said. "Went galloping off to meet the oncoming Xhosa before the commando was fully formed and of course got himself killed in a jiffy. Old Joe brought him home in a sack—bits and pieces, y'know."

There are still plenty of Shorts in the Salem–Grahamstown area today, but by the 1850s, my mother's forebears had had enough and trekked to Potchefstroom

---

*a cloth or towel (Afrikaans)

in the Western Transvaal, where they established a thriving general dealer's business known as Short Bros. on the main street. Joseph Short—son of the original settler, Joseph—even became mayor.

My grandfather, Clifton Max Short, was born in Potchefstroom in 1898. He studied medicine at Cornell University in New York State and was by all accounts a promising young surgeon with a bright future. In 1930, he married Hilda Edmunds at St George's Cathedral in Cape Town. However, from the bits and pieces gleaned from my grandmother, he had a drinking problem and died in 1935, aged only 37, from an alcohol-related illness. Shortly before his death, he performed a successful appendectomy on my grandmother, in the bush at Loskop, at night, and armed only with a candle, a scalpel and a bottle of whisky.

★

It was New Year's Day 1967. Elevenses. We had some new people coming, including children: always a testing time. The Sandys-Thomases couldn't make it as the Hunyani was in flood and they were marooned in their mud hut. Uncle Pat was 'in the studio' at the RBC and Bruce Thoms had sent his apologies as there'd been an outbreak of foot and mouth on his Battlefields ranch. I'd always wondered what foot and mouth (or hoof and mouth) disease was. I'd once looked it up at the Queen Victoria Library, and it looked vile (almost as vile as syphilis and penile warts which I'd also looked up). Sort of like the plague for livestock, cloven-hoofed ones anyway (so horses were okay). Well, at least my father was safe from Bruce's potential Lantana camara abuse. Of course, he had done nothing to deal with it and there were some rampant outbreaks down by the river near the poplars, and beautiful they were too: a riot of reds, oranges, pinks and yellows.

Bob Smith, a kindred farmer/rancher of Bruce's, was tut-tutting away in Welsh to me: That's not good, Christopher. Foot and mouth could wipe out his whole herd."

I nodded sagely. "It's a bit like rabies, isn't it, Bob?" (Our parents encouraged us to call their friends by their Christian names: "None of this Uncle Bob stuff: 'Uncle' and 'Auntie' is very common, very non-U. And if you have an aunt, you call her 'Aunt' not 'Auntie'.")

"Well, not quite, Christopher. But they're both pretty nasty."

We liked Bob and enjoyed spending weekends on his farm—technically the Bentleys' farm—out "in the Umvukwes" as my mother called it. Bob, still a bachelor, was not too fussed about what my sisters and I got up to. His record collection comprised a dozen Clancy Brothers albums, Andy Stewart's album

151

with the blockbuster hit, 'A Scottish Soldier', which I played to death (later referred to as 'on loop') and two new-on-the-block The Dubliners albums with the lead singer Ronnie Drew looking out at you from the cover like a demented Rasputin with his thick black beard and penetrating sapphire-blue eyes. That was it. Celtic stuff only, and not immune from Caroline's addiction for turning volumes up by decibels, which didn't brother Bob in the slightest.

What did bother Bob, though he carried it off well, was my all-encompassing obsession with his motorbike, a Honda 90, which he used for doing the rounds of his tobacco lands. My obsession knew no bounds and I was fully prepared to risk the wrath of Bob and my father in my relentless ambition to ride it. I nagged and nagged and nagged and, eventually, Bob gave in. After a few brief lessons—kick-start, throttle, gears and brakes—he hesitatingly pronounced me ready to go solo. Finally, after a few mishaps—I fell off and burned my calf on the exhaust but refused to let anyone see it for fear of being banned—I was off, wind in my hair. I opened up the throttle and the Honda leaped forward, hungry to complete the 500-yard sandy circuit around the homestead and the barns. It was exhilarating as the machine between my legs screamed to a halt in front of Bob and my father.

"Well done, Christopher," said Bob grudgingly. "You didn't fall off but next time it'd be useful if you changed gears. You can't stay in first gear, otherwise you'll burn the engine out. You need to listen to the engine. If it's screaming, it's in the wrong gear."

"Oh." I hadn't thought of that. I just couldn't get a grip on how the gears worked and so ignored them.

"One more circuit," said Bob, reluctantly.

I was off and after fifty yards or so changed into second gear in one fluid, grinding motion. That was better. Before changing into third, or whatever came next, I decided to take a different route and veered off the track onto a narrow path through a patch of bush. (I needed to tell my friends that I was an accomplished motocross rider.) This was more like it. Open up the throttle a bit, negotiate the next tight bend ... and WHAM! Next thing I was flat on my back on the path. I smelled the blood in my eyes, I smelled the oil and petrol from the screaming motorbike that was lying on top of my legs, burning them, pinning them to the sand.

I could hear the sound of my father's voice, I think in fright: "Christopher! You bloody little fool!"

Then Bob's more soothing tone, somewhere far off, almost dreamily: "C'mon, let's get this bike off him ... and get him patched up. Hope he's not going to lose an eye … or two."

I was taken inside, where my mother met us.

"Good GOD! What happened?"

"Bloody motorbike."

"Get him to the bathroom. Bob, have you got any mercurochrome?"

"Should have been wearing a bloody helmet," my father droned on.

And so I was repaired. Apparently, I had not seen the single strand of barbed wire strung across the path at head height between two trees: well, at eye height for a 9-year-old future motocross champion on a rampant Honda 90. The barbed wire had caught me in the face, a fraction of an inch below the eyes, and had literally torn me off the motorbike.*

Emerging from the bathroom some half an hour later, my face red, orange and black under the bandages, I was met by a wall of The Clancy Brothers and my sisters' taunts. Since that day I'd been trying to make amends to Bob, though I knew the chances of another motorbike ride any time soon were zero.

My reverie was interrupted by my mother: "Christopher, go'n get your sisters."

Standing next to her were three children, the 'new' ones we'd been told about—two boys (around my sisters' age) and a girl (around my age).

"Sarah, Caroline … this is Jeremy. Jeremy George. You remember him, don't you?"

"No."

"Of course, you do!"

"Maybe it's cos he's so skinny we didn't notice him." The twins giggled, cruelly mumbling under their breath words like 'weed' and 'skinnymalinky-longlegs'.

George? My ears pricked up. That meant Di George was here. I scanned the sea of adults under the pergola and identified Grenville George's distinctive (very loud) laugh and sure enough, there was Aphrodite standing next to him, chatting with Di and Joy who were flirting outrageously with her. I was fixated: she was wearing a white dress that was very tight and impossibly short, offsetting her tanned, toned legs. I couldn't quite reconcile how a creature of such perfection could be Jeremy's mother.

"Don't be rude, girls," censured my mother. "Jeremy is going into Standard 1 at St John's this year. Jeremy, Sarah and Caroline are the same age as you. They are going into Standard 1 at Chisipite Junior."

---

*I never established why that single strand of barbed wire was where it was.

Jeremy nodded without interest, or perhaps it was fear. He had a handsome face and a smooth, darkish complexion, but he was very skinny, almost emaciated.

"And girls, this is Stewart Buchan-Ford. He's also going into Standard 1 at St John's."

Stewart, with an impish face, was several inches shorter than the twins who scowled at him, clearly unimpressed.

"Now run along, you lot, and go'n play."

I was introduced to Jane Buchan-Ford. I liked her instinctively. She was a big girl for her age, pretty, with blonde hair, a smattering of freckles across her nose and the sweetest smile I'd ever seen. Her parents were Ann and John. Ann, from the Isle of Man, was a diminutive, homely woman, with curly hair (like my first love Shona), freckles and a hint of buck teeth. With a kind, open face and a ready laugh, I liked her immensely. She would become a close friend of my mother's. Husband John—he was 'in finance'—was the antithesis of his wife: urbane, debonair and with smoldering good looks, he was a cross between an early George Clooney and the Camel Man. I took Jane off to my room to show her my collection of *Treasure* annuals and my Ladybird Book collection, recent additions being *Robert the Bruce* and *Captain James Cook*. The twins were somewhere in the garden bullying Jeremy and Stewart.

There was a voice outside the bedroom door. "*Gogogoyi*. Knocka knock, Christopher."

"*Pindai*, Lizzie," I responded, showing off my knowledge of Shona to Jane who was sitting on my bed, flipping through a *Treasure*.

Lizzie entered, the purpose of her visit clearly to inspect Jane as a potential breeding partner for me. "Ah, but she's nice one, Christopher. Strong one."

"*Errpp* ..." from the throng of adults on the pergola. Lizzie was wanted. We followed her out and I helped Jane to a Coke.

Di and Joy were in full sail, the whisky (rather whiskey, the ersatz variety) flowing.

"So, what do you call it?" Ann asked them.

"Flat Kat Pak."

"Very clever marketing," announced John in finance. "And Pack spelled P ... A ... K?"

"Yes."

"Intriguing," added John.

I thought so too. How boldly anti-establishment was that? Deliberately misspelling words for sales purposes. Mrs Scrase would not be pleased.

Joy continued, in between bouts of a hacking cough: "We came up with the idea after speaking to an old dear who lives in a flat in The Avenues. Her biggest challenge in life is the cat litter, y'know, when they crap. Complaining that she spends her life cleaning out the cat tray and hoiking bloody great bags of cat litter up the stairs. So, we thought, 'Why not come up with something disposable? Something you chuck away when it's done with?'"

"Just ingenious," added John.

"Getting the raw material together was pretty simple," continued Di. "Got Hunyani Pulp and Paper to knock up some reasonably durable cardboard trays."

"Not *too* durable," snorted Joy. "Don't want them lasting *too* long … here, Christopher, be a darling and do something with this, will you."

I studied the still-smoldering, lipstick-smeared stompie* I'd been handed. I don't know what made me do it—perhaps to demonstrate my international-passport-to-smoking-pleasure man-of-the-worldness to Jane—but I put it to my lips, took a puff and promptly started coughing, choking and gagging, much to Jane's horror. Fortunately, my parents were out of sight, but Di and Joy thought it was very funny.

"Christopher, when I said do something with it, I didn't mean smoke it!" said Joy, snorting and laughing at the same time.

"And then we spoke to our *shamwaris*† at Vainona Quarries who came with a plan for us to use the spoil from their gravel. Perfect for cat litter. They chuck it away anyway and were only too pleased when we'd said we'd take a few tons off them. Took several truckloads and dumped it round the back of the house and got old Jairos the garden boy onto the production line.‡ Gave him a shovel and

---

*cigarette butt (S. African slang)

†friends (Shona)

‡By a bizarre coincidence, some twenty-five years later, I too was involved in a production line at 4 Borrowdale Lane—the tractor-tyre dog baskets were still there—with my friend and business associate (never a good mix), Fraser Mackay. Officially known as Loofex Enterprises—originally dealing in loofahs—the company produced snails for the Zimbabwean and Mauritian markets (mainly restaurants and hotels) under the trade name of Burgundy: bizarrely again, Burgundy snails are still on the market but from a different producer. We 'produced' the *Helix aspersa* variety, the proper, more *petits* 'French' escargots, whereas our Chinese competitors used the large *Achatina achatina* variety—the ice-cream-cone lookalike—which they diced (cheating really). When I say we 'produced', we didn't actually grow the snails: we simply shanghaied all the local gardeners—they had graduated from garden boy in April 1980 with Zimbabwean independence—and offered them a rate per kilogram. Several dozen gardeners came back a few days later with buckets and sacks bursting at the seams with live *Helix aspersa* harvested from the local suburban flowerbeds, snails being abundant—and a pest—at the height of the rainy season (zero

told him we'd pay him a tickey a unit."

"Well, I never," added John.

"And really, that's all there is to it," said Di. "Add some fancy packaging with a catchy name and we were off. Got Pat Matthews to do a voiceover for a TV and radio ad—'FLAT KAT PAK … you can't live without it and neither can your pussy' [Joy almost choked on her whiskey]—and now we can't keep up with demand. Banging out 200 units a week."

It all sounded so simple. I'd picked up on the word 'catchy' which was one of those 'groovy' new words that Mrs Scrase didn't like, and which was being applied to anything and everything, particularly songs, as in a 'catchy tune'.

"So, how long does one Flat Kat Pak last? asked Bob. "And how do you know when it's finished?"

"By the smell or if it starts seeping through the bottom."

Everyone laughed.

"Normally though, one unit will last one cat for around four days, sometimes even a week, So, we reckon a one-cat flat will need around five or six units a month … thereabouts."

"So, when it's finished, you just chuck it in the bin?"

"Yip."

"Amazing," added John, and being in finance, now a disciple. "So, what else does P&R Transport do?"

"We erect fuel depots all round the country. Massive undergound tanks for the oil companies and smaller overhead ones for government departments, like police stations, District Commissioners and so on. Those are normally around five or six hundred gallons, some even a thousand," explained Joy.

"And farmers!" said Di. "Some of them have so much fuel they don't even know what to do with it. No fuel rationing for them. It's coming out their ears. Oh Bets, you might want to hear this. We were installing some tanks for a farmer out in Enterprise this week—no names, no pack drill—who says he needs the tanks as he's just been awarded a veeery nice contract to supply roses to some of the big hotels in town on a weekly basis."

I thought my mother was going to be sick as she angrily stubbed out a cigarette into an overfull soapstone ashtray. The day had somehow lost its gloss,

---

available in the winter). We were in business. Our production manager, Jairos junior, then got things going. The snails were boiled (to death) in batches in large drums over an open fire for half an hour, in our homemade concoction of herbs and spices, before Jairos deftly removed the shells with a crochet needle and then ladled *les escargots* into big plastic bags for freezing prior to canning.

although the gloss flared briefly when Jane squeezed my hand as they were leaving. Not even Lizzie's cross observation that "*Ehe ... that one Christopher, she make strong babies*" could dampen my nascent ardour.

That night, kneeling on the threadbare Persian carpet by my bed, I said my prayers and asked God to visit eternal hell and damnation on that Enterprise farmer. I mentioned that I was a good choirboy and perhaps this might help in processing my application expeditiously. "Do you Lord not see that because of this Enterprise farmer I now have to ride nearly forty miles a week? And Lord, do you not see how this hurts my mother? It's just not fair, Lord." I knew I was pushing my luck so felt I needed to finish on a positive note: "But thank you God for the day today and bringing Jane into my life ... Amen."

★

Musically, 1967 began in the same exciting manner that 1966 closed with. The big song for January was The Turtles and their number 1 US chartbuster, 'Happy Together'. It was almost if the words had been written for me ... and Jane.

However, I was slightly nervous about going public with my new relationship, for that's surely what it was, even though I'd only seen her once. After all, I had never forgotten the pain of losing Shona or the ignominy of being jilted by Wendy in *Peter Pan* before the relationship had barely begun. One had to be careful about 'going public', which in my case entailed confiding in my sisters—always a dangerous proposition—and telling Duddo. 'Going public' created expectancy in the confidees that the relationship was more than just puff.

Talking of Duddo ... Inyanga beckoned. Richard Dudley had, as promised, negotiated with my mother about taking me up with the Dudleys to their newly acquired holiday cottage on the shores of Little Connemara, just below what Cecil Rhodes had named as World's View.* This was an event of some magnitude: Inyanga, with its clean mountain air, fresh mountain streams and reservoirs teeming with brown and rainbow trout, abundant pine forests and bracken-covered screes, is an area not unlike the Scottish Highlands, at the northern edge of the Eastern Highlands. Bordered to the south by Lizzie's homelands, the Mutasa reserve, that stretches south almost as far as Umtali; to the east by tropical rainforests and the tea estates of the vast Honde Valley that

---

*Rhodes also named the World's View in the Matopos Hills (now Matobo National P{ark), south of Bulawayo.

backs on to the Mozambican border; to the northeast by the Gairezi River that also marks the border with Mozambique; to the north the lowlands of the Mazoe River that snakes its way to the Zambezi and the border post at Nyamapanda/ Cochemane (of Império Português renown); and to the west by middleveld that encompasses Mtoko, Mrewa, Headlands, Macheke and, ultimately, Salisbury.

At the heart of the Inyanga district is the Rhodes Inyanga National Park,* once Rhodes's 472-square-kilometre personal estate that he bequeathed to the nation—well, the whites of the nation—as a hiking, climbing, fishing, swimming holiday destination, with thatched holiday cottages that dot the shores of the various reservoirs in the park. Also in the park is Mount Inyangani, the country's highest mountain at 8,504 feet, and the Pungwe River which, on the eastern slopes of Mount Inyangani, begins its epic 400-kilometre journey to the Indian Ocean at Beira with its teeming hordes of Rhodesian oiks.

I was unaware of it at the time, but there was trouble brewing on the Gairezi River, the ancestral lands of Chief Rekayi Tangwena and his people which had been designated 'white settler' land by the government. The chief had arrived at the local District Commissioner's office at Ruda in the Honde Valley to register his status as a chief but was informed by the white officialdom there that he was not a chief and that he and his people were all registered as labourers—presumably to supply a workforce to the tea estates and the Forestry Commission—and not as the tribespeople he assumed they were. Like an open wound, the issue festered—Tangwena was arrested multiple times—until 8 September 1969 when dozens of Rhodesian policemen and Ministry of Internal Affairs (INTAF) district assistants swooped on the Tangwena people in a Sophiatown-type sequel operation, and violently evicted them, burning all their huts in the process. Tangwena, with nowhere to go, took his people across the border into Mozambique, where the Portuguese authorities appeared to take little notice. Subsequently, the chief assisted in getting Robert Mugabe and his lieutenant, Edgar Tekere, out of the country to take up the armed struggle

---

*Fun fact, all conjecture/ allegation of course: when Rhodes went back to England in 1874 to study at Oxford, he had a dalliance with a woman, possibly one Mrs Norris. Mrs Norris bore a child, John, who was later dispatched, as a mere boy, to the Cape to live at Rhodes's Cape Town residence, Groote Schuur, much to the astonishment of Rhodes's retainers. On his majority, John Norris was sent up to the new colony of Rhodesia where he took up the position of Rhodes's secretary on the Inyanga estate. As a thank-you from Rhodes, John was given land in the town of Umtali, at Dangamvura, which later became a black township. John's great-grandson, Charlie Norris, was best man at my first wedding (there would be three). There are discrepancies with the dates in this account. (Source: Charlie Norris)

with ZANLA, the Zimbabwean African National Liberation Army.[*]

I was beside myself with excitement as the Mini pulled into the driveway of the Dudleys' house on the Golden Stairs Road, Avondale. And there it was, on its trailer already hooked up to Richard Dudley's white Simca 1000: the *Tyke*, the Optimist sailing dinghy that Richard had bought in the Christmas holidays to take up to Little Connemara—where it would live in a small boathouse. In the back of the dinghy were the mast, the boom, the rudder and tiller, the centreboard, the sail in its bag, oars, paddles, ropes and several fly-fishing rods, landing nets and other tackle.

"Ahoy there, Mate Cockso!" welcomed Duddo. "Stow your gear aft, you scurvy dog!"

"Aye aye, skipper!" I retorted. It had been agreed beforehand that as Duddo was the boat owner, the cottage owner and an accomplished fly-rod fisherman, he would be skipper for the trip and I'd be the mate. I had not done any fly fishing before and was quite nervous about making the cut. Forbes Davies had kindly lent me his fly rod and reel—it was an Orvis bamboo rod: "Don't break it; I've had it since 1936"—and had given me a couple of casting lessons on the lawn next to the swimming pool. I had not coped too well; it was fiendishly complicated.

"Christ … a … pher!" Ice tinkling, it was Meg. "Don't … waste … your time … with that silly casting nonsense. When I was in Turkey, I went fishing for sea trout at Karadeniz on the Black Sea and we just dangled the rod out of the back of the boat and trolled."

"Were you rowing?" I asked.

"Don't be a silly billy. Of course not, you can't row *and* hold a G&T at the same time."

"Oh Meg," snorted Forbes. "For goodness' sake, don't fill the boy's head with such rubbish. And anyway, it's illegal to troll here. Just not cricket."

My mother kissed me goodbye as Richard came out the house, laden with provisions. "Right, you poxy landlubbers. Here's the grog and salt beef. Get it all stowed sharpish or you'll be tasting the cat! We cast off at ten bells."

"Aye aye, Admiral!" Richard had been appointed the expedition's Honorary Admiral of the Fleet.

During the holidays we'd spent a few mornings rigging out the Optimist on the lawn, sort of a dry run, under Richard's guidance. Not just a fighter pilot but an old salt too, he taught us how to fit the mast and the boom and how to

---

[*]The armed wing of ZANU. ZANU/ ZANLA are used interchangeably for the movement's guerrillas.

set the sail (and to fit the Perspex batons to stiffen it), how to fit the rudder and how to use the tiller and what the centreboard did (important as the Optimist has no keel). We learned how to control the sail using the mainsheet, which is the rope that runs on a block (a small pulley thing) between the boom and the skipper's hand. We got to understand what it meant to go about and what it meant to tack. We spent hours learning the knots: the reef knot, the running bowline, the clove hitch and many more. The Admiral then pronounced the crew of the *Tyke* as ready to sail when we arrived at our port of embarkation: Little Connemara.

Apart from the naval training, we crammed as much relevant reading in as we could, specifically the twelve-book Swallows and Amazons series, which was what the *Tyke* was based on. I'd managed to get onto book 4, *Winter Holiday*, having raced through *Swallows and Amazons*, *Swallowdale* and *Peter Duck* in a year. Duddo was on book 5, *Coot Club*. *Tyke* was naturally more attuned to the *Amazon*, being more martial than the *Swallow*, and like *Amazon*, we'd even persuaded my mother to knock up a skull-and-crossbones pennant which we could run up (and down) the mast.

"To your stations!" It was the Admiral. "Wench approaching on the starboard bow."

It was Fay coming out the house to bid us adieu. My heart skipped a beat and I immediately felt guilty. Was this what was called 'two-timing'? Was I being unfaithful to Jane?

"Hello Cockso," she beamed, genuinely happy to see me. "You boys all set?"

I nodded dumbly. I felt myself blushing furiously.

It transpired that 'the wenches'—the lovely Fay, Duddo's sister Susan—referred to by Duddo as 'Period Pain'—and Susan's friend Janine Park (her brother Charlie was in our class at St. John's)—were only joining the expedition in two days' time as they had "important stuff to do", no doubt involving sulky, unsmiling, spotty teenage boys, and at any rate three wenches plus two ratings and an officer would not have fitted into the Simca. This suited Duddo fine: Susan regarded boys our age as a sub-species to be disregarded at best and demeaned at second best.

It was a blissful week, perhaps one of the happiest weeks of my life. A mere twenty-five yards or so from the lake, the thatched cottage was everything that I'd imagined, and more. No electricity but with a wood-burning AGA cooker, it was cosy and functional. Portable gas lanterns provided light while a wood-burning forty-four-gallon-drum Rhodesian boiler—aka a 'donkey boiler'—

round the back supplied the hot water. Wood was cut and the boiler and AGA fires maintained by the cottage live-in majordomo who had two names, a Shona one, Garikayi, and a biblical one, Abel, pronounced 'Uh–bell'.

Very possibly from the luckless Tangwena clan, his other duties included cooking (only breakfast), cleaning the cottage, preventing the small patch of Kikuyu lawn from being invaded by the adjacent bush grass and bracken, planting and watering a few optimistic Namaqualand daisies, Mexican marigolds and busy lizzies and ensuring that the small wooden jetty into the lake didn't rot; likewise, the small log-cabin-type boathouse with a corrugated-iron roof that was to be *Tyke*'s future home. Garikayi/ Abel also did the laundry, washing in a big galvanized-iron tub next to the boiler (with what must have been five pounds of Persil per tub). The drying was done on a wire clothesline strung between the boiler and a lone pine tree, while the ironing was done on the kitchen table with a heavy box iron filled with hot coals.

Our day started at dawn when we two ratings and the officer would be down to the lakeshore to catch the morning rise, that period of an hour or so after dawn when the fish are active, feeding on the surface and then plopping lazily back under. Even though it was summer, it was cold at that time of the day, with a ghostly mist rising off the mirrorlike surface. I had scanned the flies in Forbes's fly box the night before and tied a Walker's Killer onto the leader. That apparently was the fly of the moment, with Coachman, Invicta, Bloody Butcher, Black Gnat and Mrs Simpson as worthy backups. But casting I could not master, and I'd watch with envy Duddo effortlessly throwing his line a good dozen or more yards into the middle of lake to lightly kiss the surface and settle ever so gracefully. My casting did improve over the course of the week, but nine casts out of ten ended up whipping the water into a frenzy, with the one out of ten managing to achieve a respectable distance of seven or eight yards and without too much surface violence. Then there was the inevitable 'bird's nest' when the line overran and snarled up into a tangled mess. I was exasperated and almost chucked it in, but seeing Duddo catch a two-pound rainbow on the third day kept my motivation alive. Perhaps Meg's idea of trolling had some merit, though I was quite uneasy about mentioning it. Richard was serenity personified as he studiously went about his business and landed one or two trout every morning (and evening), which ensured a splendid dinner that night.

At 9 o'clock-ish it was back to the cottage for Garikayi/ Abel's 'hearty breakfast of bacon, fried eggs, sausage, mushrooms, fried tomato and toast, followed by lashings of hot, sweet tea'.* Garikayi/ Abel would also take possession of any trout and gut and clean them outside the kitchen, probably in the galvanized-iron laundry tub. Breakfast was a social affair, with Fay quizzing us menfolk on the fishing and quizzing Susan and Janine who were still in their dressing gowns, hair in curlers, about what they were planning on doing today, other than sunbathing on the lawn in their bikinis and listening to LM Radio on the portable wireless.

"Taxing stuff," muttered Duddo, not quite under his breath.

Susan's eyes narrowed to almost-closed status. "You little cave-dwelling, mutant pre-human," she hissed.

"Well," added Fay with levity. "I'm going down to Troutbeck store later on for bread and milk, if anybody wants to come with me. We can then pop in to Troutbeck Inn for some tea and scones."

I'd been pondering the idea of seeing the girls in their bikinis—the bikini was a revolutionary form of bathing suit that was taking the world by storm—but it was not to be, not today anyway: the wenches were all heading off down the hill to Troutbeck while we chaps would be launching *Tyke* for a day's naval manoeuvres.

Richard as Admiral went out first with Duddo to ensure that the new ensign was fully au fait with his craft; in any case, the dinghy could only take two. My job was to hold the painter (the rope tied to the bow) and toss it in the boat as they got underway. The sail flapped idly in the breeze as Richard took up his position by the tiller, his left hand loosely holding the mainsheet. Duddo began paddling up near the bow to get *Tyke* into deeper water to be able to lower the centreboard as I threw the painter into the boat while they drifted away from the jetty. A gust of wind caught the sail which billowed and tightened with a *thwack* and they were off. Sailing. While dropping the centreboard in place, the jolt of acceleration had caught Duddo off balance and he nearly toppled in. But they were sailing: it was a fine sight. Slowly at first before Richard hauled in the boom to sail closer to the wind as the sail bit, tight, and *Tyke* almost lunged out the water.

I can say that by the end of that week, unlike casting a fly road, I knew how to sail. It was glorious. We spent the days tacking up the lake and running back with the wind astern, letting the sail out to ninety degrees and feeling the power of the dinghy in perfect harmony with the elements. At times it felt like *Tyke* was a living thing, like a racehorse. Unfortunately, there were few, if any,

*paraphrased from Enid Blyton's *The Famous Five*

other craft on the lake, so we had no *Swallow*-type enemy to engage. Nor could we practise our rules of the road: steam gives way to sail, or if two craft are approaching head on, both vessels alter course to starboard and pass each other port side to port side. We did, however, discover a small island in the middle of the lake. We ran up the skull and crossbones, armed ourselves with a paddle each and stormed the beach, where we ruthlessly dispatched what poxy scurvy dogs we could find.

Closer to home, a frosty truce between Duddo and Susan had unfolded after the cave-dwelling, mutant pre-human slight. I did get to see the girls sunbathing in their bikinis, but the sight was marred by the dreadful sunburn they had both suffered. Inyanga is like that: at altitude and with a constant cooling breeze, it's common to disregard how brutal the sun can be. Their necks, shoulders (especially at the straps), chests, hips and backs of their legs were almost burned raw. It looked very painful, and I was unable to witness any beauty therein.

And then it was all over, the week gone in a flash and a blur. It was left for us to make our way back to Salisbury, *sans Tyke*, with a sense of deflation. School was starting in a few days—Standard 3—which did little to alleviate the general sense of gloom. The twins were starting Standard 1 at Chisipite Junior School, up Hindhead Avenue past Délice Bakery. That reminded me: perhaps the time was approaching for what had been formulating in my mind for some while now: a raid on Délice, a shoplifting raid. Spiro's time was nigh.

★

No relation to Howie, the Standard 3 teacher was Mr Gardiner. Youngish, maybe late twenties/ early thirties, with a neat black beard and a twinkle in his eye, he was the epitome of Rhodesian man-cool what with his confident swagger, his tight pale-green polyester trousers held up by a built-in striped polyester belt, a white polyester shirt with a neat array of biros in the pocket and an old boys' club tie. With Mr Gardiner we would be starting Latin, a daunting prospect.

We would also experience Mr Gardiner's style of discipline: sadism. He was a master of his craft and had no end of variety of punishments in his armoury, nothing overtly brutal, mind; in fact, it was all quite subtle, almost civilized: no blood, no bruising. An example was the recalcitrant boy called up to stand next to Mr Gardiner seated at his desk and subjected to the gentle-but-firm tapping of a ruler on the back of an exposed leg, behind the knee. For half an hour. After five minutes it was irritating, after ten it was mildly painful and after fifteen minutes it was excruciatingly painful. All the while,

Mr Gardiner, oblivious to the victim next to him, continued with his class. A similar punishment, also involving a ruler, was the boy victim kneeling at Mr Gardiner's desk with his hands palm down on the desk. Mr Gardiner would then employ the thin edge of the ruler—the bit with a thin strip of metal embedded into the wood, presumably to assist in drawing a straight line—to gently tap on the boy's knuckles. For half an hour. Cruder forms of punishment included a straightforward beating (with the whippy three-foot steel ruler this time) where the victim would be made to bend over with his head tucked under the little wooden chalk and duster tray at the bottom of the blackboard. One sharp blow of the ruler against the back of the legs was enough for the boy to cry out in pain and instinctively snatch his head upward only for it to make violent contact with the little wooden chalk and duster tray at the bottom of the blackboard. Quite crafty, I thought: one cause, two effects, or as Di Edmunds always said, "Two *nyonis* with one *dombo*."[*] And last, the infamous sideburn lift: no ruler involved with this—just Mr Gardiner's thumb and forefinger gripping a chunk of a boy's hair above the ear and lifting said boy a sixteenth of an inch[†] at a time and ever so slowly … upward. Until the boy was standing on the extreme extremity of his tiptoes. Mr Gardiner later confided in us that his goal was to be able to lift a 9- or 10-year-old boy entirely off the ground using only his thumb and forefinger. I do believe that he achieved this one day with Ian Moss, a short sometime-friend of mine who had an aviary at home and collected bronze mannikins, finches, canaries and budgies (lots of them—I spent a day with him once learning all about small aviary birds). He was then to repeat the feat a few days later with future jockey Ronnie Lawrence who was even shorter than Ian Moss, this time suspending Ronnie for a good couple of seconds off the ground by about half an inch.[‡]

Well into the term, I was to become one of Mr Gardiner's victims. We had a Latin test looming and I had not revised for it. How to get out of it? I know! I'll forge my mother's handwriting and send Mr Gardiner a sick note. That'll do it. The snag was that this could not be done retrospectively—that is, after the event of calling in sick—as it would be almost impossible to get my mother to accept that I was really sick (in vain, I had tried this before by bashing my head against my bedroom wall to induce either a migraine or a coma, but had only ever managed a lumpy skull and a headache). I pondered the options and came up with a convoluted plan: I would write my mother's sick note to Mr Gardiner

---

[*]two birds with one stone (English and Shona)
[†]1.5875mm
[‡]12.7mm

for the following day and once this was accepted, I would inform my mother that the class had been given the day off because of an outbreak of mumps. So it was that the following day I presented Mr Gardiner with my mother's sick note, written in block letters to highlight the severity of the illness (with only one tiny ink blot):

DEAR MR. GARDINER.
CHRISTOPHER IS FEELING VERY SICK. I THINK HE HAS MUMPS. SO HE WILL NOT COME TO SCHOOL TOMORROW.
BYE.
BETTY COCKS

I thought the employment of mumps at either end of the ploy really quite crafty. Mr Gardiner didn't.

"How old is your mother, Cocks?"

"Ummm, I think she's thirty-four, sir."

"Did she go to school, Cocks?"

"Yes sir! Diocesan School for Girls in Kloof ... in Natal!" I stated proudly.

"Well, perhaps Diocesan School for Girls only went up to Standard 3?"

A sneaking feeling that I was about to be rumbled overcame me. I think I could see where this was heading. Panic. Adopt the defence of absolute silence and look downcast.

Silence.

I could feel Mr Gardiner's eyes boring into me. Very slowly he placed the note in front of my face (half and inch from the tip of my nose) and, in a series of measured digital movements, tore it up into little bits and dropped it like confetti into the waste-paper basket next to the desk. It wasn't over though.

"Hands on the desk, palms face down."

Ruler-tap-tap-tap-tap-tap-tap-tap-tap-tap-tap-tap-tap-tap-tap-tap ... for half an hour.

Apart from the pain, I was concerned that this might get back to Mr Hickman, in which case I'd be facing the headmaster's butter pat, the official school instrument of punishment, and the subsequent ignominy, and worse, that it might get back to my parents and I'd be facing my father's leather slipper. In the event, it went no further than the Standard 3 classroom, Mr Gardiner content to manage his own in-house punishment regime.

Apart from Latin and our new teacher's sadism, also new were two fresh arrivals: Paul Stobart and Russell Franklin. 'Stobes' immediately upset the comfortable status quo of the Top 5 pupils in the class by coming first in every subject and at the end of the term, first in class overall. The Top 5—formerly Graeme Fleming, Duddo, Mark Bushnell, Ming Majo and me—was now relegated to Within the Top 6, with each of us slipping occasionally to sixth in a subject or two. Paul Stobart, with bones seemingly made of some type of rubberized material and a soft-as-a-baby's-bottom complexion, was notably unathletic (though he was always up for a game of cricket) and an only child. He carried himself with an air of supreme self-confidence, underscored by the coquettish hint of a moue which, coupled which his probable four-figure IQ, endeared him to all the teachers. His parents too, George and Carla, also with probable four-figure IQs, soon slotted in with the other parents and became quite friendly with mine. Russell Franklin took over the role of tallest boy in the class from Jamie Beaton, the man mountain. I liked Russell and spent a fair amount of time at his double-storey house—double storeys were regarded as posh in the colonies—in Colne Valley. His father was a dentist. They were everywhere.

Standard 3 was also the Year of Stationery when we were inducted into the world of the fountain pen, inkwells and blotting paper. Each desk was blessed with a ceramic inkwell inserted into a hole at the top right corner of the desk, just above the hinge where the desk lid opens and closes. Naturally, the area in the immediate vicinity of the inkwell was an ink-stained disaster zone from years of boys either overfilling the inkwell or overfilling their fountain pen while recharging it. By 1967, however, inkwells were redundant: they were just too messy, and the boys were expected to provide their own small bottles of ink—or better still, the new-fangled plastic ink cartridges—with the surviving inkwells becoming mini rubbish receptacles to accommodate pencil-sharpener shavings, tiny balls of rolled-up blotting paper and a cross-section of dried snot. I used the Parker pen Granma Teddy had given me at Christmas and it was to provide many years of unblemished service, even taking me into my high-school years. Biros, or ballpoints as we later knew them, were taboo that only idlers and wastrels with no sense of pride used. Writing, especially the joining writing that Mrs Scrase had taught us, was only to be done with a pencil for rough work and notes and a fountain pen for formalized work.

Other stationery accoutrements included a Lakeland & Cumberland set of twenty-four crayons in a tin with pictures of Lake Windemere on the top, two Staedtler pencils, one HB and the other 2B, a rubber (called an eraser by Americans and South Africans) and a metal pencil sharpener. (The class also boasted its own more industrial pencil sharpener that was bolted onto Mr Gardiner's desk, a strange apparatus into which you inserted your pencil and cranked the handle several times. However, it had long since given up the ghost with several pencil stubs clogging up the internal mechanism. Either that or it was formerly one of Mr Gardiner's instruments of torture and had a few Standard 3 pinkies lodged therein.) Last came the geometry set—compass, protractor and set square—which we were still trying to master. Other than using the compass to gouge a girl's name into the desk lid, it was a nasty little weapon that had been used as such by millions of schoolchildren since its invention by Galileo Galilei in Padua in 1597.

At the beginning of one our Latin classes, Mr Gardiner was scratching away on the blackboard, tapping the chalk vigorously against the blackboard with a flourish when he was done, like a sonic full stop:

Caesar had some jam for tea. Brutus had a rat.

We were about to be introduced to *the only* Latin joke in the world. Mr Gardiner looked pleased with himself: "Right, you lot. Your challenge today. The original Latin is *Caesar adsum iam forte. Brutus aderat.* I want to know what this means in English. A shilling to the first boy who gets it right." With that, he sat back in his chair, put his legs on the desk and started reading *The Rhodesia Herald*, probably scanning the Vacancies smalls.

In a flash we grabbed our Latin grammar textbooks from inside our desks, flipping the pages in random and futile haste.

"It's all Greek to me, old boy," whispered Duddo, with a snigger. It was terribly witty.

Of course, it didn't take long before Stobart had his hand up. I was stuck on '*adsum*'.

"Sssssssss ... stobes," another whisper from Duddo.

Mr Gardiner peered over his newspaper, perhaps slightly irritated that he hadn't made it as far as the sports pages. "Okay, Stobart, what is it?"

"Sir ... I, Caesar, am already here, as it happens. Brutus was here also." He half turned to the class with that triumphant, supercilious pout of his.

"Well done. Here's your bob." Mr Gardiner tossed a one shilling coin at Stobes.

"Thank you, sir ... I know the rest of the verse ... *Caesar sic in omnibus* ..."

"Siddown."

Equally perplexing as Latin were imperial measurements, most of which, it seemed, came directly out of the *Domesday Book*. I had the money more or less under control—still Federation of Rhodesia and Nyasaland coinage and still LSD, which I thought was medication that hippies took—starting with the halfpenny and penny, the tickey (3d.), the sixpence, the shilling (1/-), the florin (2/-) and the half-crown (2/6). Then came the 10-shilling note, the £1 note (20 shillings to a pound) and the £5 note (the 'biggie'). (There was even a guinea that was 21 shillings, but I never saw any of them.) Then, two years later, the country 'went decimal',* as South Africa had done with its currency in 1961 when one pound became a two-rand coin, the one shilling a ten-cent coin and the three pence a two-and-a-half-cent coin.

I was okay to a point with lengths: inches, feet, yards, fathoms, rods, furlongs, miles, nautical miles and leagues (there was a chain in there somewhere, too). When the country went metric, the 440-yard race changed to the 400 metres, a distance at which I later became something of a specialist; regardless, I still vomited after every race—in both distances. Weights were tricky with ounces, pounds, stones, hundredweights (for fun, two types, short and long) and tons (again, two types, short and long). Liquid measures started to get complicated with fluid drams, fluid ounces, gills, pints, quarts and gallons, with dry measures being pecks and bushels. Add to the overall complexity, the Americans had their own measures, similar to the English system, but not quite the same, while the Europeans were the most sensible of all with the decimal-based metric system. I mean, what was an acre-foot? Or a board foot? Just one example, there were four variations of a ton: the English short ton and long ton, the US ton and the metric tonne. This is before we even started on cooking measurements, Fahrenheit and Centigrade, horsepower and acres and hectares.

In February, two notable musical events occurred. First, the Beatles' 'Penny Lane' hit the charts. I loved it immediately and considered it my favourite Beatles' track, on a par with their 1965 hit 'Girl'. Obviously, the Beatles had been dominating the airwaves for several years and would continue to do so for a few more: they were just part of your life, ubiquitous and all-encompassing, so it was inevitable that you'd have to like one or two of their songs. The year before, my mother had taken Duddo and me to see the new Beatles' movie *Help!* which was showing at The Palace. I was disappointed with it but didn't want to appear ungrateful; however, my mother's critique was more straightforward:

*Coins started at ½ cent, 1 cent, 2½ cents, 5 cents, 10 cents, 20 cents and 25 cents. Notes were $1, $2, $5 and $10. After much soul-searching, the Ministry of Finance unimaginatively decided on the (Rhodesian) dollar.

San Francisco (Flowers in Your Hair)—Scott MacKenzie, 1967

"What a load of bloody rubbish. Waste of bloody money."

The other notable event in February 1967 was that the Standard 5 teacher, school pianist and choir mistress Mrs Law—'Ma Law' to us—was recruiting for the junior choir that was made up of standards 3 and 4 (standards 5 and 6 supplied choristers to the senior choir). More of a pressgang selection process than any conventional recruitment, only boys who were clearly tone deaf or whose voices were breaking (unlikely in Standard 3, though Jamie Beaton wasn't far off) were exempt. Unlike St Mary's church choir, I liked the St John's choir practice and twice a week after lunch we'd gather in the hall with Ma Law at the piano and sing (trebles and descant) a selection of traditional, mainly English (and Scottish plus the odd Welsh and Irish) folk songs and sea shanties, harking back to a more uncomplicated time that predated even Music Hall: anything twentieth century was considered too avant-garde for Ma Law's taste: 'Westering Home', 'Bobby Shafto', 'Pretty Carolinka', 'The Ash Grove', the stirring 'Drake's Drum', 'Cockles And Muscles', *Dashing Away with the Smoothing Iron' and the rollicking-everyone's-favourite* 'What Shall We Do with a Drunken Sailor?' are songs that still resonate with me today, even though most have slipped off the radar and been consigned to history barring a few traditional choral societies in Britain that gamely soldier on and still perform them.

★

My father had relatives in Salisbury: an uncle and first cousins. We saw them only very occasionally; they lived "across town" as my mother had said, implying that petrol was an issue. Uncle Eric Lamond (my grandmother Esmé's brother) and his wife Aunt Phyl lived in Milton Park, an older suburb just north of the city, while their children, my father's cousins Esmé Mackintosh (married to Mac) and Ian Lamond (married to Elizabeth) lived out toward the suburb of Mabelreign on the northwestern outskirts of the city. I liked them all, even if we didn't know them too well. (It took me some time to work out that my grandmother Esmé who lived in Toronto was not one and the same as Esmé from Mabelreign, that she was in fact her aunt.) Esmé and Mac (who was a police driving instructor) had two children roughly the same age as the twins and me, Donald and Fiona. Like their mother who was an accomplished tennis player, they too were very sporty. Talented in a more musical/ artistic way were the Lamond clan, Ian, Elizabeth and their children, toddler Murray and baby Ceri (two more would be produced in the coming years, Daryl-Anne and Douglas). Elizabeth was a talented pianist/ organist while Ian was the drama teacher at Prince Edward High School, the oldest government school in Salisbury. His nickname at school was 'Spike', possibly from the auburn Lamond hair that was usually awry or the slightly untamed auburn beard. Every year, Ian was responsible for putting on the school stage production of a Gilbert and Sullivan musical, something he did for around twenty-five years. I was proud of my relations.

But never far away, humming menacingly, constantly, as a backdrop to our sheltered suburban lives, was what the whites referred to as "the security situation". It just wouldn't go away and although government communiqués— via Rhodesian Broadcasting Corporation newsreaders like Uncle Pat—kept telling us that it was all under control, that it was a minor "police action", somehow, I never quite believed it. Why was there not a definitive endpoint? Why did the killings keep happening again and again and again?

In the autumn and winter of 1967, the Rhodesian security forces were involved in no less than five military operations in the Zambezi Valley. It was quite clear that not much had improved in the nomenclature stakes since the choice of *Yodel*. Operation *Glamour* saw the Rhodesian African Rifles (RAR) capturing a complete group of nine ZANU guerrillas at the Sebungwe Narrows on the Zambezi, assisted by local two-toes-per-foot Batonka tribesmen. Just over a week later, during Operation *Pantechnicon*, on 26 May, Special Branch (SB) and the SAS eliminated a group of ten ZANU guerrillas hidden in a pantechnicon* near Chirundu: this was the notorious 'Suicide Squad' who were on their way to Salisbury to open fire on the crowds in First Street on a busy Saturday morning. Two weeks later, it was the turn of Operation *HUSK*—why the sudden upper case?—near Chirundu where the RAR and the Rhodesian Light Infantry (RLI)† killed one and captured eight ZANU guerrillas. It transpired that another ZANU cadre was shot dead by a comrade in a fight over money. Then came operations *Isotope and Isotope II*,‡ also near Chirundu, where respectively five ZANU and eighteen ZAPU guerrillas were accounted for (three ZAPU escaped).

I felt powerless, more frustrated perhaps. I sort of knew that the Rhodesian security forces would always win. But for how long? Can you keep winning forever? It was sometimes too much to absorb, so I buried myself in music, as always. It was my go-to place.§ There were three massive hits in April/ May

---

*a very large removals van
†A whites-only regiment formed in 1961 to counter the growing threat of black nationalism.
‡in modern parlance ... WTF!
§It still is. I give thanks to God every day for YouTube (and Spotify).

1967 that grabbed my attention. First, Manfred Mann's 'Ha! Ha! Said the Clown' with front man Mick d'Abo belting it out, a solid, punchy song with some 'catchy' arrangements.[*] On the back of that came 'The Boat That I Row',[†] with the vivacious Lulu, ever the consummate performer, hooking me good and proper with her raunchy, high-octane voice, those big round eyes ... and that miniskirt. And then, the irrepressible Supremes—like the Beatles, they were always 'around'—with 'The Happening', which to me was their greatest-hit-of-all-time song. Written by the legendary Holland–Dozier–Holland and Frank De Vol combination, I just couldn't get enough of the high energy, the melody, the joyous, bouncy, noisy, raucous celebration.[‡]

But then the clouds of war returned. First with the Arab–Israeli Six-Day War (to the Israelis) or the 1967 War or Naksah (to the Arabs) when in six short days, between 5 and 10 June, the Israelis defeated three Arab armies and captured territory four times the country's original size, becoming the unrivalled military power in the region. White Rhodesians were ecstatic, perhaps comparing their own situation of underdog squaring up against a vastly superior force. Moshe Dayan, the iconic eye-patched Israeli defence minister and conqueror of East Jerusalem, was hero of the hour. For more than a year, at every fancy dress party in Salisbury there were at least two or three Moshe Dayans.

Bang in the middle of the Six-Day War, on 8 June, Procol Harem's 'A Whiter Shade of Pale' reached number 1 on the UK singles chart where it stayed for six weeks. Worldwide, over ten million copies were sold, a staggering number. Undoubtedly, despite the incomprehensible lyrics, romantic as they might seem, it is one of the greatest pop songs ever written, with the miller telling his tale and sixteen vestal virgins heading off to the coast. How could you not be completely and utterly enmeshed?

Ushering in the next significant new conflict, the Biafran War or the Nigerian Civil War, was 'Groovin'' by the Young Rascals that shot to number 1

---

[*]Manfred Mann, né Manfred Sepse Lubowitz, is a Lithuanian Jew from Johannesburg who left South Africa in 1961 to escape apartheid. He moved to London and in 1963 was signed by EMI. Mick d'Abo later sang the part of Herod on the first recording of *Jesus Christ Superstar*, which, coincidentally, was the first LP (and a double at that) that I ever bought.

[†]written by Neil Diamond

[‡]Writing on YouTube in 2022, Brock Reynolds said: "This performance is just electrifying. Mary is so gorgeous and perfect on point. Florence looks dignified and amazing ... and Diana just lets loose and rides this song like a wave. When her head gets to boppin', you know it's gonna be a great performance."

on the Billboard Hot 100. (I was curious what Mrs Scrase might have thought of it.) Simple lyrics, gentle Afro-Cuban beat that was so different from the rock 'n' roll fare plugging the airwaves, I immediately fell in love with it. That it was an accidental soundtrack to the horrific war in Biafra was not its fault. Following the secession of the Biafran state in southeastern Nigeria, the Nigerian Civil War officially started on 6 July 1967, and like Vietnam, I followed it closely in *LIFE* and on *Roving Report*. It dragged on until 15 January 1970 by which time the war had produced 100,000 military casualties and a cruel harvest of between half a million and two million civilians, mainly Biafrans and mainly children who died of starvation. Other than the sheer scale of the numbers, I was staggered by the margin of error. What was the real figure? Half a million or two million? How could you not account for one and a half million people? How? They hadn't been vaporized, so where were they? Apart from the images that had come out of the Holocaust, those to emerge from Biafra were perhaps, until then, the most disturbing ever encountered. Gaunt, fly-smeared faces of desperately malnourished children (many my age) stared off the pages of *LIFE* and *Time*, their eyes deadened, their bellies bloated and who were likely dead by the time the magazines were on the newsstands. I studied the images in a kind of macabre trance, unable to take my eyes off these children, guilty about feeding my dinner of kedgeree to Pluto, guilty about being a privileged white boy on a continent which wasn't mine.

★

Southern African schools generally have three terms of three months a year, each punctuated by a month's holiday. The first term at St John's, roughly early January to Easter, being summer, was mainly given over to athletics and some cricket (for the second half of the term). The second term, May into early August, was the winter term with rugby and hockey the two main sports. The third term, mid-September to early December, was cricket only. Tennis was played year-round.

So it was that in the second term of Standard 3, in June 1967, we were inducted into the world of rugby, as the junior year in the Colts rugby team, the senior year being Standard 4. I remember in the Easter holidays being taken by my mother to buy a brand-new pair of Bata rugby boots from legendary school suppliers McCullagh & Bothwell next door to Barbours on Stanley Avenue, where we were attended to by Mr Davis who Bruce Thoms said had been there since the rinderpest.* The rest of the kit—emerald-green jersey, emerald-green socks and white shorts came from the school's second-hand shop, so it was understandable that the emerald green was no longer its original vibrant green. Equally exciting and something that never failed to intrigue me was the pneumatic-tube payment system that McCullagh & Bothwell employed. Once my mother had written out the cheque for the purchase, Mr Davis would slot the cheque and the order chit into a small tube, about nine inches long and with a two-inch circumference, screw closed the lid on the tube, then pop it into a miniature space docking port of about one cubic foot, close the door, pull a lever and *whoosh!*—the tube got sucked like a rocket up to an invisible accounts department several floors up, while Mr Davis carried on nattering to my mother, his left hand poised lightly on the door handle to the mini space docking port. Then a few minutes later another *whoosh!* and a *kadunk!* as the tube came back to earth. Mr Davis then opened the port door, unscrewed the lid from the tube and with a "Thank you for you custom, Mrs Cocks," presented my mother with the receipt. (My sisters thought the whole pneumatic-tube payment system was magic and would peer up into it like meerkats.) And every time as we left the store, my mother would say: "What a *nice* man that Mr Davis is." Then, before the new rugby boots could even touch sides, let alone be fondled and admired, it was off to Mr James's surgery to have the dreadful 'orthopedic' inserts fitted.

Mr Stansbury, the Standard 4 teacher, was our Colts coach. We liked him immensely. With several Standard 4 boys, veterans led by Simon Gray, the supreme athlete, supreme scholar and Colts captain, we gathered in a bunch on the Little Field, whence I could see Mrs Gooch's cottage across the vlei. The light was gloomy and it was cold: perfect rugby weather, apparently.

And so began my journey into the world of rugby union and I relished every minute of it. The physicality was a part of it, of course, but it was more than that: it was the strategy, the tactics and the skills, which when combined, manifested holistically into a thing of beauty.

The field was measured imperially, so 25-yard lines and 10-yard lines. The scoring was straightforward: 3 points for a try, 2 points for a conversion (so 5 points for a converted try) and 3 points for a penalty goal or a drop goal. There were four types of kick: place, drop, punt and grubber. Place kicks were used for all kick-offs and shots at goal, where the ball was placed on the ground in an upright position with the kicker positioning himself in a straight line directly behind the ball and kicking the ball with the toe of his boot—none of the round-

*the highly contagious, fatal bovine virus that annihilated most of the southern Africa's cattle population in 1896/7

the-corner football style employed today. Drop kicks were only ever used for attempted drop goals and a punt was an ordinary kick out of hand to either gain ground (such as an up-and-under) or put the ball into touch. (An accomplished kicker like Simon Gray could 'torpedo' the ball which achieved extra distance and never failed to impress.) Grubber kicks were tricky to get right and involved kicking the ball along the ground so that it bounced unevenly making it awkward for the opposition to pick up. But a perfectly flighted grubber kick through the legs of the opposition might create all sorts of mayhem for them and then sit up nicely for a flying winger. Kicking for touch could take place anywhere on the field with no forfeit of ground gained for kicking outside of one's 25-yard line—so no 'directly into touch'.

Rules were far simpler then. High tackles or a dangerous tackles were not penalizable let alone recognized—simply bring the man down any which way, spear tackles included—though tackling the opposition player just above his knees was encouraged as a surefire way of immobilizing him. Yellow and red cards—football aberrations—were unknown in ruby union with players never sent off. The only time a player left the field was if he was so badly injured that he was physically unable to continue. There were no substitutes so a less-physical team might start a game with fifteen players and at full time walk off with ten, with the other five either incapacitated in their parents' cars or in hospital.

Lifting in the lineout was illegal. There were two types of scrum: a tight (or set) scrum and a loose scrum (none of those poncey rucks and mauls which came many years later). Setting a scrum was simple: the referee would say "Bind" and the two packs would lock and scrum down together with the scrum half putting the ball in at his discretion (which had to be put in as straight as an arrow, not under his locks' or eighth man's feet). Today, setting the scrum is an epic palaver with a complex register of instructions coordinated by the referee: "Crouch, bind, set" has replaced "Crouch, touch, pause, engage" which in turn replaced "Crouch, touch, pause for a wee think, scratch your armpit, engage" by which time the props had forgotten why they were there. Loose scrums were simply a grand mêlée involving sixteen players wrestling for the ball, with zero referee supervision. A loose scrum could sometimes last for twenty minutes, a quarter of the match, which gave the backs time to draw breath and have a chat. Unlike in the modern game, playing the ball on the ground was taboo; however, holding on (to the ball), the tackler not rolling away, off your feet at the breakdown— are all modern concepts—as are the ball-carrier and the first receiver. An HIA (head injury assessment) didn't exist: if a player's head was bleeding profusely and he was comatose, then it was a reasonable assumption that he should depart the field. Gum guards hadn't been invented, though primitive scrumcaps had. The hooker was permitted to wear shinpads.

A game lasted for ninety minutes, forty minutes a half and ten minutes for half-time when the oranges (segmented) were brought on by the linesman on a plate. Drinking water during the game and at half-time was strictly forbidden (for fear of players cramping). Offside and obstruction laws have not really changed, though the knock-on/ knock-forward law has: it is now permissible to not catch the ball cleanly and even juggle it as far as you like, as long as you don't drop it. "A player must not attempt to kick the ball from the hands of the ball-carrier" is another modern law.

As I appeared to have impressed Mr Stansbury with my tackling ability, my first position was blind-side flanker; the open-side flanker had more responsibility and was allocated to Ryan Fry, a Standard 4 boy. Ryan's brother Richard was a tall Standard 3 boy and linked up with Russell Franklin as the lock combination. Simon Gray was one of those multitalented boys who shone at anything he put his mind to. On the rugby field, apart from being blessed with an innate rugby brain, he was the second fastest player (Ming Majo on the wing was by far and away the speediest), the best tackler and the best kicker but at one session I managed to get one over him.

After practising the various phases and skills of the game—scrummaging, lineouts, tackling, passing and kicking—we would usually have a twenty-minute game with the squad divided into two teams: vests versus shirts. The opposing team, Simon Gray's team, was on the back foot and we were mere yards from the try line. It was a given that somewhere during the next phase, we would score. Scrum down, good hooking work by Duddo, ball out to the scrum half who passed to the fly half who passed to the inside centre three-quarter who passed … but, oh no! an intercept by none other than Simon Gray who took off, unopposed, toward the try line at the other end of the field. Instant deflation from my teammates. In a flash, I made up my mind that we should at least try and catch him, but there was no support for the 'we' concept, so I alone took off in hot pursuit. As he was approaching our 25-yard line, Simon, assuming no one was on his tail, tapped off to a canter. Five yards short of the line, I hit him with a flying tackle: ball knocked on and try saved. Simon took it well and I was hero of the minute.

We started playing matches against other schools: in Marandellas against private schools Springvale and Ruzawi (where we clashed with my old friend and nemesis Simon Brewer who was bulking up the Ruzawi front row). Also

175

in Marandellas was Digglefold, a government primary school. In Salisbury, two regular opponents were Highlands Junior School, a government school, where Joughin played scrum half, and Hartmann House, a private Jesuit school that was the feeder to St. George's. The classification of a school as private or government was important: private schools were multiracial but non-white children were not permitted to play away against white government schools.

I remember the first time we were to play away, against Highlands, when Ming Majo was not selected. In fact, Ming Majo was absent that practice session when Mr Stansbury announced the team. I immediately noticed the omission but there was no explanation why Ming Majo had been not selected. Mr Stansbury liked me and so at the end of the session I felt comfortable approaching him.

"Excuse me, sir. Please may I ask you something?"

"Yes, Cocks, of course."

"Why is Ming Majo not playing on Saturday?"

Mr Stansbury stopped dead in his tracks. With a look of utmost profundity, he looked me in the eyes. "Christopher, Ming Majo cannot play because he is classified by the government as non-white. And the law states that there shall be no mixing of races at government schools."

I could read the pain in his eyes. "So, sir, is Ming Majo a non-white?"

"Yes, Chinese are classified as non-white."

That evening as I rode home on my bike, I tried to digest it all. I felt physically sick, that feeling when you get kicked in the crotch whiteout, nausea and bile superseding the excruciating pain. I didn't know what emasculate meant but it's what I felt. It was an unidentifiable, visceral anger. Anger at Mr Ian Smith and his Rhodesian Front cronies, the "damnable, bloody right-wingers" as my mother called them. What had Ming Majo ever done to them? What? (Not only that, on a practical level, we had no reasonable replacement winger and would have to make do with Ian Moss.) The next day at school, it was like nothing had happened. No one asked Ming Majo how he felt about it, and I'm ashamed to say, me included. But it was a deep-seated, low-key rage in me that would persist. It never went away. Over the following years, at St John's, and at my private high school, the cruel segregation laws never changed—unbending— and I was to see an array of black, coloured,* Indian and Chinese friends denied participation at school sporting events at white government schools.†

---

*people of mixed race (Rhodesian and South African racial classification)
†Springvale beat the system with Ashok Bardolia, a paler-skinned Indian who was passed off as Portuguese. However, it was not uncommon, particularly at high-school level, when a white government school played a private school at the private school, that some white

San Francisco (Flowers in Your Hair)—Scott MacKenzie, 1967

I clearly remember my father driving me to Highlands Junior School that Saturday in his Citrëon. The Tremeloes were on the radio with their blockbuster hit 'Silence Is Golden', with mournful, soaring falsetto harmonies that even today evoke that hurt, that crass injustice. Of course, on the rugby field, it all fell by the way as whites competed against whites and such matters were consigned to the dustbin of irrelevance. But I could not help looking at the Highlands boys askance, that they were so seemingly oblivious to it all. That day my trademark tackles had that little bit of extra needle.

★

On 1 August 1967, Operation *Nickel*,* or the 'Wankie battles', opened in the northwest of the country near the coalmining town of Wankie, adjacent to the vast Wankie game reserve. This was the first major crossing of the insurgency to date. Rhodesian security forces—RAR and RLI again—made contact in a series of running battles in Northern Matabeleland with a combined force of around ninety ZAPU–MK[†] insurgents. (I always struggled with the term 'contact', as in 'contact the enemy', initially thinking making contact was something people did by writing to each other or phoning each other, sort of keeping in touch.) What was apparently an interesting departure, apart from the size of the group, was ZAPU guerrillas joining forces with MK. The plan had been for the ZAPU guerrillas to infiltrate Matabeleland and its capital Bulawayo, while the MK fighters continued south to infiltrate South Africa from across the Limpopo River. The South African government was so alarmed that it dispatched South African Air Force (SAAF) Alouette III gunships under the guise of 'police helicopters' to Wankie to combat the insurgents.[‡] The final tally of seventy-seven was messy: on Rhodesian soil twenty-nine guerrillas were killed, seventeen were 'arrested' (i.e. captured) and one escaped. Twenty-nine fled into neighbouring Botswana but were all arrested—Botswanan cooperation

---

government school parents would direct abuse at the non-white players on the field, with 'kaffir', 'nigger', 'munt' and 'All Black' being run of the mill. The private school white boys were not immune either, referred to as 'kaffir boeties' (lit. kaffir brothers) or 'kaffir lovers'.

*Not original, the codename *Nickel* was used by the RAF in 1939/40 as the overall campaign to replace bombs with leaflets urging German civilians to give up the fight. Who knew?

†uMkhonto we Sizwe—Spear of the Nation (Xhosa)—or MK for short, was the armed wing of the South African African National Congress (SAANC), Nelson Mandela's party.

‡This South African helicopter support would remain on Rhodesia's northern border, essentially the Zambezi River, until 1975.

would not last—and one was arrested in South Africa. The ZAPU guerrillas were commanded by Dumiso Dabengwa who later became the ZIPRA* supremo, while the MK's Luthuli Detachment was led by Lennox Lagu and Chris Hani, the latter becoming the charismatic leader of the South African Communist Party (SACP). However, unheard of until then, the Rhodesian security forces suffered twenty-two casualties, including eight killed in action and fourteen wounded, even with the full cooperation of the local tribespeople. White Rhodesians were stunned and suddenly had to get used to the security forces communiqués on RBC and RTV that began, "Rhodesian security forces headquarters regret to announce the deaths of ... "

At the same time that Rhodesian security forces were chasing after ZAPU and MK cadres in Matabeleland, Aretha Franklin hit the airwaves, not with a bang but more of an explosion. Otis Redding wrote the song 'Respect' and Aretha Franklin launched it into the stratosphere, at the same setting herself on the path to superstardom. Like 'Paint It Black' and The Animals' 'We Gotta Get Out of This Place', it soon became a signature song for the Vietnam War and the soundtrack to the images coming out of Saigon, Hué, Pleiku and Da Nang of black and white Marines and GIs fighting, bleeding and dying together.

In September, my father, after a year's break from hockey and cricket at Salisbury Sport's Club, decided that 35 was a good age to take up golf, much to the delight of Meg and Forbes who were both avid golfers, Royal Salisbury being their home course. It was from the resident pro at 'Royal' that my father bought his first set of clubs and a bucket (a big one) of second-hand balls. Of an evening, he would tip the bucket onto the lawn for chipping practice. This was a time my sisters and I attempted to make ourselves scarce: we would be roped in for ball collection, perhaps one of the deadliest-dullest chores in the country at the time—picking up a ball and tossing it into the bucket, maybe 200 or 300 times. When full, the bucket was recycled and the whole painful experience would begin again, relieved only by eating oxalis.

On a more exciting note, September was when I bought my first two 7 singles—'The Letter' by the Box Tops and 'Itchycoo Park' by the Small Faces, fronted by Steve Marriott† and Ronnie Lane. I proudly handed over the money I'd saved to the cashier at Kingstons who nonchalantly handed me the paper packet with the two records inside. I was now officially an owner of vinyl,

---

*Zimbabwe People's Revolutionary Army, the armed wing of ZAPU. ZAPU/ ZIPRA are used interchangeably for the movement's guerrillas.
†In my opinion, Steve Marriott had the best rock voice in Britain, but in a photo finish with Paul Rodgers of Free.

which in decades to come would become a trendy epithet. Naturally, they were played to death on the multi-record-spindle gramophone. I was particularly drawn to 'Itchycoo Park' which was an atypical combination of psychedelia and heavy rock. But, oh man! did it rock, what the Scotch (my father's term) would call 'a belter'.

Spiro was getting out of hand. He was becoming insufferable, particularly with his seedy behaviour toward my mother. It was time for The Great Raid. An orders group was called for with my sisters and the plan of attack drawn up: it was to be a blitzkrieg-type operation. In and out. We would ride up to Délice, ensuring we had ample hiding places on our persons in the form of bulky coats with lots of pockets, even though it was summertime. Timing was important. It couldn't be during a busy time as there'd be too many customers/ potential witnesses in the shop. Friday evening just before closing was decided upon. The fresh bread would all be gone and so less customers/ potential witnesses.

With a sense of trepidation, much like the start of the 440 yards, we duly set off and arrived at the bakery to find Spiro's Lambretta gone. Good news! We dropped the bikes on the pavement and like we'd done hundreds of times before, casually entered the café, trying not to look too furtive. Spiro's father was on the till by the door, busy cashing up. Perfect. There was no sign of mama: probably in the bakery at the back. And there were no customers. Also perfect. We split into two assault groups, the twins making up the principal strike force, their target the sweets aisle, where chocolate bars, jelly babies, apricots, liquorice strips, gobstoppers and sherbet were the booty of choice. I made for the crisps and peanuts aisle where sugared peanuts were king. Go, go, go, go, go, go, go. Like a well-oiled machine, we were in and out in under two minutes, in the nick of time too as the distinctive sound of a Lambretta drawing up outside created minor panic in the ranks. Uh oh. We bustled out as casually as we could, the cheese-and-onion Willards crips packets making an almighty scrunching sound in my pockets. I took a deep breath and sauntered past Spiro who was hitching the scooter onto its stand. No eye contact.

Not so Caroline who stuck her tongue out at the Greek playboy: "Nah na na nah nah!"

I was almost apoplectic. "Caroline!" I shouted angrily to defuse a dangerous situation. "We have to get home … NOW!"

And with that we were on our bikes, peddling furiously out of Hindhead Avenue and across the Enterprise Road onto the bicycle track, half expecting at any second to hear the scream of a Lambretta bearing up behind us. Nothing. And as we swung into Midvale Road, I knew we were home free. In the twins' bedroom we emptied out our pockets onto Sarah's bed to split the plunder three ways. Altogether, there must have been the equivalent of several weeks' combined pocket money. It exceeded our wildest ambitions, and it was a glorious victory.

That night when I said my prayers, I asked God to forgive us our sins, though I did cite 'an eye for an eye'. Clearly the Lord heard my prayers for it was at the Sunday service two days later that I was pleasantly surprised with the presentation of my surplice.

★

On 3 December 1967, at Groote Schuur Hospital in Cape Town, cardiac surgeon Dr Christiaan Barnard successfully performed the world's first human-to-human heart transplant. Successful because the recipient, one Louis Washkansky, survived eighteen days with his new second-hand heart. I wondered what would have warranted a failure: a survival rate of a day? Or a week? Helpfully, because of his chiselled good looks, Dr Barnard became an instant media celebrity with hundreds of thousands of middle-aged white women across southern Africa falling for his languid charm and charisma, my mother and Granma Teddy included. Sadly, for the hordes of middle-aged white women, Dr Barnard set his sights a mite higher and married Barbara Zoellner, a former, very recent Miss South Africa.

The day before the groundbreaking heart transplant, on 2 December, The Monkees rocketed to number 1 on the Billboard Hot 100, with 'Daydream Believer' which stayed at the top for four straight weeks. Davy Jones—a pre-David Cassidy heartthrob—sang lead vocals, though he admitted later he never really liked the song and felt that drummer Micky Dolenz's vocals were better suited to it. I, on the other hand, absolutely loved the song and still do. For me, it must rate as one of the top pop songs of all time, up there, almost, with 'A Whiter Shade of Pale'.

Almost unnoticed, and certainly with no great fanfare, on 28 December, 126 ZIPRA guerrillas slipped across the Zambezi River. So began Operation *Cauldron** which would drag on for several months. On 31 December 1967, it was stated on *Roving Report* that 385,000 troops were on the ground in Vietnam, 'in country' as they called it, with another 60,000 en route at sea.

---

*Again, not an original: the first Operation *Cauldron* took place in Britain in 1952, to do with biological warfare.

6
Eloise—Barry Ryan, 1968

A t half past midnight on 31 January 1968, 80,000 North Vietnamese regulars and Viet Cong guerrillas attacked around 100 towns and cities in South Vietnam, to coincide with the Lunar New Year festival, Tết Nguyên Đán, in an operation that became known to the world as the Tet Offensive. It caught the Americans and South Vietnamese completely off guard. As inconceivable as it was, the US embassy in Saigon was invaded shortly after and only retaken later the same morning. Apart from a few isolated pockets of resistance that held out, the ancient city of Huế fell to the communists swarming across the Perfume River. Huế would see some of the bitterest fighting of the war with American and South Vietnamese marines clawing their way back, block by block, to recapture the ruined city. But it was the images of the war that stunned the American public. And me. The photograph of wounded and dying US Marines, bloodied and bandaged, draped over each other on a tank in Huế, was Renaissance art at it most horrible. The image of the South Vietnamese policeman Nguyễn Ngọc Loan summarily executing Viet Cong guerrilla Nguyễn Văn Lém, a revolver bullet to the temple at point blank and the grimace of the guerrilla, captured in a split-second of timelessness, something that would endure as one of the images of the century and beyond. I sat glued to *Roving Report*.

I was entranced by the pages of *LIFE*, still struggling to come to terms with the difference between Tet Vietnam and Tete Mozambique. The Lemon Pipers' psychedelic-folk 'Green Tambourine' was an unlikely Billboard Hot 100 number 1 on 3 February—with its electric sitar, signature bass line and tape echo on the word 'play'—'plaaay plaaay plaaay plaaay plaaay'—which provided the perfect score to the horrors of Tet. It still does. On 18 February the US State Department announced the highest US casualty toll of the Vietnam War: 543 Americans killed in action and 2,547 wounded … in a week. That's over 441 casualties a day or 18.4 an hour or one every three and a quarter minutes.

1968 remains for me a watershed year. It was big in every respect, of a world gone utterly mad, at the same time as my Standard 4 year with Mr Stansbury at the helm. As my sisters and I were starting work on our latest project, a treehouse in the big fig tree, on 7 March three members of the so-called Crocodile Gang—James Dlamini, Victor Mlambo and Duly Shadreck—were hanged in Salisbury Central Prison, with Ian Smith defiantly showing the world that they were not glorious freedom fighters but nothing more than murdering criminals. The world condemned him.

On 16 March, but unbeknown for a year, Lieutenant William Calley and Charlie Company, 11th Brigade, murdered over 500 civilians, from babies to old women in the hamlet of Mỹ Lai, in Sơn Mỹ village. The massacre was only stopped when American helicopter pilot Major Hugh Thompson, with crewmen Glenn Andreotta and Lawrence Colburn, landed their Hiller OH-23 Raven helicopter between the rampaging American troops and the fleeing civilians. On 20 March 'The Legend of Xanadu' by Dave Dee, Dozy, Beaky, Mick & Tich reached number 1 on the UK Singles Chart, with some sublime Spanish guitar picking and the clever sound effect of Dave cracking a (big) whip *à la* Zorro. I could never work out whether it was the five-man band of Dave Dee, Dozy, Beaky, Mick & Tich or the six-man band of Dave, Dee, Dozy, Beaky, Mick & Tich, Dee seemingly an unusual Christian name.

On 4 April, Martin Luther King was assassinated by another three-name killer, James Earl Ray, in Memphis. Protest riots across America left forty-six dead, mainly black. In April/ May 1968 three songs made their indelible marks on music history on the Billboard Hot 100, with 'Young Girl' by Gary Puckett & The Union Gap achieving a number 2 position, a week stuck behind Otis Redding's '(Sittin' On) The Dock of the Bay' and then three weeks wedged behind Bobby Goldsboro's monster tearjerker, 'Honey'. 'Young Girl', one of the most vocally powerful hits of all time, did deservedly get to number 1 in the UK.

On 6 May, a Monday, Paris erupted as 5,000 students marched through the Latin Quarter, calling for revolution. Violent running battles with riot police soon followed, the day being dubbed 'Bloody Monday'. Within a fortnight, nine million workers were on strike, in sympathy with the student unions. The revolutionary furor was only eliminated when President de Gaulle sent in the army to restore order.

On 31 May, Rhodesian security forces declared Operation *Cauldron* over. Fifty-two ZIPRA guerrillas were dead and fifty-eight had been captured. The leader of the group, Moffat Hadebe, escaped but was later captured by the Portuguese in the Tete Province.

A week later, Bobby Kennedy was assassinated by Sirhan Sirhan, or Sirhan Squared as Mr Gardiner referred to him, a 24-year-old Jordanian living in Los

Angeles, in retaliation for a pro-Israeli speech Kennedy had made recently.

The twins and I were sitting in our treehouse a few days after this, discussing Project Go-kart,* which had long been on the agenda but had never met with any resolution, being shuffled from one any-other-business to the next since it had first been mooted many months before. The treehouse had taken up most of our resources—time, planks of wood, nails, pocket money and enthusiasm—and had ended up disappointingly low off the ground, not much higher than around ten feet above the now-collapsed Matabele-ant tunnel. During the planning phase, we had envisioned something like a ship's crow's nest fifty feet up whence we could pelt the Saunders boys with rotten figs without fear of reprisal. The go-kart project needed to be more measured with all the component parts in situ prior to construction.

"So far, we've got all the wood and enough screws and nails. We even have the two front wheels."

"Those ones from the Treasure Trove?" asked Sarah.

"Yes, the second-hand pushchair wheels." They had cost me a shilling for the pair. "But," I continued, "what we haven't got are the back wheels which need to be bigger and stronger."

"Ummmm," pondered Caroline.

"Oh! You mean like those trike wheels at James's *khaya*?"† suggested Sarah brightly.

"*Voilà! C'est ça!*" I confirmed, French now another language chalked up into my repertoire which now included German, Afrikaans and Shona, with Xhosa knocking at the door. "Those are absolutely perfect. About a foot radius and with good rubber tyres."

"So, why don't we just ask James if we can have the trike?" suggested Caroline not unreasonably.

"What if he says no?"

"Well, then we could just pinch it."

"Then he'll know it's us," I concluded.

Silence.

Lingering silence.

"Then we'll just have to steal it."

Motion carried.

The next issue was when to do the deed. Except when it rained, during his time off, James was always sitting by the fire outside his *khaya*. We agreed

---

*Also known as a soapbox

†Mrs Roos's gardener, the bloodshot-eyed, unsmiling James the Manyika tribesman

a daytime raid was not on: James would be somewhere in the garden and even with those bloodshot eyes, he appeared to have the vision of a weasel. It would have to be at night after he'd turned in. The problem here was that this would be way past our bedtime, so it was agreed that it would have to be during our parents' next party—with no bedtime at these events, we pretty much had free rein—which, fortuitously was a week on Saturday. We also agreed that once uplifted, the wheels needed to be stripped off the frame as soon as possible and the chassis returned to its former position next to James's *khaya* as soon as possible, where James would be none the wiser that it had ever gone missing.

In the manner of the Cockleshell heroes, we donned balaclavas, ensured we were wearing dark clothing and through the back door slipped like thieves into the night. We hadn't gone ten yards when we came across Bruce Thoms, next to the Pride of India, in a passionate clinch with one of his more attractive co-guests.

"Nah na na nah nah," sang Caroline. "Bruce is a kissing a lady, Bruce is kissing a laydee."

"G'wan. Piss off you little brats," Bruce hissed.

This we did and came to the scraggly boundary fence of straw, most of which had been utilized by James for kindling. Dying embers indicated that James had indeed called it a night. With my heart racing, I took a deep breath, stepped over the straw and snatched up the trike in one fluid movement. We hurried back to the kitchen door, ignoring Bruce and *femme* who now looked to be wrestling in the geraniums. In the light of the kitchen, I could see that it was a straightforward operation to remove the back wheels which were secured by a circlip. I dispatched Caroline to my father's toolbox to bring back a pair of pliers, a hammer and a screwdriver and, in a jiff, I had the wheels off and safely stashed under my bed. It was decided that—no time like the present—we would return the trike, *sans* back wheels, to its former position and so we did, disregarding Bruce and his wrestling partner now writhing in the geraniums trying to pull each other's tongue out with their mouths.

Construction of Mark 1 was not that taxing and I was able to produce a template that served us faithfully for several years. The key this time was to find a decent piece of round bar to serve as the back axle: the front wheels had come with the pushchair axle which was solid enough. With my father's various on-the-go building projects, there was always a pile of timber, wood offcuts and bits of steel lying round the back and, fortuitously, I found a length of round bar of the correct diameter, more or less. Attach the front axle to a length of wood (with bent-over 4-inch nails to secure it) a few inches short

184

of the wheel-to-wheel width and drill a hole in the middle where the steering bolt went through (so the front axle could turn). (Drilling was a tedious process as we had to make do with my father's manual drill.) Then join the two axles with a length of plank around four or five feet—this was the load-bearing piece of wood and needed to be strong enough to take a driver's and possibly a passenger's weight—and drill another hole that matched the one below on the front axle plank. Insert the pre-purchased bolt complete with washers and a lock nut and tighten securely but not so tight that the axle cannot move. The steering system was now done barring the piece of rope that allowed the driver to steer, left and right. This would be attached at the end of the process to match the driver's reach. Then the actual bench seat which consisted of several pieces of wood cut to size and nailed crossways on the load-bearing plank. We decided against sides. And brakes: "Just use the heels of your shoes," I advised. And that was it. Time for a test run.

The problem was to find some tarmac on a slope. We couldn't use Steppes Road or the Enterprise Road: just too busy. Eventually we found a nice steep hill that had recently been paved: Sunridge Road which was off Steppes Road just beyond Ellman-Brown's perennially empty reservoir across the other side of the Umwindsi. We duly arrived at the bottom of Sunridge Road, having dragged Mark 1 up along the bush track from the river. We couldn't see the top of Sunridge Road, it was that steep: at least a 45° incline to our eyes. The other issue was that at the bottom of the hill, the road took a 90° bend to the right. That would take some handling, I thought to myself. We climbed the hill and at the summit positioned the go-kart. It was agreed that I would go first. The twins pushed me off.

It was absolutely exhilarating if a bit scary. Mark 1 was handling like a dream, gathering momentum as the bend at the foot of the hill loomed up suddenly. Hit the brakes! I slammed the heels of my brand-new Bata *veldskoene* into the tarmac, pulled the rope steadily to the right and took the corner on two wheels, coming to a gentle stop fifty or so yards later. Wow! Wow! Wow!

Arriving back at the top, we had to wait for a car. The twins did not look confident.

"Gee, that was really fast," said Caroline nervously, her face ashen.

"Did you have to use your brakes?" asked Sarah.

"Yes. You must slow down before the bend." I showed them the heels of my *veldskoene*. Uh oh. The heels had had a large wedge of rubberized sole ground off.

The twins had decided to go down together. Sarah took her position as the driver and Caroline climbed on behind, clinging to her like a monkey.

"Ready?"

Sarah nodded, teeth gritted, lips dry.

I pushed them off. Like a racehorse, the go-kart barrelled off. Sarah was doing well keeping it straight. No steering wobbles. The bottom of the hill, the bend, was fast approaching. No one seemed to be applying any brakes. Maybe Sarah had things under control. She didn't. With no attempt to negotiate the bend, the go-kart carried on straight, ramped the ditch on the side of the road and, airborne, flew into the long veld grass before it was gone from view. Vanished.

Uh oh.

I shot down the hill and several yards into the bush found the badly damaged go-kart and two badly damaged sisters entangled beneath it, James's trike wheels still spinning furiously. It was an unhappy mess of blood and tears and dirt and snot and torn dresses, but seemingly no broken bones. I helped them up, their hair dishevelled and matted with grass seeds, and took them home for a mercurochrome drenching.

Round 1 to Sunridge Road.

On the sports field, we were now the senior Colts year in both cricket and rugby. The government's racial policies still applied. (It must have affected Springvale and Hartmann House more than others as they had several black boys in their teams.) We were invariably beaten—but not always thrashed—by Ruzawi and Springvale who seemed to have no end of talent, Springvale boasting the likes of Marc Scholvinck, John Chalk and Tom Small, with Ruzawi superstars being Gordon Chance, Graham Smith, John Wilson, Henry Rudd and Rob Bentley (the Umvukwes lot), a graceful left-hand bat and a precocious child two years our junior who was impossible to get out, ever, and probably had a batting average somewhere in the low thousands. We shared the honours with Highlands and Hartmann House.

At rugby, we discovered that Ryan and Richard Fry had a distinguished pedigree. Occasionally, their father Alec would come and coach us. Alec had played for Western Province and was a fine player in his day but, not to be outdone, Alec's one brother, Denis, had been a Springbok fly half and when he was up visiting from Cape Town, he too would come and coach us. We were in awe of these men as they casually tossed the ball between them while imparting their skills. I later discovered there were five brothers, all having gone to Bishops in Cape Town where they all played 1st XV rugby. They had also all served in the war, but in different regiments. Alec had a twin brother Robert. The eldest brother, Anthony, flew Hudsons with RAF Coastal Command but was shot down, missing, presumed dead, over the North Sea. Another brother, Stephen, was also a Springbok, a flanker, and in 1955 captained the Springboks in the four tests against the British Lions, drawing the series 2–2. Stephen had served in the South African 6th Armoured Division during the war. Just how stellar could one family get?

On the cricket field we did okay. Park and Bushnell were ferocious fast bowlers, particularly Charlie Park who had a vicious round-arm-type action, emulated a few decades later by the legendary Sinhalese* speedster Lasith Malinga. One of our regular opposition teams was Lilfordia School, situated twenty miles west of Salisbury in the white farming district of Nyabira. It was the oldest private boarding school in the country but was something of an anomaly in that it was named after 'Boss' Lilford, the founder of the Rhodesian Front and architect of the country's segregation policies. The school was even smaller than St. John's and was unable to field a rugby team but did manage a cricket team which included their star opening bowler, opening bat and captain: a girl! Bigger than all the players on the field, Glenda was a daunting prospect.

At one home game, against Lilfordia, the visitors were batting. Glenda had just belted Charlie Park for four fours in an over, an unheard-of humiliation before playing on to one of Duddo's wily off-spinners.† Being the last man out, once she'd unpadded, ungloved and presumably unboxed (no helmets then), Glenda took over the scoring duties as Lilfordia were unable to supply a specialist scorer, which with many schools was normally the class dork. With us, our scorer was Bushnell who was nursing an injury, apparently a sprained toe. The scoring desk—as opposed to the scoreboard which was situated on the far side of the field and manned by whoever happened by—consisted of two school desks placed side by side in the pavilion which doubled as a shady plane tree. The form was for both scorers to cross-reference each entry so that there would be no argument at the end of the game. So, if an umpire signalled a four, for example, both scorers would say "Four" and then raise an arm in acknowledgement to the umpire.

Fleming was bowling his leggies. A loose ball. The batsmen ran two leg byes and the umpire, Mr Stansbury, signalled leg byes.

"Two leg byes," stated Bushnell, raising his arm in acknowledgement as a matter of course,

*Sinhalese = the major ethnic group of Ceylon. The country became the Republic of Sri Lanka in May 1972.
†A played-on was not credited as a wicket to the bowler back then.

Silence.

"Two leg byes," repeated Bushnell.

"No, it was two byes," said the Lilfordia captain.

"Definitely leg byes signalled," replied Bushnell.

Another silence.

"Well, I've marked down two byes, so you better do the same," said Glenda. It was clear she liked to get her own way.

"It was leg byes, I promise you," said Bushnell.

A further silence, this one pregnant with menace before Glenda turned to Bushnell, glowering, and socked him with an almighty punch to the nose, sending him and his desk sprawling. The contretemps attracted so much attention that the players and umpires on the field were looking at the uptipped scorer's desk and floored scorer with bemusement. Shortly thereafter, Lilfordia were all out for 28, with Glenda top-scoring on 22, as well as taking 8 wickets. Bushnell, his blood-encrusted nose and pride irreparably damaged, came second in the scorers' stakes.

★

In August, 'Lady Willpower', another smash hit by Gary Puckett & The Union Gap, had to settle for the number 2 spot on the Billboard Hot 100 (again!) behind South African trumpeter Hugh Masekela's 'Grazing in the Grass'. Another catchy band name was Herb Alpert & the Tijuana Brass, also a trumpet-driven outfit, which reached number 1 on the Billboard Hot 100 the previous month with 'This Guy's in Love with You', another outstanding creation from the Hal David–Burt Bacharach partnership that just seemed to churn out hit after hit after hit.

Undeterred by any musical magic, on 20 August the Soviet Union invaded Czechoslovakia with some 200,000 Warsaw Pact troops, putting an end to Alexander Dubček's enlightened 'Prague Spring' and ushering in an era of communist oppression. Was there no end to Soviet rule? To Vietnam? To the Zambezi Valley insurgency? These things caused me much angst.

'What a Wonderful World' by Louis Armstrong became the top-selling single of 1968 in the UK and was ultimately ranked at number 171 on *Rolling Stone*'s 'Top 500 Best Songs of All Time'.* It was a fine song to accompany the exciting news that we were going on holiday in September to visit Granma

---

*It flopped in the US because the president of ABC Records, Larry Newton, loathed the song and declined to back it.

Teddy for a month, the 'we' being my mother, my sisters and me (my father apparently had too much work on). And, what's more, we were going by train, Rhodesia Railways, a wonderful three-day journey of steam and soot from Salisbury to Addo via Bulawayo, Francistown (in Botswana), Gaborone (the shiny new capital of Botswana), Mafeking, Johannesburg, Bloemfontein and then Addo (just short of Port Elizabeth). We were in a second-class carriage, complete with a three-tiered bunk, the twins sharing pole position, the top bunk, and me wedged in in the middle one.

We disembarked at Addo, the only passengers to do so, and there on the hot, windswept platform was Granma Teddy wearing white slacks, a yellow blouse and a big white floppy-brimmed hat. She always managed to look so chic. This was the first holiday where we'd be visiting Granma Teddy in her new house, Polo Cottage, on Willowtree Farm which was owned by her friend Jean Butter. She had soldiered on for a couple of years with Nutcombe Farm after Granpa Roy had died, but in 1967 gave up the fight and sold it. Polo Cottage, named after the adjacent polo field, was technically in Sunland and not Addo, as Sunland had its own post office—well, a corner in Deysel's General Dealers— and a telephone exchange in a small office at Sunland Station (the train didn't stop at Sunland) next to the stationmaster's office. The telephone exchange, host to only a handful of party lines, was manned by the *nommer aseblief*[*] lady, Mevrou du Preez, who knew all the Sundays River Valley gossip. Granma Teddy's Sunland phone number was 2.

We hugged Granma Teddy, with that special smell of hers.

My mother was struggling with the suitcases at the same time trying to light a cigarette. "Christopher, give me a hand, won't you darling ... bloody suitcases. Oh, hello, mama."

"How was the trip, darling?"

"Not too bad. A bit bloody long and too much bloody soot."

We piled into Teddy's 'new' car, an automatic Austin Westminster—"a cross between a damned tank and a hearse" according to Granma Teddy—which had been a gift from her brother Bob up in Jo'burg when the Hillman Minx had caught fire and perished at Dead Man's Gulch, a godforsaken stretch of road on the badlands before Port Elizabeth. It did sound like it had been torched by marauding Pawnees.[†] The demise of the Hillman Minx coincided symbolically with the demise of the British motorcar industry—as so accurately predicted

---

[*]number please (Afrikaans)
[†]The evidence of the inferno—a large black patch of melted tar—is possibly still there today.

by Hans Wiedemann—which in the space of a few short years plunged from the second biggest producer in the world to 'not applicable' in the rankings. Even the Austin Westminster got in on the act a couple of years later when its brakes failed at the top of Brickmakers Kloof Road in Port Elizabeth … during rush hour. The black beast hurtled down the hill at breakneck speed before embedding itself into a bollard just before the bridge over the Baakens River. Teddy was unharmed and managed to extricate herself with a succinct "Damned car".

Polo Cottage was delightful, immaculately maintained by Xhosa gardener Porky, and Eunice, Granma's Teddy's Xhosa housekeeper, companion and co-chef in the outside catering business that Teddy ran: they catered only for the Port Elizabeth elite at select dinner parties. Eunice's husband Daniel would get shanghaied from his regular Addo Citrus Co-op job to serve as the waiter, complete with white uniform, red sash and red fez. Being in the catering business, Granma Teddy introduced my mother to the newfangled kitchen utensil that was taking the world by storm: the rubber spatula, which I spent many hours studying. She introduced my sisters and me to her lip sync* version of 'Puppet on a String', the Sandie Shaw hit that won Eurovision in 1967 and which all the older adults, especially Teddy, adored: "Just so light and gay, she'd say, impersonating a nodding, wobbling puppet.

There was so much to do, from exploring the vast Willowtree Farm and its acres and acres of citrus trees to swimming in the Sundays River with Eunice's children, twins Sondile and Sandile, who taught us their favourite song 'Isonka Ngesenti Enye'† and its accompanying dance, and how to avoid the huge *leguaans*, the water monitors, that lived in the river. We helped Arthur, the 'St Helena boy' who stuttered and who mucked out the stables every morning, loading up the night's straw and manure into the back of the donkey cart pulled alternately by the donkeys, Two Pounds and Two Rand (the amount Jean paid for them).

I learned to ride, with Granma taking me to riding lessons in Port Elizabeth once a week and at Willowtree, I'd occasionally be allowed to ride Happy, my mother's horse since she was a girl. Happy, a solid piebald, in semi-retirement at Willowtree with his own paddock, was banned from mixing with Jean's yearlings.‡ We assisted Peter Burton, the farm manager, and his son Kenneth when it came to docking the sheep's tails. I shot doves on the next-door farm

---

*known as mime in 1968
†Bread for One Cent (Xhosa)
‡One of Jean's yearlings, Dragon Prince, would win the Durban July, South Africa's most prestigious horse race.

with the owner's son, William Rogers, who taught me how to use his .22 rifle, how to defeather and clean a dove and then how to cook it over an open fire in one of the orchards. We visited Herbert and Albert at The Poop on Swartkops River, we swam at Bluewater Bay and King's Beach and I learned the Lexington advert off by heart, with the tag line, 'After action satisfaction':

When you've had your action
And you've faced your facts
You'd do a lot better than just relax
'Cos work is work and fun is fun
And man* ... relax with a Lexington

Near the end of the holiday, my mother nearly killed us all. We were on the way to Deysel's General Dealers to buy bread, milk and ice lollies and play with Mevrou Deysel's mongoose that had the run of the very long sales counter when my mother stalled the Austin Westminster in the middle of the rail crossing, on the hump. I've no idea why my mother was driving as she'd never driven an automatic before. Sitting in the back with my sisters, I could almost sense her fear it was that palpable.

"Just keep calm, Betty," said Granma Teddy. "Don't panic. Put the gear in N, then restart the car. Then put the gear in D and accelerate."

The twins were starting to whimper. And rightly so, for coming down the track some three or four hundred yards off was a train, billowing smoke and sounding its whistle. My mother was getting flustered, starting to panic, as the twins' wailing grew exponentially in volume.

The train was now some two or three hundred years away and sounding its whistle in one shrill, unbroken blast.

"BETTY!" instructed Granma Teddy deliberately. "DON'T PANIC. PUT THE GEAR IN EN ... START THE CAR ... PUT THE GEAR IN DEE ... ACCELERATE."

The train was now little more than a hundred years away, and I, being locomotive side in the back, realized the end was imminent. I closed my eyes, invoking the Catholic "Holy Mary, Mother of God"—why, at my hour of death, did I forsake my Anglican faith?—and braced myself for impact.

It never came.

Instead, I could hear the car engine racing and then the *thuk* as the Austin Westminster engaged D for drive and shuddered its way off the tracks out of

---

*coupled with a deep, satisfying exhale

harm's way, with the train passing at speed mere yards away in a malevolent slipstream of steam, smoke and heat and the driver leaning out the window waving his fist at us and shouting something about *"Jou fokken bliksem!"** My mother then managed to stall the car again. And there we sat with my mother lighting up a cigarette, her hands trembling violently, and my sisters extricating themselves from the floor behind Granma Teddy's seat.

Apart from the odd sniffly whimper from the twins and a deep inhale from my mother, the silence was absolute, almost surreal. I'd opened my eyes by this stage, taking in the world around me like it was something new, with the tall gumtrees along the side of the polo field waving gently in the breeze, the blue cloudless sky, the cicadas' omnipresent chorus never far away. Life. The cicadas, mine.

I felt now was an appropriate time to put in for an ice-cream upgrade request. "Mummy, instead of ice lollies, d'you think we could maybe have Eskimo Pies instead?"

Long exhale. "Yes, of course, darling. Anything you want."

★

In October, what became known as the Fearless Talks took place, again on a Royal Navy frigate off Gibraltar, this time on HMS *Fearless*, between British Prime Minister Harold Wilson and his Rhodesian counterpart, Ian Smith. What was it about talks on frigates? Smith was accompanied by a smaller delegation this time, Jack Howman and Desmond Lardner-Burke, who, being more right wing than Hitler, were presumably there to ensure Smith did not agree to anything. Which he didn't of course and even I as an almost-11-year-old political observer knew that the talks would fail. As long as the Rhodesian Front persisted with its racial segregation on the sports field where Ming Majo was forbidden to play, nothing would change. Ever. As if to reinforce the chasm between black and white, the Summer Olympic Games in Mexico were boycotted by thirty-two African nations to protest South Africa's participation.†On 18 October, Tommie Smith and John Carlos, American athletes and medal winners in the 200 metres, raised their arms in the black power salute during the 'Star-Spangled Banner' at the medal ceremony.

While Republicans were still choking on their Southern Comforts, Lionel Bart's musical *Oliver*, the film, opened at the Rainbow Cinema. I simply could

---

*Very roughly, "You fucking bastard!"
†It was a given that Rhodesia, with its pariah status, was forbidden to participate.

not miss it and implored my mother to take Duddo and me to see it which she did. It proved to be everything and more that I could have wanted: extravagant song and dance numbers and a fine cast that included Oliver Reed as the menacing Bill Sikes, Harry Secombe—I knew him from *The Goon Show*—as Mr Bumble, Ron Moody as Fagin, Jack Wild as the Artful Dodger* and the vivacious, gorgeous, beautiful, stunning, magnificent, effervescent, divine goddess Shani Wallis—I was much taken with her—as Nancy. The only slightly sub-par performance was by the lead Mark Lester who played Oliver. As always, my mother was blunt: "Didn't much like that Oliver. Thought he was a bit of a bloody wet."

That month, like a ballistic missile, 'Eloise' hit the airwaves and got to number 2 in the UK charts, selling an astonishing three million copies worldwide. Written by Paul Ryan in three days and sung by his twin brother, 19-year-old Barry, it was a song of epic proportion, being over five minutes long. In this Paul had emulated Richard Harris's 'MacArthur Park'—though Barry could sing and Richard Harris couldn't—and proved that a pop song could be longer than the normal three minutes and a bit.[†] I first saw the album cover when we were visiting Bruce Thoms at his ranch in Battlefields. It was the only album cover without a semi- or zero-clad girl on the front. His LP collection consisted mainly of Dan Hill and His Sounds Electronic. Dan Hill was a talented South African multi-instrumentalist and apart from his clear musical ability, his album covers all featured naked girls draped with a scarf or an unclipped bikini top. This alone ensured Hill's enduring success. The album on the turntable, evicted to make way for 'Eloise', was the 1967 *Dan Hill and His Sounds Electronic Play Music to Watch Girls By*. I remember the naked girl on the cover had a squint which, strangely, I found quite fetching.

Apart from celebrating my eleventh birthday in November, it was also the fiftieth anniversary of the Armistice and the third of UDI, the latter unworthy of celebration. October had morphed into November and the rains were pressing. Like clockwork, they normally broke around the second week of November, and 1968 was to prove no different. It had been a hard, dry winter aggravated by the black frost of August that had laid waste the ordinarily hardy perennials.

---

*Bart had tried to get Steve Marriott to play the part but he turned it down: he would have been brilliant.

†John Paul Jones and Jimmy Page were two of the session musicians during the recording. With 'Bohemian Rhapsody', Queen too proved that a pop song could go on and on and on … and on.

.

For my birthday that year my parents decided to have it at Domboshava, a granite whaleback mountain, more of a dome really, and a national monument some twenty miles northeast of Salisbury on the Bindura/ Shamva road. The name derives from the Shona *dombo* (rock) and *shava* (pronounced *shawa*, meaning red, possibly after the ubiquitous red and orange lichens that cover the rocks). It is a vast area, some twenty-five miles square, crisscrossed with gigantic balancing boulders, fresh streams and ancient Stone Age and Bushman caves with a plethora of rock art. At the base on the southern side a sacred forest, Rambukurimwa ('the land that cannot be tilled') loomed large. The biggest cave is home to the Rain Spirit to whom the local Chinamora community made their offerings, and perhaps still do. We were advised that the cave and Rambukurimwa were off-limits. Nevertheless, the area was one sprawling playground, with a thousand and one hiding places.

Half the class had been invited and it was an impressive convoy of half a dozen cars carrying the revellers that pulled up at the base of the dome. There were no amenities, nothing, though today there are ablutions, an interpretive centre and a picnic and braai area.

In short time, the cars were disgorged of boys, camping chairs (for the parents) and tables, picnic blankets, flasks of tea, cooler bags with cold beers (for the parents) and Cokes and Fantas plus baskets and baskets of food: cakes, sandwiches, crisps and sweets. While the parents were making themselves comfortable, cracking open Lion Lagers and mixing G&Ts, we boys were organizing the two sides for the forthcoming war. It was to be Kiowa versus Arapaho, the treacherous Kiowa armed with catapults and spears in the form of sharpened sticks about which Audrey was having minor conniptions and the wily Arapaho armed with bows and arrows (poisoned tips) made from poplar saplings, about which Audrey was also in a flap. The two teams were decided upon, eight boys in each. I was to lead the Arapaho and Anthony Murdoch-Eaton was appointed chief of the Kiowa as his parents farmed in the area—Jimmy Murdoch-Eaton was a renowned mushroom grower—and who was thus blessed with some local knowledge. Duddo had found the remains of an old braai fire and was busy blacking up with war paint, daubing his face and any exposed skin—neck, arms and legs—with charcoal. Soon all sixteen boys were following suit accompanied by Audrey's desperate mewling.

Cramming pockets with sweets and sugared peanuts, Anthony then led his band of Kiowa warriors off into the granite hills to establish their base camp and presumably prepare an ambush. We Arapaho would follow half an hour later, in the meanwhile getting stuck into the cakes and Cokes, paying little heed to the girls milling about the food table: Sarah, Caroline and Anthony's sister Deborah who was the same age as the twins.

One of my braves sidled up to me. It was Ian Moss, his freckly face artistically streaked black. "Cockso," he mumbled *sotto voce*, "I don't know what to do. I need a dak."

"What? A job? A number two?"

"Shhh. Not so loud!"

Now this was a conundrum. What to do? My leadership was required. Hmmm.

I went over to my mother sitting in a camp chair eating a cucumber sandwich and nattering away to Faysie. "Mummy," I whispered, "Ian needs to do a poo."

"Oh … hang on … Jimmy!" she called loudly to the group of fathers standing about drinking beer. "Ian needs to do a poo. Did you bring that shovel? And some loo paper?"

"Yes, Betty, I did … Ian, it's in the back of my truck, Go'n grab it."

Sheepishly Ian retrieved the shovel and loo paper. "What do I do?" he asked.

"I dunno. Just go into the bush and do your business," I replied. "We'll wait for you."

After what appeared an age, Ian emerged from the bush holding the shovel in front of him and on which was perched a freshly laid turd, neatly curled too, with fat blue flies squabbling for pole position.

"Mr Murdoch-Eaton, what must I do with this?"

Jimmy turned, taken aback. "Goodness me, Ian … I don't know. Flambé it?"

Audrey was gagging with what appeared to be an onset of the vapours. The other six Arapaho and the three girls were sniggering, which I felt was inappropriate.

"Here, come with me, young man." Jimmy put his arm around Ian, leading him back into the bush. "Let me show you how we deal with this puppy."

Ablutions done, we began the trek up the granite mountain, wary of an ambush along the way. I kept the warriors spread out and in the open to avoid any nasty surprises from the notoriously cunning Kiowa. Some two hours later and there was still no sign of them. We were taking a break in the lee of a rocky overhang when they pounced with a deadly barrage of stones and javelins hurled at us. They came at us like a Roman legion. In some disarray, our bows and arrows useless at such short notice, I sounded a retreat.

"Flee, my warriors, flee. All is lost!"

My warriors took up the call. "Run away, run away!"

And so we fled, across the baking granite toward the stream in the valley where I felt we might regroup and make a stand. However, the Kiowa were not giving chase, instead feasting on the booty of sugared peanuts and cheese-and-onion crisps that we'd left behind and taunting us with chicken impressions as we ran.

"Buk buk buk bukk ... erk! Buk... kerrrrk!"

Breathless but undaunted, we arrived at the stream. I prepared the braves for the final battle. Drawing on some sketchy military history, the shallow stream, only ankle deep, evoked the burn at Bannockburn. There was even a soggy vlei on the far side, its depth deceptive (knee deep in fact as I'd sent Dan Winch in to test it and he'd got sucked in up to his knees, stuck good and proper). If I could position two warriors on the other side of the vlei to lure the Kiowa across the river ... and position two ambush parties of three warriors each in the bushes on either side of the vlei to spring the ambush when the Kiowa were stuck in the morass, then it might just work. I instructed my two trusty lieutenants, Duddo and Flemo (now bedecked with guinea fowl feathers in his floppy hat), to take two warriors each and assume positions on the flanks, while I would take up the bait position on the other side of the vlei with Ian Moss who was a still a bit whiffy and had been unkindly labelled *Picannin Chief Bos Kak*[*] by the other braves.

We didn't have long to wait. We heard them long before we saw them, their cockiness preceding them. The plan worked like a charm. As soon as they arrived at the stream, they spotted Ian and me sitting some distance off and, unaware of the treacherous *vlei* between us, sounded the Kiowa war cry—"*Whoop, whoop, whoop, whoo ... oop*"—and charged with reckless abandon. In mere seconds, all eight of them were foundering in the bog, the signal for the two ambush parties to spring the trap, which they did with panache. No mess, no fuss, the six Arapaho braves, with bowstrings anchored taut and arrows set for flight into Kiowa torsos, methodically encircled the hapless enemy.

"You are surrounded, Kiowa dogs," I called out. "If you value your scalps, you will cast your weapons onto the bank and surrender."

They had no choice and so the Great Plains War of '68 closed with a glorious Arapaho victory as sixteen weary warriors made their way back to the rendezvous. It had been a splendid day.

★

---

[*]Little Chief Bush Poo (Shona/ Eng./ Afrik.)

Ma Law had decided that Standard 4 was going to put on *A Midsummer Night's Dream*. There was no reading for parts: Ma Law had us all precast as it were and I got Hippolyta, Queen Hippolyta, Queen of the Amazons and engaged to Theseus, the Duke of Athens, played by Mark Bushnell. I was briefly confused, mixing up the Queen of the Amazons with Nancy Blackett of *Swallows and Amazons* fame. As with *Lawrence of Arabia* and *Peter Pan*, my mother put together the costume and fine a costume it was too: a flowing white gown with gold beading around the edges to match the tiara-like crown on my head. And as with my two earlier productions, the taunts, particularly from the homophobic, voice-breaking, scrotum-dropping Standard 6s, came thick and fast: I was a "homo", I was a "fag", which I thought was a cigarette, and I was a "queen"—well, yes, of course I was: Queen Hippolyta! We were assured by Ma Law that this was one of Shakespeare's finest comedies and that the audience—mainly dutybound parents and siblings—would be rolling in the aisles. I really did try hard to appreciate the humour but there was nothing in it that came remotely close to *The Goon Show*, *Hancock's Half Hour* or the *Carry On* films (which we were forbidden to watch—too risqué, I was told—but which we did anyway).

Even Di and Joy came to watch. "This we just have to see, Bets," said Di, trying not to laugh.

"Got yourself a ladyboy, Bets," said Joy, winking at me through a cloud of fag smoke.

It was clear my mother had no idea what a ladyboy was. Nor had I.

"Wasn't Hippolyta Queen of the Amazons?" inquired Di.

"Yes, she was," I responded earnestly.

"Bit like us, eh, Joy?" quipped Di.

The play was a resounding success, warranting two curtain calls and one vulgar catcall which did sound like it came from Joy.

Within a day, however, the glory of the stage was forgotten, with yesterday's star of stage becoming today's stingers bait. Yes, stingers and open gates were taking breaktimes by storm: stingers particularly as there was more opportunity to inflict pain than in open gates. More edgy. One person was 'on', facing the herd of boys cowering on the brick steps at the corner of the Big Field, where the retaining wall ended. This was 'den' where the herd was safe from the marauding boy with the tennis ball who was 'on'. (The retaining wall ran down the one side of the field and was there to stop the plane-treed embankment sliding down onto the field.) The herd had one minute's grace before they had to leave the sanctuary of 'den' and try and make it to the other end of the field without being stung by the tennis ball hurled mightily by the boy 'on'. It was a question of safety in numbers, hence the herd, one of whom would undoubtedly get stung, but most would make it. The one or ones stung would then be obliged to join the 'on' side until such time as there was only one man left unstung, the last man standing, who would then claim victory.

It so happened that one breaktime a few days after my birthday I was 'on'. I could sense the herd's fear as they tentatively stepped out of 'den'. At any second the rush would begin. My tactic was to split the herd. Let the fleet-footed ones get away then pick off the stragglers who without any leadership would mill about in a bunch, stupidly. The tactic worked and I closed in on the pathetic little group of stragglers, like a lion going in for the kill.

But lo! One straggler, braver than the rest, raised his arms and like a wounded buffalo issued a roar of rage and charged directly at me. The wounded buffalo was none other than man mountain Jamie Beaton. It was terrifying but in a nanosecond my mind considered the options: fight or flight? Flight was simply not an option: I would become the laughingstock of the class, the chicken who ran away. It would have to be fight. With man mountain not five yards from me and clearly intent on tearing me limb from limb, I raised my right arm, took aim at Jamie's face and unleashed a throw of terrestrial force. The tennis ball achieved maximum velocity as it contacted Jamie's face which exploded on impact. Man mountain stopped dead in his tracks, disbelieving, sinking slowly to the ground, his big hands clutching his big, bloodied face.

The silence that enveloped Big Field, and Little Field for that matter, was almost ethereal. I paid it no heed. Man mountain had been stopped. My limbs were intact. My honour was intact. That was what mattered. But Jamie wasn't done. Like Thor, he rose to his feet, his face glazed with blood and mucus and tears. He looked straight at me and bellowed a bellow of such visceral intensity that surely terrified even Valhalla.

Uh oh.

This was serious. I frantically cast about for the tennis ball but it was nowhere to be seen. Probably still lodged in Jamie's skull. This time the only option was flight. With utmost immediacy, I took off like a greyhound to the other side of the field, with the wounded buffalo—no acting this time round—in hot pursuit, baying for my blood. I knew I was faster than Jamie but did I have the stamina? Did he? We were on our second 440 yards and he was still going but starting to flag. The baying for blood had tailed off and now it was just straightforward survival of the fittest. Literally. The bell went in the distance. Breaktime over. And still Jamie wouldn't let up. I mixed it up a bit and took a circuit round the Little Field, hoping it would throw him off the scent. It didn't. The boys were now all in class. Only the distant figures of Mrs Dickinson and Alfred observing the curious spectacle from under the plane trees could be seen. We ran and we ran and we ran. I would run forever if I had to: my limbs meant much to me. Then, several hours later—probably twenty minutes more accurately—Jamie stopped. He didn't look at me. He just turned and trudged back to the classroom.

It was over.*

In December, the Umwindsi came down in flood and in places burst its banks. Ordinarily an innocuous stream, empty more often than not, it was a terrifying sight to behold. Laced with dirty froth, the brown floodwaters surged and grumbled, carrying away everything in its path: logs and detritus, natural and not. My usual crossing point was impassable, with the river a good twenty yards across and some ten to twelve feet deep. "Such a bore," as my mother would say, as I'd have to take the long way round to school: Enterprise Road, left into Drew Road and then left onto Steppes, a diversion that added a mile and a good twenty minutes to the journey.

One morning on my way to school, at the top of the drive I noticed a swarm of wild bees had set up hive in a hollow at the base of a bauhinia tree. HONEY! That evening when we were all home from school, I invited my team—Sarah and Caroline—on a reconnaissance mission to inspect the hive and a motion was carried that a honey raid would take place on the weekend. I had read somewhere—possibly *The Famous Five*—that a smoking paraffin-soaked rag put the bees to sleep or at least made them drowsy enough for a raider to plunge his hand or hand-held implement into the hive and extract a whopping great wadge of honeycomb dripping with golden honey.

At 0900 hours on Saturday morning, we assembled at the top of the drive. As insurance, we were all wearing our bee-proof safety clothing: plastic raincoats, gloves, long pyjama trousers and masks which were fashioned out of an old pair of my mother's pantyhose and pulled tight over our heads like gangsters. I lit the rag which immediately burst into flames. *Woof.* Flapping the burning rag against the trunk of the bauhinia, I managed to put out the flames and the rag was engulfed in smoke. The bees were getting agitated, the buzzing increasing in intensity.

It was now or never.

---

*Still, I was careful for the next few days, even weeks, and watched my back, ready to take off in a flash.

"I'm going in!" I cried out and bending over into the hollow, waved the smoking rag about. Much bee anger followed. Much, much anger. I was being stung in the face—so much for the gangster nylons—and I was being stung through the pyjama bottoms, but the raincoat and the gloves were holding firm. I found a small recess in the hive into which I jammed the smoking rag and then withdrew. The mask was causing acute claustrophobia. Dashing into the road, I ripped it off, gasping for breath. I was sweating like a sauna under the raincoat.

Armed with their beach spades and buckets, the twins were standing by. Even beneath their Great Train Robbery outfits, I could sense their disquiet.

"Can we go?" Sarah asked.

The hive was calming down with only a few diehards patrolling the entrance. I was concerned that the inactivity wouldn't last. The retrieval squad would suffer a few stings, but such was the nature of the operation.*

"Okay, go!"

Like ferrets, the girls were in, bravely ignoring the stings that came their way. Plunging their arms and spades into the interior of the hive, they hacked away at the honeycomb and were able to fill their buckets in double-quick time before conducting a tactical withdrawal at speed. There was an alarming increase in bee activity. Word had got out. Like me, the pantyhose masks were causing the girls much distress. They tore them off but this time round the bees had locked onto them and went in for the attack. Caroline was screaming as she fled down the road, arms flailing, swastika style. Like an armadillo, Sarah cleverly pulled the raincoat over her head and rolled herself into as small a ball as possible.

I inspected the plunder in the buckets and was sorely disappointed. The honeycomb was dirty and blackened, filled with the corpses of sundry flies, mosquitoes, Matabele ants, worker bees and an array of unidentifiable bugs. What little honey there was looked like grey, watery gruel. The operation had ended in ignominious failure and all we had to show for it were a couple of dozen beestings per pax. I mean, what sort of bees were these? Had they no self-respect? What sort of ship did the Queen think she was running? Dirty, low-class, trashy bees.

Like pox victims, we trooped down the driveway to be treated by mother in the bathroom, our ardour for such projects dampened indefinitely. It was while my mother was smearing me with calamine lotion that I noticed her uncharacteristic quietness. Normally she'd have a comment—"You bloody little fools. What on earth did you think you were doing?"—but there was no

*collateral damage in today's parlance

hint of censure. I glanced up into the mirror and for a moment it appeared as if she had been crying.

The reason became clear that evening.

At around 6 o'clock, my mother popped her head round my door: "Christopher. Your father and I need to speak to you and the twins. In the sitting room." It was all so formal. Mary Hopkin's 'Those Were the Days' was playing softly in the background. I loved that song.

"When?"

"Now, please."

Like marmosets, the twins were sitting squashed up together on the pouf. My father was standing at the fireplace, a whiskey on the mantelpiece. My mother was sitting on the edge of the rocking chair, under the standard lamp in the corner. A faint frown creased her brow, her lips dry and pursed, her gaze downcast.

This was serious.

My father kicked off: "Christopher, twins … we have something important to tell you."

"What, daddy?" It was Caroline.

"Your mother and I have decided to get divorced."

Silence.

My mother's gaze was still locked on the parquet flooring.

Sarah broke the silence: "Why?"

"Your mother and I have decided that it would be for the best."

Caroline was sniffling. "So, you and mummy don't love each other anymore?"

Another silence, an awkward one.

"I suppose you could say that," replied my father. "We—your mother and I—will not be living together. We want to know who you children would want to live with."

"Who will live here?" I asked.

"Your mother will carry on living here. I will probably rent a house or a flat in The Avenues."

"I want to stay here," I said.

"So do we," added Sarah.

Still staring fixedly at the floor, my mother had not said a word,

That was it. There was nothing more to be said. We went back to our rooms. I had some prep to do. I switched Radio Jacaranda on to listen to the hit parade.

Although my sisters and I lived every day expecting it to be the last as a cohesive family unit, the subject was never brought up again. Never. As if it had never been mooted in the first place. And we were too nervous to bring it up in case it rekindled the matter.

There was a distraction: the Buchan-Fords were coming over for Christmas Eve drinks. For background ambience I turned my radio on, hoping Radio Jacaranda had not become slave to the monster that was the Christmas carol. It hadn't: The Foundations were on with their smash hit, 'Build Me Up Buttercup'. Stewart ensconced himself in the rocking chair with a *Beezer* while Jane came into my room as was her custom. Before she sat on the bed, she'd wander around the room looking at everything, inquisitively, in case there was something new since the last time. She was wearing a loose yellow cotton dress that simply complemented everything about her: her sunniness, her blonde hair, the sprinkling of freckles across her nose, her tanned legs and always that enigmatic smile which I could never make out but loved nonetheless.

She sat, patting the bed next to her. "Come sit, Christopher." (She only ever called me Christopher.)

I sat. I loved her smell.

She took my hand. "My mum told me that your mum and dad are getting divorced."

I nodded.

"Is it true?"

I shrugged. "I don't know … they haven't said anything for a while."

Mary Hopkin, the beautiful Mary Hopkin, was singing.

Jane rested her head in the crook of my neck. She let go my hand and put her arm around my waist and gave me a squeeze.

Awkwardly, I put my arm around her waist and squeezed her back.

She looked up at me and smiled. I wanted that moment to last forever.

Epilogue
Look for the Silver Lining—
Marion Harris, 1919

Look for the silver lining
Whene'er a cloud appears in the blue.
Remember somewhere the sun is shining
And so the right thing to do is make it shine for you.

A heart full of joy and gladness
Will always banish sadness and strife.
So always look for the silver lining
And try to find the sunny side of life

Betty Short, now a young woman, had finished her schooling and was ready to face the world. In 1952, she was sent to Europe as a debutante. Her coming-of-age was reported in the social pages.

'Judith', in her regular column 'A Woman About Town' in the Eastern Cape's *Evening Post* of Tuesday, 18 August 1953, gives notice of a Round Table cocktail party to be held that Thursday at the Walmer Club. Under the sub-heading 'Braaivleis', Judith's Uitenhage correspondent reports on Mr and Mrs Derek Kleinschmidt's sixth-anniversary celebratory braai and mentions

> There were some glamorous braaivleis fashions—Mrs Pat French [not the Banda connection], in a gay marina twin set with a tweed skirt, Mrs C. Green in lilac nylon, Mrs Sheila Elliott in a brick-coloured suit and Mrs Thwaites was smart in navy.

Under another sub-heading, 'Gay Rhodes dance', Judith's Grahamstown correspondent reports that "men of Founders' Hall, the oldest dining hall at Rhodes University, held their annual dance on Saturday". However, Judith allocates the bulk of her column to my mother, with the leader 'Betty Short returns after 16 months overseas':

203

Miss Betty Short, daughter of Mrs Roy Matthews, returned to Port Elizabeth this week after 16 months in Britain and Europe.

She has had a wonderful time—saw the Coronation, was presented to the Queen at Buckingham Palace, attended a Coronation Ball at Londonderry House, a coming-of-age party in Paris, motored all over Ireland and Scotland, ski-ed in Austria, took a three months' Cordon Bleu course and worked in an antique dealer's shop.

She went over originally for six months but stayed 16. The highlight of her stay was the garden party at Buckingham Palace.

She and other debutantes were put through their paces in the Gold and White Ballroom, made their curtsies in the small Throne Room and, later, again saw the Queen at the garden party.

Miss Short spent three months with a French family in Paris learning French. It was while she was with them that she attended the coming-of-age ball of the daughter of the house.

She also worked for a few months with an antique dealer in Bruton Street, and while there, attended the opening of the Antique Dealers' Fair, which was opened by Princess Margaret, who came and chatted at their stall.

She took the Cordon Bleu course because she felt she should know something about cooking and was most intrigued with it all. The course is very comprehensive and she now knows how to prepare a good plain dinner and how to prepare a five or six course dinner for a formal party.

She learnt, too, that sauces are one of the most important frills to any dish and that the manner of serving a meal is half the battle.

In London she saw Penelope Thoms, Shirley Bengough, Mary Johnson, Paula de Kock, all from Addo, also Nico McBean, whose party she attended just before she left.

She is thrilled to be home again, but is already making plans to return to England later, this time to study antiques, which she has found most absorbing and interesting.

Betty was indeed ready for the world. It was during her time in London that a young man knocked on the door of her digs. He'd come courting Betty's flat mate, but the flat mate was out at the time. Quick as a flash the young man asked Betty whether she'd accompany him on the date instead. Betty agreed—and promptly fell in love with one Michael George Cocks, my father.

Teddy, no doubt horrified that Betty had fallen in love with a sallow, young insurance clerk with little prospects decided to take the bull by the horns.

Rather than lose her daughter to the vastness and drabness of an anonymous London, she made up her mind to bring the 23-year-old Englishman out to Africa. She found him a position with a firm of Port Elizabeth insurance brokers and booked his passage on the *Windsor Castle* as 1954 drew to a close.

★

My parents celebrated their fiftieth wedding anniversary at Fairways Homes for Aged Persons, Bodle Avenue, Eastlea, in Harare on 25 January 2006, though 'celebrate' would hardly seem appropriate under the circumstances. I phoned that evening from Johannesburg to congratulate them on their achievement, as hollow as it was and as sad as it was.

Still, in some strange, unidentifiable way, I was proud of them and proud for them.

I tried for two hours to get through—the lines to Zimbabwe are always hit and miss. But this time I didn't give up. This time it was important. Eventually at around 7 o'clock, pleasantly but nervously surprised, I got a ring tone—a dull *brrr brrr*. It rang for a long time and I was about to put the phone down—either my mother was out visiting my father in the Frailcare section of the home, or she was in the bath, or asleep—when she picked up.

"Hello?" The voice was flat and tired.

"Hello? Mum? Can you hear me?" I spoke loudly.

"Hello? Christopher? Is that you?" The voice was more animated now.

"Yes, mum," I shouted. "Have you got your hearing aid in?"

"Hang on. I can't hear you. Let me put my bloody hearing aid in. Got another bloody power cut."

I heard the *thuk* of the handset as she put it down on the table. I heard muttering and clattering as I visualized her scrabbling around in darkness. I wondered if she had any candles lit.

After several long minutes, I heard her pick up the receiver. She was breathing heavily. I could see her fitting the hearing aid, clumsily cranking the volume control.

"There. That's better."

"Hi, mum. Can you hear me now?"

"Yes. Much better. How are you, darling?" The hearing aid squealed faintly, like a short-wave radio being tuned.

"I'm fine, thanks mum. Happy anniversary. Congratulations."

"Thank you darling. Actually, had quite a good day even though there's been no bloody electricity for three days. That nice nurse Violet brought dad up to the cottage at five o'clock for a drink. Bit naughty but Mike had a whisky, but you know, poor old dear doesn't have very much to look forward to these days."

"And you, did you have a drink?"

"Oh yes! Also had a whisky. We had a little bit of that bottle of Teacher's left that Sarah brought up which I was keeping for a special occasion. Fifty years … quite something, I suppose," she said, a trace of pride in her voice.

There was a momentary silence. Never a good thing as we'd both start speaking again at the same time.

"So … how is dad?" I got in quickly.

"Actually, quite 'with it'. He was joking about putting up with an old bat like me for half a century."

I smiled. That was good. A hint of normality, of how things once were. "Has he had any more … you know … any more …" I scratched for the right word, "… any more episodes?" I blurted it out. It wasn't the right word but she'd know what I meant.

"No. Not since last week when he hit one of the nurses. Violet was telling me about it. They had to get three nurses to hold him down."

I winced inwardly. That wasn't my father. That wasn't my dad. That was the Alzheimer's. He'd also taken to hitting my mother—that was when he was still living with her in the cottage, before she'd been forced to get him admitted to Frailcare—for her own safety. It had come out, inadvertently, in a previous conversation and I could sense that she'd regretted mentioning it as she'd immediately tried to change the subject. Even after all this time, she still protected him: her man who could do no wrong. But it was out now.

"Poor old darling kept asking when he was coming home. And you know, I feel dreadful about it but I lied to him and said it'd be soon. As soon as he got better."

"That's quite understandable, mum. 'Bout time you took care of yourself."

"It's just that I simply can't cope." She sounded mildly apologetic, guilty almost. "He's too much work and I'm absolutely exhausted all the time."

"You've done the right thing, mum. What have you been eating?" I changed the subject quickly, steering her away from any self-recrimination. Not that there'd be any; she was far too practical for any kind of self-indulgent emotion.

"Oh, nothing wildly exciting. Can't do much without electricity. Had a tin of sardines on some bread this evening."

"Cold?"

"Yes."

I felt the lump rise in my throat. Now I was getting emotional … self-indulgent. I turned it off immediately. "Oh, well. Maybe the power will come on tomorrow," I said. A useless statement.

"They say it will."

I didn't know what to say. I didn't want to continue the conversation. It was too draining. But I didn't want to hang up either. I didn't want to leave her there, alone, in the dark.

"Okay, mum. I better go …" I stammered, limply.

"Alright, darling. Thanks for phoning." Her voice was small and I could hear it starting to crack.

"Are you okay, mum?" I hesitated. I couldn't leave her like this.

There was a silence. Then I could hear her breathing, more heavily. Now she was crying. Softly at first then louder and more intense. Then the sobs, gut-wrenching sobs. The handset clattered to the floor but still the sobs came—in a desperate, primordial wailing, like a wounded beast bellowing in pain. It was cry of such utter despair and such utter anguish.

I'd never known my mother like this, if in fact this was my mother. I sat transfixed. This was surreal, a hideous nightmare.

"Mum! Mum!" I yelled into the phone. "Mum! Please talk to me. Pick up the phone. Please, mum." I felt the panic in my voice. For the first time in my life, I wanted to hug my mother and squeeze her tight and wipe away her tears and tell her that everything would be alright, even though it wouldn't.

After what seemed an eternity, I felt her pick up the phone.

"I have to go and lie down." Her voice was lifeless, dispossessed.

"I love you, mum, I love you," I blurted out. She must hear it, she must. "You have to know this, mum. I love you."

But the phone was dead.

I gently put down the receiver, staring vacantly, unblinking. I willed the tears to come but they wouldn't.

Four days later, on 29 January 2006, my father died. He was seventy-three. It happened at 5.30 a.m. as he was having his early morning bath in Frailcare. I'm not exactly sure what happened, but I suspect he had an epileptic seizure which induced the fatal heart attack. It was quick. His last words were to Nurse Violet: "Tell Betty to come quickly." But by the time my mother had hobbled the hundred or so yards from her cottage to Frailcare, he was dead.

The entry in the death registration book kept at Harare Market Square records the causes(s) of death as 1) Multi infarct dementia, 2) Hypertension and 3) Arterial fibrillation.

It was almost fifty years to the day that my father, a fresh-faced young immigrant from England, with prospects of an exciting future, had arrived in the booming colony of Southern Rhodesia. He did everything right and to the best of his ability. He worked hard, he rose through the ranks to become the managing director of the firm he worked for for forty years, he educated his children, he clothed them and fed them and he took them on regular holidays, he paid his taxes, he saved diligently, he contributed to many life insurance and pension schemes.

Yet in his last few years he was destitute, living off food parcels and the charity of his children. He died of a broken heart, a pauper.

My mother's passing was not quite as straightforward. After my father's death, determined to maintain a semblance of independence, she soldiered on for a few weeks at Fairways but it was an unequal fight, in spite of the ministrations of Colleen, my first wife, who visited her almost daily. One evening, during a blackout—we suspect that this is what happened—she suffered a series of minor strokes and collapsed, dislocating her hip as she fell. (She'd had a hip replacement several years earlier but the procedure had been fraught, with an ensuing spate of subsequent dislocations.) A neighbour found her the following afternoon prostate on the kitchen floor and barely conscious. She never walked again.

Colleen impressed on me the severity of my mother's situation and so I flew up to Harare. I found her in Frailcare, her condition alarming. With chronic pneumonia, she had not had a bowel movement in over a month, nor was she able to eat or drink, instantly vomiting when the nurses tried to force anything down her throat. I decided to take my mother away and managed to book a British Airways flight to Johannesburg, omitting to advise the BA staff of my mother's condition: they surely would not have permitted her to fly had they known. I went down to the Fairways office to inform the administrator and settle the final account. The elderly secretary was clearly relieved.

"Probably for the best, Christopher," she quipped. "She never really fitted in here, you know."

"I'm sure," I replied curtly.

Colleen had kindly agreed to pack up the cottage and store all Betty's effects in her garage. In the meantime, we had to get Betty into Colleen's car and onto an aeroplane: no easy task. Manoeuvring the dead weight of her body—her legs rigid with pain from the hip-replacement to-do—into the front of the car with the seat tilted all the way back, we eventually arrived at Harare airport where the process was reversed into an awaiting BA wheelchair as Colleen bid a tearful goodbye. I was a bundle of nerves at the check-in, hoping against hope that they wouldn't notice her condition but, being comatose, it appeared that she was asleep so it was not an issue. What was an issue was the four-hour delay—the plane had a puncture and the Air Zimbabwe technicians did not have the right tools to change the tyre—expecting at each interminable minute in the transit lounge that a BA crewmember might spot my obviously un-airworthy mother. Changing her nappy in the airport toilets was an equally harrowing experience.

We landed at Johannesburg International—now O.R. Tambo—at midnight to be met by Kerrin, frantic with worry as she'd been unable to contact me or ascertain the reasons for the delay or indeed the whereabouts of the aircraft. Repeating the procedure of wedging my mother into the front seat of our small hatchback, we finally made it home where Kerrin had made up the spare room into something of a private hospital ward. We were obliged to employ a home-nursing service, represented by two no-nonsense Scottish nurses who promptly dealt with the pneumonia (a course of antibiotics) and the compacted bowel (a fearsome hosepipe contraption) and for two weeks Kerrin nursed my mother back from the brink, at her side every waking minute, feeding her, changing her nappies, washing her, changing her linen until at last my mother came back into the world. She had absolutely no recollection of the events of the past month, and it took some time for her to appreciate that she was even in Johannesburg.

"I'm sorry I'm such a bloody nuisance," was all she could manage.

Kerrin, as equally forthright as the Scottish nurses, would respond, "Oh shut up, Bets. We quite like having you here."

It was good to see my mother smile again.

And so it was. We secured a place for her in the Frailcare section of an old-age home—Huis Hoëveld—round the corner in Albertsville, literally a two-minute drive from our house. It was adequate and for me and my sisters, affordable. I won't say she was happy there but she was content, developing a special bond with one of the matrons, Sister Kotze. We spent money on a physiotherapist in an effort to regain the use of her legs but it was futile. My sisters visited as often as they could but it was difficult for them: Sarah lives in Cape Town and Caroline in France. Once a month we'd bring her home for the day, plying her with ice-cream and filter coffee or take her on an outing to the park in Emmarentia for a picnic, where she'd sit in the sun in her wheelchair and squeeze our hands: simple, happy times.

I was away when she died on 18 December 2012, receiving the call from Sister Kotze to tell me that she'd gone peacefully. I had last seen my mother ten days before when she had told me she was scared, that she didn't want to die. I didn't know what to say; I could do nothing but hug her tightly and tell her that I loved her, over and over and over. And as I had turned to leave, numb with sadness, I saw her head had dropped onto her chest and she was weeping quietly.

The only consolation, I keep telling myself, is that my father was there to meet her when she crossed over, with a large bunch of red roses in his hand. Kerrin had seen this.

It's eighteen years since my father's death and eleven since my mother's and it's only struck me now that I am, I suppose, the head of the family. In older times I'd be the patriarch. That's a peculiar thought. Patriarchs are supposed to be imposing old men, men of authority and distinction, aren't they? Apart from the fact that my immediate family is scattered across the globe—in South Africa, Zimbabwe, UAE, Kuwait, Australia, England and France—I don't feel patriarchal. If anything, part of me is still that child of all those years ago.

The Bee Gees' 'I Gotta Get a Message to You' is playing on the radio and it transposes me, instantly, with a detached sense of melancholy, back to the sixties and back to my childhood. At once it's as if it was yesterday and then it's another world—dreamy, wispy, intangible—and I am merely a distant voyeur looking down on something that isn't real, was never real, with events that never really happened.

Postscript
The Promise—Tracy Chapman, 1995

Boss Lilford was murdered on his farm in Zimbabwe in 1985, bound with barbed wire, beaten, tortured and then shot. Ian Smith retired to the Cape. Fortuitously, his wife Janet had managed to export her cattle herd *in toto* (it's unclear what happened with her husband's). Smith managed to write his memoirs, *The Great Betrayal*, before his death in 2007. He gave me a signed copy. Granma Teddy died in bed at my parents' home in 1995, ravaged by shingles. She was ninety-three. Pat Matthews died in Johannesburg in 2010, impoverished and alone. Both Meg and Forbes Davies have long since passed on, with Meg spending her last years at Nazareth House. Unaware that she was even Catholic, I'm ashamed to admit I never visited her. Di and Joy retired to George in the Western Cape where Joy died in 2009; Di followed her seven years later. Clans Lamond and Mackintosh, in a localized version of the Highland Clearances, have all dispersed across the globe—New York, Buckinghamshire, Perth (WA), Johannesburg, Cape Town—apart from die-hard Donald who still lives in Harare. Murray Lamond suffered a fatal heart attack in New York and I still ache for Ian and Elizabeth. Lizzie's daughter, Eva-May Mutasa, became a highly qualified nurse and moved to Minnesota in the United States, managing to wangle a green card for her mother. Michael Sandys-Thomas took his own life in 2010. Charlie Park hanged himself in his teens. Also in his teens, Oliver Grey took his own life. Ian Gillespie died from cancer in his late forties.

Although some went on to high school with me, I have lost almost all contact with my childhood friends from St John's. Chris Dudley did his national service in 1976 as a subaltern in the Rhodesian African Rifles before becoming a doctor; he was working in the Renal Department at a National Health hospital in Bristol. I have no idea what happened to Paul Stobart though it's not beyond the realms of possibility that he's a billionaire and consults to the likes of Elon Musk, Bill Gates, George Soros and sundry heads of state. Mark Bushnell did his national service in the BSAP in 1976 and also went into medicine, a surgeon with his own practice in Harley Street, London. His mother, the irrepressible Audrey, was murdered in her Colne Valley home in the mid-1990s. Derek came home to find the blood-soaked gardener sitting next to Audrey's body on the carpet in the lounge. Declared insane, the gardener was nonetheless hanged. Richard Fry qualified as an engineer and lives and works in Johannesburg. Dan Winch pursued a military career and was commissioned into the British army; on retirement he became a carpark mogul. Ronnie Lawrence became a top-flight jockey but lost his fight with cancer in 2023. Graeme Fleming followed his father into accounting and still lives in Harare. Ian Moss, who also did his national service in the BSAP, qualified as a Chartered Accountant before suffering a fatal heart attack playing squash at the age of forty-two. Russell Franklin was a national-service sergeant in 1976 when his base camp at Inyanga came under a ZANLA mortar attack: a tiny shard of shrapnel hit him in the eyes and blinded him. Dean Wood and the Wood clan all moved to Australia. Simon Brewer lives in the Eastern Cape. I would like to take this opportunity to apologize to Jamie Beaton: I truly am sorry, Jamie. The Buchan-Fords, in a cruel stroke of irony, got divorced not too long after my parents' pseudo-divorce. I remember seeing the heartache in Ann's eyes. I was not there to comfort Jane. Ann, Jane and Stewart moved to Australia. Sarah has lived in Cape Town since 1978 and Caroline lives in Gouvieux, north of Paris. I remember Theresa with great affection, and sadness.

Printed in Great Britain
by Amazon

43573323R00128